I0881676

Leonard J. Arrington

Leonard J. Arrington

A Historian's Life

Gary Topping

THE ARTHUR H. CLARK COMPANY
An imprint of the University of Oklahoma Press
Norman, Oklahoma
2008

Also by Gary Topping

Glen Canyon and the San Juan Country (Moscow, Idaho, 1997)

(ed.) *Gila Monsters and Red-Eyed Rattlesnakes: Don Maguire's Arizona Trading Expeditions, 1876–1879* (Salt Lake City, 1997)

(ed.) *Great Salt Lake: An Anthology* (Logan, Utah, 2002)

Utah Historians and the Reconstruction of Western History (Norman, 2003)

(ed.) *If I Get Out Alive: World War II Letters and Diaries of William H. McDougall, Jr.* (Salt Lake City, 2007)

Library of Congress Cataloging-in-Publication Data
Topping, Gary, 1941–
Leonard J. Arrington : a historian's life / Gary Topping.
p cm.
Includes bibliographical references and index.
ISBN 978-0-87062-363-9 (hardcover : alk. paper) 1. Arrington, Leonard J. 2. Mormons—Biography. 3. Church of Jesus Christ of Latter-Day Saints—History 4. Mormon Church—History. I. Title.
BX8695.A77T67 2008
289.3092—dc22
[B] 2008010959

The paper in this book meets the guidelines for permanence and durability of the Committee on Production Guidelines for Book Longevity of the Council on Library Resources. ∞

Copyright © 2008 by the University of Oklahoma Press, Norman, Publishing Division of the University. Manufactured in the U.S.A.

All rights reserved.
No part of this publication may be reproduced, stored in a retrieval system, or transmitted, in any form or by any means, electronic, mechanical, photocopying, recording, or otherwise—except as permitted under Section 107 or 108 of the United States Copyright Act—without the prior written permission of the University of Oklahoma Press.

1 2 3 4 5 6 7 8 9 10

Contents

Illustrations

Preface

In 2003 the University of Oklahoma Press published my *Utah Historians and the Reconstruction of Western History*. Originally it included a section on Leonard Arrington that consisted of a lengthy biographical chapter followed by brief essays on specific historiographical problems. Two circumstances kept me from completing the Arrington section at that time and forced me instead to substitute in the conclusion what now seem some pretty perfunctory observations about him and the New Mormon History. One was the fact that the immense Arrington collection at Utah State University was not processed and opened to the public prior to the completion of my research. The other circumstance was my irritation as I became increasingly aware of the degree to which Arrington's books after *Great Basin Kingdom* (1958) were written by "research assistants" at Utah State University or staff members at the History Division of the Church of Jesus Christ of Latter-day Saints. What was I evaluating, I grumbled, a man or a committee?

Happily, those inhibiting circumstances no longer apply. The Arrington Papers are now not only open to research but are efficiently administered by one of the friendliest and most encouraging special collections staffs I have ever encountered. And the reader will see that I have made a complete reversal in my attitude toward Arrington's relationships with his supporters and coworkers, to the point that I actually admire and perhaps even envy their system.

Having established a happy relationship with the University of Oklahoma Press editors, it was my thought to ask them for a second edition of the original work, revised and enlarged, which would include the originally planned Arrington section. Imagine my surprise and delight, then, when editor-in-chief Charles Rankin called to suggest instead that I write an entire biography of Leonard Arrington! It need not be a lengthy book, he continued, but it would afford me sufficient space to give Arrington the same extensive consideration I gave to the subjects of the previous book. After overcoming my astonishment, I agreed to undertake the project and applied for the sabbatical leave that would enable me to complete it within a reasonable span of time.

This is a biography, but it is a particular kind of biography. Most of our interest in a historian, I think, lies in his historical work rather than his personal life. Important as one's involvements in family, church, and civic activities are, they are comparatively mundane in relation to the historical work. So while I have not shunned consideration of purely personal matters, I have tried to keep consistently in mind that this is, as the title promises, a *historian's* life, and I have tried to pare such considerations down to those that bear directly on his work.

Also I ask the reader to realize that this is an essay in historiography, not bibliography. The combined energies of Leonard Arrington and those who contributed to his work added up to an immense dynamo of literary production that, in my judgment, varied considerably in quality and significance. Thus I have confined my attention to those works that strike me as most important and also from which I can most efficiently and persuasively make the points I wish to make. So there are a number of works, such as the histories of W. W. Clyde Co.,

American Linen Supply, and Tracy Collins and First Security Banks, that receive little or no mention here. Nor do I deal with Arrington's massive history of Idaho except as a source for his own life. Bibliographic completeness, I have thought, would extend the length of the book considerably without a corresponding increase in insight, and David Whitaker's bibliography of Arrington's writings is available elsewhere. On the other hand, some readers are no doubt going to dispute the lengthy analysis I give, for example, to his history of the beet sugar industry, which I think is a fascinating and unfortunately neglected little masterpiece, besides being one of the few books he apparently wrote with no assistance.

In my documentation of sources in the Arrington Papers, I have chosen to cite the date of a letter or diary entry precisely but to give only the series in which that document may be found instead of the exact box and folder number. I believe that by using my citation and Utah State University's excellent register to the papers, anyone wishing to check a particular document will have little trouble locating it. In all citations of either published or unpublished sources, Leonard J. Arrington is indicated simply as "LJA." Finally, readers will see a few citations to Lavina Fielding Anderson's unpublished "Doves and Serpents: The Activities of Leonard J. Arrington as Church Historian" and many citations of Leonard's personal diary, both of which are restricted parts of the Arrington Papers. I have not sought, nor have I been offered, a dispensation from those restrictions. The selections I have cited were photocopied by Leonard himself and placed in the unrestricted part of the collection, so I have felt at liberty to employ them in my research while still abiding by both the spirit and the law of the restrictions.

I first met Leonard Arrington by mail in 1978 when he wrote to thank me for an article I had written in graduate school in which, in passing, I had corrected (I hope humbly) an assertion he had made about western novels. It was one of those gratuitous gestures of humility and kindness one never forgets. Nor was my own humility diminished when, during the research for this book, I occasionally came across in his papers a photocopy of something I had written that he had carefully read and underlined. Leonard Arrington took *everyone* seriously! If, in the following pages, I balance effusive praise with relentless criticism, both are my way of honoring my memory of him.

Acknowledgments

Ordinarily, in the course of writing a book like this, one accumulates so many debts that finding a place to begin acknowledging them is a bewildering task. Happily, that is not the case in this instance, for although I have incurred many debts, my acknowledgments must begin at the beginning, with Charles E. Rankin of the University of Oklahoma Press. Chuck not only suggested that I, a practicing Catholic and an employee of the Roman Catholic Diocese of Salt Lake City, should write a biography of an icon of Mormon culture, but he also wrote a most flattering letter in my behalf that helped me get the sabbatical leave that enabled me to complete the research and writing within a reasonable period of time. This book would not exist without him; indeed, the *idea* of the book would not exist without him.

That sabbatical was also made possible by several supportive administrators at Salt Lake Community College who creatively construed the rules to grant a sabbatical for which a literal reading of those rules would not have rendered me eligible. I refer to my then Division Chair, Dr. John Fritz, my dean, Dr. John S. McCormick, and the then Vice President for Academic Affairs, Dr. David Richardson. I am grateful for their belief that research and writing are legitimate activities for community college professors.

The Merrill-Cazier Library of Utah State University, where the Leonard Arrington Papers are housed, is one of the most accommodating places in which I have ever done research. I am grateful to Ann Buttars, Steve Sturgeon, Brad Cole, Liz Kline, Dan Davis, and many others who cheerfully and efficiently produced materials for me.

But my debts extend to other institutions as well. At the Utah State Historical Society I was assisted by Linda Thatcher, Greg Matthews, Doug Misner, and Susan Whetstone. Walter Jones and Roy Webb of the Marriott Library of the University of Utah put my request for scans of two dust jackets on the fast track, making me ever more grateful for our ancient friendships. Ron Watt, of the Library-Archives of the Church of Jesus Christ of Latter-day Saints, also assisted me in my search for photographs.

At the University of Oklahoma Press, it was my good fortune that my manuscript fell into the hands of Bob Clark of the Arthur H. Clark Company, an imprint at that press. He and Chuck Rankin sped the manuscript on to acceptance against considerable odds. And the seven thousand words that Bob's editorial dexterity docked from what I naively thought was a tightly written text will never be missed! Editorial assistant Jessica Walker deftly handled organizational matters and deadlines while tutoring both Bob and me in the use of the press's splendid software. After moving into the copyediting phase, it was a pleasure to work once again with the editor of my previous book on Utah historians, Alice Stanton. Thanks, too, to Crystal Yoesting for planning the marketing strategy for the book.

Last, my gratitude goes once again to Marianna Allred Hopkins, my colleague, friend, and now my wife. Our almost constant dialogue over the past decade about words, grammar, style, and many other literary matters has improved my writing and my thinking more than she can ever know or would ever acknowledge.

Leonard J. Arrington

Chapter 1

Idaho Farm Boy

Some called it "Camelot," and in certain ways that legend was an apt analogy for the History Division of the Church of Jesus Christ of Latter-day Saints under Leonard Arrington's leadership in the 1970s. In their less romantic moments, though, Arrington and others of his staff realized that some of the biggest dragons the knights and ladies of their Round Table had to slay were within the walls of their own castle. As the division's King Arthur, it was Leonard Arrington who had to bear the brunt of the frustration of dealing with midlevel church administrators who poorly understood the work of professional historians and who conspired to undermine projects they should have been defending. The ever-optimistic, jovial, and diplomatic Arrington was the perfect buffer to shield his staff from the ravages of their administrators, but on rare occasions the frustration boiled over even within him. Upon learning that the division was to be transferred to Brigham Young University in 1982, he realized that this would mean the end of Camelot, and in his diary he succumbed to a moment of despair: "The only thought in my mind is whether to take up the options that I have to go to the U of Utah or USU instead of running down to BYU in 1982. Or, maybe going up to a little two-and-a-half-acre plot on the family farm in Twin Falls and pitching hay and showing chickens."[1]

Pitching hay and showing chickens? It seems a strange option to be considered by a man at the top of his profession, universally regarded as the greatest of all Mormon historians and author of *Great Basin Kingdom*, an acknowledged classic of United States historiography.[2] The possibility was certainly there, for the Arrington siblings still ran the old family farm in Twin Falls, Idaho, as a family corporation, but there is no reason to believe that he seriously thought of such a monkish renunciation of his career and status within his profession. If his expostulation was, then, a passing outburst of frustration, it was more than just that, for it was a telling revelation of who and what Arrington really considered himself to be, and where he would retreat to, if only in his imagination, to define life in its bare essentials. Whatever else he had become—and he had become a *lot*—Leonard Arrington was at his innermost core an Idaho farm boy. "I do feel that, in a sense, I have not been living 'in the real world' since I went away to college at age eighteen," he wrote during the 1980s. "The world in which I was brought up was the real world. I try to keep connections with it in a variety of ways: by having artifacts showing chickens, by having a little plow, by having paintings of natural scenes on the wall, by keeping my 'kid's things' in my file, by keeping photos and clippings of my doings as a boy."[3]

To some, even to some of those who knew him best, Arrington's farm boy persona was posturing. His son Carl, for example, once chided his father for selling his sophistication short, for his "insistence at playing the country bumpkin after five decades" of academic and scholarly attainment.[4] Some of it, no doubt, *was* posturing, a defense mechanism against his discomfort with certain demands of the modern world and of the church administration within which his family had not been socially prominent and for which he had never served a mission. But all of that misses a fundamentally important point: it was the farm that shaped Leonard Arrington's personality, formed his values, and even focused his scholarly interests. All understanding of him has to begin with that small farm in Twin Falls County, Idaho, in the early years of the twentieth century.

He came by his love of farming naturally, for his ancestors on both sides had been pioneers on the trans-Appalachian frontier in Tennessee and Kentucky. "They were mountain folk," he said of his Arrington forebears. In fact, they resembled classic comic-strip hillbillies, for his grandmother smoked a corncob pipe, never wore shoes until she was married, and remained illiterate to the day of her death in the 1940s.[5] They were also classic American pioneers, on the move west in search of more abundant and better land and the economic opportunity it offered. Following their conversion to Mormonism in the 1890s, the Arringtons naturally sought that opportunity in Utah, but after a brief try, they found farming in Spanish Fork no more profitable than in Tennessee and they returned to their previous home. In 1906 a redistribution of Indian lands to white homesteaders in 160-acre plots lured the Arringtons to Faxon, Oklahoma. Prosperity remained elusive and they stayed only a few seasons. It was during this time, however, that the Arringtons met the Corns, who had come to Oklahoma from Kentucky via Indiana in search of the same kind of opportunity. In 1913 son Noah Arrington and Edna Corn married. They would have no fewer than eleven children during the long course of their marriage, the third of which was Leonard James Arrington, born July 2, 1917.[6]

At about the time of his marriage, Noah Arrington learned of an immense tract of 350,000 acres in the Snake River Valley of Twin Falls County, Idaho, which had been made irrigable by the privately built Milner Dam. The tract was intended to create fifteen thousand new farms, and Noah and Edna Arrington were determined to get one.[7] Starting out with a twenty-acre tract, the Arrington farm was, as Leonard remembered it many years later, "a pretty self-sufficient agricultural economy not too different from that of frontier America for 200 years. We did not fear Indians, but the plowing was still done with a hand-plow and one horse or mule; we did not suffer from periodic famine, but my mother did handwashing on an old washboard; we took baths Saturday evening in tubs filled with water heated by our old wood stove; we did not have one-room schools, but we were driven to school each morning in sheepwagons with hot rocks in the middle of the floor to keep us warm on cold mornings." Twin Falls County contained only a few hundred white settlers. Although they were largely self-sufficient, Noah found it necessary to supplement his farm produce with a few odd jobs for cash, such as driving a school "bus" (a sheep wagon), laboring on road construction, and working in the sugar beet factory. On the farm itself, Noah diversified his crops among "potatoes, garden beans, corn, wheat, and alfalfa," as Leonard remembered. Livestock, in the form of draft animals and milch cows, primarily served the family's needs, but they also raised chickens—later a specialty of Leonard's—for a cash income.[8]

Young Leonard found life on the farm highly fulfilling and later in life wrote about it (no doubt feeling a tug of nostalgia) with a warmth that echoes Robert Frost or even Virgil. His reminiscence of threshing wheat evokes the heat of southern Idaho's open skies and the smells of wheat chaff, sweat, and animal manure:

> We'd cut the wheat (or oats or barley) with a binder, put the sheaves into shocks, and, when ripe and dry, pitch the bundles onto wagons and drive our team up to the noisy, fearsome thresher . . . where we'd fork bundles into the feeder. Chaff and straw was blown out onto a stack, while appointed persons sacked the grain that came from the spout, sewed up the sacks, and loaded them onto a wagon to be hauled away to the produce buyer. The delightful time came at noon when everything was suspended while we watered our teams, unharnessed them to feed, and went to the house, washed up in a tub, and sat down to enjoy the homemaker's best dumplings, vegetables, and pie.[9]

The heavy work on the Arrington farm was done by animals in keeping with agricultural practice since the time of Charlemagne. "My principal jobs on the farm each summer were to drive a team, although I also weeded, irrigated, and assisted in the harvesting. I was good with horses, and my father used me as a horseman most of the time. . . . I was a kind of specialist . . . with horses and cows and chickens, and got along well with animals. . . . This was good training for me as a diplomat or politician, keeping things calm and pleasant. I did not 'fly off the handle,' as the expression went."[10]

It was only after Leonard went away to college in the 1930s, costing Noah his best horseman, that the Arringtons began turning to mechanized farming, and by 1939 Noah had sold the last of the horses. Although Leonard by that time was going to college year-round and thus was not directly involved in farming, the selling of the horses was a profound disappointment to him. It was an odd reversal of the roles one might expect of father and son: while Leonard, the agricultural science student at the University of Idaho, was the romantic who preferred traditional farming techniques, Noah, the lifelong one-horse farmer, wanted to move to the greater efficiency of mechanization.[11]

Thus the seasonal rhythms and the primeval struggle of man and animal to wrest a living from the earth were bedrock elements in Leonard Arrington's life. Equally important were the very different role models provided him by his parents. After struggling as a young man on unpromising farm plots in Tennessee, Utah, and Oklahoma, Noah Arrington found in Idaho the environment he needed for real success as a farmer. No doubt marriage and agrowing family lent a new urgency to his efforts, but it seems that these circumstances only enhanced an ambition and energy that were already inherent to his personality, and under the Arringtons' labors the sagebrush plains of the Snake River Valley—"Magic Valley" it was popularly called—

brought forth in abundance. More than simply a farmer, Noah Arrington was a self-made agricultural entrepreneur whose frugality, wise investments, and long hours of labor were a classic fulfillment of the American Dream.

Although Noah had to supplement his meager farm income by taking on other jobs, he disliked working for others and tirelessly planned to expand his holdings and to earn his livelihood by the work of his own hands—once again fulfilling the American ideal of the self-made man. "He wanted to be a farmer, work for himself, and make money on his own labor and resourcefulness, and frugal living," Leonard recalled. "As he worked, he earned money to buy a cow, then a horse or mule, then a down payment on some land. He continued that pattern throughout his life, so that by his death he had acquired some 500 acres of highly productive irrigated land, and a good deal of machinery." Noah's almost frenetic energy, always on the go, always with a new project ready to launch, impressed itself deeply in the personality of his son, who only had to redirect that momentum into scholarship. "I did not expect writing to be easy," Leonard wrote in his autobiography, "but, growing up on a farm, I learned the habit and joy of work. Work did not seem onerous or burdensome, but, as I remember it now anyway, a source of pleasure and accomplishment." Writing to his children in something of an apologetic mood on a Father's Day many years later, Leonard admitted to having neglected family outings and recreation, as his own father had, in the interest of professional development: "If my father's chief goal was land, mine was attainment as a teacher and writer. If I had an extra $100 I went to an econ. convention; or a trip to a historic site."[12]

Noah gave his sons much more than just a hard-driving work ethic and a love for the soil, for he was, with all his ambition, a most generous, cheerful, diplomatic, and life-loving person. No grasping, unscrupulous materialist determined to feather his own nest at any cost, Noah Arrington went about his enterprises "always with a pleasant expression, good disposition, geniality, enthusiasm. Launching into something new with excitement and anticipation." Leonard also inherited and emulated his father's gregariousness and love of people: "He treated everyone with respect, with dignity. My father enjoyed being liked. Did not want to disappoint people. Was not condescending or patronizing. Was not insensitive. Was not cruel. Did not laugh at people's problems." And on another occasion he noted that "some persons are born to be mediators; I may have been one of them. My father tended to be one of these, and I may have emulated him. Studying about Jesus tends to reinforce that attitude—at least I have felt that it did. Persons who become angry almost never achieve as much as they think they can. If my writing seems calm and unimpassioned, this is not just the result of studied effort, but my natural tone. There are exceptions, I'm sure, but not often."[13]

What role did Mormonism play in the Arrington home? In the first place, with the exception of their brief sojourn in Spanish Fork, Utah, Mormons were always a minority in the communities in which the Arringtons lived. It was not until Leonard had finished his Ph.D. coursework, completed his service in the army, and accepted a position in the economics department at Utah Agricultural College in Logan that he first had the experience of living in a Mormon community. Thus, although the Arringtons' faith was secure and their commitment to the church was solid, they never experienced the all-pervasive presence of the church in their lives and the level of church regimentation common in Utah and other Mormon-dominated areas. The Arringtons' brand of Mormonism was much more individualistic, gleaned from their own reading of church literature and adapted to their local circumstances, than they would have known in a largely Mormon community.

Also, Noah Arrington's Mormonism was rather nominal until his marriage and the move to Twin Falls. Edna Corn Arrington, his bride, did not become a Latter-day Saint until she sought baptism, shortly after arriving in Twin Falls.[14] The enthusiasm of Edna's new-found faith rekindled that of her husband. That, and the death from spinal meningitis of a baby, Thelma, drove both Arringtons into deeper church involvement. Noah was ordained an elder and the couple journeyed to Salt Lake City to have their marriage solemnized in the LDS temple (they had previously been married by a Presbyterian minister). Finally, Noah's faith was further deepened in the 1920s when he served a mission in his ancestral home of Tennessee. Not only were his proselytizing efforts a faith-building experience, but his mission president, Charles A. Callis, was a most zealous Mormon who became a lifelong friend of Noah Arrington and a continuing spiritual mentor. Even at that, as Leonard recalled, church involvement was not pervasive in the Arrington household: "Our primary responsibility was to work—school was secondary—even church. . . . My father was on the Twin Falls High Council from 1919, but I do not remember that church played an important part of our life. He went on trips to give talks and inspect wards from Hollister to Buhl and Castleford, but he left us behind. I remember clearly going to church, but think that we did not go during the worst part of winter, or during the heavy work part of summer. We occasionally worked on Sunday, but not often."[15]

Despite Noah's mission and his long service on the Stake High Council, then, the Arringtons' brand of Mormonism was largely a home-brewed concoction, incorporating aspects they found useful and enriching—mostly the spiritual and ethical aspects—but which bore only occasional resemblance to the more institutionally uniform variety emphasizing externals. As Leonard's biographer Rebecca Cornwall observes, "The Arringtons were not products of Mormon folklore and culture to the extent that many Latter-day Saints were, particularly those who grew up in dominantly Mormon communities in Utah, southeastern Idaho, and Arizona."

We shall examine the content of Leonard's own faith in greater depth, but two conspicuous external features stand out. First, he had little interest in "temple work," the secret institutionalized rituals such as baptism for the dead which often occupy large portions of zealous members' time. From time to time, he would "go through the temple" as a special favor to a friend or to participate in a wedding, but otherwise his religion was something he practiced out on the street, in his family and daily living. He had a particular disdain for pharisaical outward shows of piety that he knew to be at odds with private practice, such as his own love for Coca-Cola, which was a violation of the dietary rule of the Mormon Word of Wisdom.

A second deviation from standard Mormon behavior, which resulted in a serious conflict with his father, was that he refused to serve a mission, the church-sanctioned pattern for college-age Mormon males. Noah became insistent about the matter, evidently for two reasons. One was that his own mission had been a profound experience. The other (and one has to speculate just a bit here) is that Noah hoped it might deflect Leonard's interest from college (he had just completed his first year at the University of Idaho) and back to the farm. The Arringtons, to follow Rebecca Cornwall's reading of the family, had always been ambivalent about Leonard's educational aspirations. "For some reason," she suggests, "perhaps because he had always done well in school, college for Leonard was an assumption. His older brother LeRoy did not go, nor was there any pressure or particular urging from his parents for Leonard to go. In fact, his father's opinion was that he would be a better farmer if he stayed home and obtained practical experience." Leonard became irritated at his father's offer to pay for a mission, in view of the fact that he had refused to pay for college. For his part, Leonard thought that his university training suited his scholarly nature better than a proselytizing mission and that it could be brought to good purpose for the church. "I thought I could serve the Church and the Kingdom by getting a good education," he protested. "I didn't understand why the Church couldn't give credit to people for missions who studied and wrote and taught the Gospel in the context of higher learning. I felt a strong sense of mission in my schoolwork and felt the need to continue it for the present."[16]

The conflict culminated in an automobile trip to Salt Lake City, where Noah had set up an interview for his son with his old mission president, Elder Callis, whose well-tested persuasive abilities, so he thought, exceeded his. But Leonard stuck to his guns during the interview, protesting, out of his own Twin Falls brand of Mormonism, that because his family had contributed nothing to his college expenses, they could ill afford to send him on a mission (a clever polemical twist!), and that "there were many ways a young man could serve the Church and that missions were not the only way." Even Elder Callis could not prevail against that combination of obstinacy and logic, and Noah had to reconcile himself to defeat. For once, too, Noah's good grace failed him; Leonard's younger brother Kenneth, who had accompanied them, remembered that their father silently sulked behind the steering wheel during the entire long journey from Salt Lake City back to Twin Falls.[17] In the end, Leonard paid for his entire college and graduate work with scholarships and part-time jobs.

Education was the one issue on which his parents somewhat disagreed. Neither of them had much formal schooling. Noah was inclined to think that practical experience was more important for his children than formal education. Leonard recalled driving a horse pulling a clod masher when he was just six years of age, and doing similar farm work as a young boy, but added that "this was only in the summer and on Saturdays in the spring, for we never were kept home from school to do farm work. That was my mother's influence, I suspect. I think my Dad would have done so if she hadn't been adamant on the point of us getting all the schooling we could."[18]

As we have seen, the brand of Mormonism Leonard Arrington learned in his parents' home did not always conform, at least in its external manifestations, to official church norms, and even some of his theological ideas struck his son Carl as "clearly unorthodox." However, it is best to heed the words of Rebecca Cornwall, who cautioned that "Leonard's self-characterization as a practicing Mormon but doctrinal non-conformist was probably overstated."[19] Leonard identified two contrasting traditions in Mormon thought and practice, one emphasizing dogma and authority and the other emphasizing ethics and reason. Without making a judgment on the relative validity of either, he placed himself solidly in the latter:

> One of them begins with Joseph Smith's statements of his later years, particularly the King Follett discourse, proceeds through Brigham Young to B. H. Roberts, and is best expressed in our day by Sterling McMurrin and Lowell L. Bennion. This school emphasizes man's potential, the law of eternal progression, the importance of learning and knowledge, the tolerance of different points of view, and so on. This is the view I was brought up on. It was commonly expressed by LDS intellectuals and teachers during the 1930s and 1940s. We may call it the progressive or liberal school of thought.
>
> The other school derives from the Book of Mormon, early revelations, and early statements of Joseph Smith, proceeds through some statements of Brigham Young to Orson Pratt, Joseph Fielding Smith, and is best expressed today by Bruce R. McConkie. This school emphasizes the dependent and depraved status of man, the absolute power and perfection of God, the importance of "works," such as temple work, ordinances, following church regulations, discipline, obedience, "nar-

row is the way," and so on. This philosophy is emphasized in the New Orthodoxy which emerged at BYU in the 1950s and has continued among some people there, particularly in the College of Religion, as a sort of Mormon Fundamentalism like Protestant Fundamentalism. It emphasizes Biblical literalism, rejects the Higher Criticism, the law of evolution, the New History, and cultural approaches to an understanding of Mormonism.

> I have been all along, and continue to be, in the first school, but find the going very hard, considering the implacable opposition of Elder [Ezra Taft] Benson, Elder [Mark E.] Petersen, Elder [Boyd K.] Packer, Elder [Bruce R.] McConkie, and perhaps others who agree with them.[20]

In the tradition with which Leonard identified himself, there was no disharmony between secular and sacred thought, between science and religion. As a young man, he recalled,

> there was a pleasing continuity between my religious and professional life. The gospel included all truth and encouraged the energetic search for truth. At no time did I experience any great tension between my Mormon upbringing and my exposure to other cultures and ways of life. There was no youthful rebellion, no wrenching intellectual conflict. I had always thought that secular studies were of value, could be harmonized with and incorporated into Mormonism.[21]

With that kind of theology, it is no wonder that Arrington found no conflict between what he learned in church and what he learned in school, and that he thrived in both settings. But then he ascribed that harmony to the fact that he had no Mormon teachers at any time during his formal education: there were none at Twin Falls; only three at the University of Idaho, none of whom he studied with; and of course there were none during his graduate work in North Carolina. Later, as an adult and a parent living and rearing children in the Mormon communities of Utah, he caustically contrasted the schools of his youth with the Utah schools: "Knowing, as I do now, of some of the inadequacies of schools in Utah, I can be grateful I was born and raised in a non-Mormon town. And I do mean this. . . . My present impression is that Mormon communities placed such stress on right thinking and right behavior that they did not always insist upon academic excellence and intellectuality. The people of Twin Falls insisted upon right behavior, perhaps, but did respect training and intellect and obtained some of the finest graduates of colleges and universities [as teachers].[22]

In addition to church and school, two institutional affiliations profoundly affected the young Leonard Arrington. One was the Boy Scouts of America, which he joined in 1930 through the troop sponsored by his ward, and the other was the Future Farmers of America, which he joined slightly later in high school. While each organization influenced him in its own way, the two taken together resonated with his native Mormon ethos of group effort, the idea that people working together can accomplish more than the total of their individual labors. It would be difficult to overestimate the importance of that group ethos in Arrington's life: it made him a proverbially gregarious joiner and even founder of professional organizations; it was the inspiration behind the History Division of the LDS Church, which he headed during that celebrated "Camelot" decade; and it was the central thesis of his books, especially his masterpiece of Mormon economic history, *Great Basin Kingdom.*

It might seem at first glance that the Boy Scouts would offer an almost redundant experience to an Idaho farm boy who spent most of his waking (and, as we shall see, even sleeping) hours in the outdoors, immersed in the primeval rhythms of nature. While that experience might have put Arrington ahead of some city-bred youths, the Boy Scouts greatly enlarged his understanding of nature by encouraging the study of wild animals in addition to domesticated ones, and by developing camping, hiking, and other outdoors coping skills. Leonard thrived as a Scout, earning merit badges and enjoying outings with other boys, and eventually he rose to the rank of Star Scout. The highest level of Eagle Scout was denied to him only because he failed to develop the requisite competence in swimming, despite arduous solo practice sessions in an irrigation canal after the day's work.

Less happily, the Boy Scouts provided the young Leonard with his first experience of prejudice. It gave him a lesson he would later find useful in his dealings with church administrators in Salt Lake City—that institutional ideals are not always realized in practice. The occasion was a camping trip with some other, non-Mormon, troops. During a swim, one of Leonard's cousins got into difficulty and was rescued by another Mormon Scout. Although the Mormon Scout clearly deserved the credit for the rescue, one of the non-Mormon adult leaders pulled him off during the resuscitation so that a non-Mormon Scout could be given that honor. Arrington was outraged, but the experience was an unforgettable lesson in the historical fact of anti-Mormon prejudice as well as in the frailties of human nature.[23]

One of the happier effects of Leonard's Boy Scout membership was a widening of his literary world to include books on nature. Always a reader, Leonard had devoured the Bible, romance novels such as *Ivanhoe*, and the Sherlock Holmes mysteries—most of which would have been fairly standard fare for a boy of that generation. The Boy Scouts added the *Boy Scout Handbook*, for one thing, a fascinating repository of outdoor lore set in a context of lessons in patriotism, loyalty, and other moral concepts. Among Arrington's favorites, though, were the works of Ernest Thompson Seton, a naturalist who had been an American cofounder of the Boy Scouts with the British army officer Robert Baden-Powell and whom Arrington credited with shifting the emphasis of Scouting, in America at least, away from Baden-Powell's militarism and toward a focus on nature.

Arrington's reading time was greatly increased by a decision he made when he was twelve years old, during the summer of

1929, to transport his bed out into the middle of the orchard, a considerable distance to the west of the house. The summer heat in the Idaho farm house and the increasing size of the Arrington family led to Leonard's decision to move to the orchard for a cool and quiet place to retire and read after supper. As any outdoors person knows, the quietness and motionlessness of reading or awakening from sleep are ideal for observing wildlife: "Sleeping under the stars, and feeling a certain kinship with them since I could now recognize and identify the various constellations [from the *Boy Scout Handbook*]; watching the blackbirds fly to their nightly roost in the cattails in Snake River Canyon below the Falls; spotting the mother skunk and her six or seven baby skunks as they moved through the orchard early in the morning; picking fruits just to munch on as they matured; it all seems idyllic now."[24]

Idyllic, indeed. One night, though, the impressionable boy's communion with nature became more than that—a transcendent experience that profoundly reoriented his life. Similar to the angelic visitations claimed by the young Joseph Smith, which led to the writing of the *Book of Mormon* and the founding of the Church of Jesus Christ of Latter-day Saints, experiences of that kind are relatively common among young Mormon men throughout Mormon history. Arrington experienced three such transcendent experiences as a boy and young man. All three were life-changing experiences of such sacredness that he rarely spoke of them and recorded them in writing, so far as I have been able to verify, only once. The first of these occurred in his orchard bedroom in 1930 when he was thirteen, and I shall describe the others as they fall naturally into the chronology of his life.

On that evening, Leonard had gone to bed at twilight after a hard day's work on the farm. He read for a time in his favorite Ernest Thompson Seton book, *Two Little Savages*, then put the book down to watch the nightly flight of the blackbirds to their roosts below Shoshone Falls. "Suddenly I was overwhelmed by a feeling of connectedness," he recalled many years later, "an intimate kinship with the world and its human, bird, and animal inhabitants. I was on a higher or deeper level of consciousness, present in an affectionate environment that seems now to have been transcendental. God was smiling on me; I had a feeling of acceptance and self-validation. I was having an enhancing experience of the holy, and the holy was happy, festive, even playful. I was smiling—even chuckling with pleasure. How fortunate to get this feeling of intimacy with the universe!"[25]

What did the experience mean? For one thing, it enabled him to understand Joseph Smith's angelic visitations; now this Idaho farm boy with wheat chaff in his hair and chicken droppings on his boots would know that the line between the eternal and the quotidian realities of daily life was permeable, that the spiritual could infuse and sometimes break through the surface of the material: "This almost mystical illumination . . . made it easy for me, in the years that followed, to integrate personal religious experiences and intuitions with the more formal affirmations, practices, forms, and ceremonies of the organized church."[26] Beyond validating his Mormon beliefs, though, the experience had deeply personal meaning as well, for it gave him the confidence to go ahead and attempt the things he wanted to accomplish in life. That self-assurance sustained him to the end of his life.

The first step in the direction of those larger goals came to him through his involvement in the Future Farmers of America (FFA), which after 1932 came to occupy an ever larger role in his life and ultimately crowded out the Boy Scouts.

Not only was participation in the FFA more convenient because it was part of his regular school day, it was simply something that pointed in a more adult direction than the Boy Scouts, for it was designed to instruct young farm boys in the techniques of scientific agriculture and effective business practices. It was, in other words, a gateway to a career. It was also a gateway to participatory citizenship, for it provided debate meets and writing and speechmaking opportunities that cultivated the tools of politics. It was, as farmers had learned through bitter experience in previous generations, ignorance of those basic economic and political tools that had kept them out of the pilot house in American life, and Leonard Arrington was no doubt encouraged by his teachers to see himself as one of the leaders toward a new day for American agriculture.

That American farmers needed some new leaders with political and economic know-how was an easy point to demonstrate to a farm boy growing up during the Great Depression, and Leonard Arrington, in his first research project in economics, had already collected data to prove the point. As agricultural prices fell into the basement, Leonard and his father were presented with prices for their potatoes that hardly made them worth harvesting. As an experiment one evening in October 1932, during the potato harvest, Leonard prepared several slips of paper with a note giving his address and the information that he was selling his potatoes for five cents per hundred pound sack. He invited whomever would purchase and open that sack to write to him and tell him the price he had paid. The next day he dropped those slips into several sacks as he was sewing them up. No doubt to his surprise, and certainly to his delight, several people responded. While the prices they reported varied, all were many times what the Arringtons had received; one person reported, for example, that he had paid two dollars. "This was Leonard's first observation of agricultural economics," his biographer writes, "and it left a permanent impression." More specifically, as Ronald W. Walker observes, "It was enough to confirm to the boy the ruthlessness and inequity of the market place."[27] Perhaps also it was the dawning of a realization that action must be based on information, that research can have more than an intellectual significance, though the teenager had little idea at the time of a way to make use of his findings.

FFA membership involves instruction by practicum as well as by precept, and each student is required to have an independent project in which he or she puts classroom principles to work, with the goal of actually making a profit. Leonard had acquired from his father a love of birds, both wild and domestic, and the Arrington farm always had a variety of poultry running about, so it was natural that he settled upon raising chickens for his project. Although Noah Arrington had to help his son with the initial expense of the chicks (as an adult farmer would have to borrow from a bank), Leonard demonstrated as much of a gift for chicken raising as he had shown with cows and horses. Rhode Island Reds were the breed of choice. Leonard learned such things as how to caponize the roosters so they could be raised and sold for meat, and the hens' big brown eggs became a significant income producer for the family during those hard depression times. As a high school senior Leonard had a flock of four hundred adult chickens and two thousand chicks.[28]

Arrington's Rhode Island Reds were not only a welcome source of income, but a status symbol as well, for they won him a blue ribbon at the Idaho State Fair in 1934—an artifact still proudly displayed as part of the Arrington Collection at Utah State University. Thereafter the chicken became a symbolic presence throughout his life, including a chicken logo on his private stationery and a six-foot-high chicken statue in the front yard of his Salt Lake City home, proudly reminding visitors that his honors as a historian did not trump his youthful attainments on the farm.

A blue ribbon was impressive enough, but his FFA involvement and scholastic record led to something even better than that: a scholarship to the University of Idaho. The second phase of Leonard Arrington's life was about to begin.

Chapter 2

Scholar and Soldier

In retrospect it might seem an act of audacious courage and determination for Leonard Arrington to journey north from Twin Falls to Moscow, Idaho, in 1935 to enter the University of Idaho during the dark days of the Great Depression. Certainly he was launching onto uncertain waters as the first of his family to venture beyond a high school education, and he also merits admiration for his determination to support himself with scholarships and his own resources. Placed within the context of Idaho economic history in the early twentieth century, though, Arrington's great venture actually came at an auspicious time.

Almost from the time of his birth in 1917, Idaho agriculture had been in a depressed condition. Although the collapse of European agriculture under the ravages of World War I had created a flourishing international market for American farmers at the war's end, it proved to be an ephemeral prosperity. American farmers had been tempted by that international market to expand by purchasing new land and building new irrigation projects. Postwar production was far beyond the capacity of the domestic market, and as a result, surpluses mounted and prices plummeted. Although moved by the plight of the farmer, the business-oriented Republican administrations of the 1920s acted by raising tariffs on three different occasions. Tariffs, which were the time-honored way of supporting domestic industry by raising the prices of competitive imports, were exactly the opposite of what the farmers needed, for they had products they needed to sell abroad. One buys where one can sell, and when American markets for foreign goods became restricted, foreign markets for American goods closed down proportionately.

Thus the onset of the Great Depression, which began with the stock market crash of 1929, was, in the words of Idaho historian F. Ross Peterson, "the second act of a disastrous economic drama that began after World War I."[1] But by 1935 this second act was working toward a happier denouement than the first one because of the more effective recovery measures applied by the Democratic gubernatorial administration of C. Ben Ross and the national administration of Franklin D. Roosevelt. Although the opportunistic Ross was no New Dealer and opposed most of Roosevelt's programs that did not directly benefit Idaho, New Deal funds flowed into the state anyway: by Peterson's calculations, only seven states had received more New Deal assistance by 1939 than Idaho. The effects of that assistance were dramatic; during Roosevelt's first term in office, for example, prices for Idaho's agricultural products almost doubled.[2] Paradoxically, when Arrington set out for Moscow during the midst of the Great Depression, he was riding a rising economic tide.

The University of Idaho, founded in 1889, was the state's first and most prominent institution of higher learning. Even today, despite the presence of major universities in Boise and Pocatello (as well as smaller church-related colleges in Caldwell, Nampa, and Rexburg), the academic stature and the social contacts one acquires with an Idaho degree are useful tools. Especially when coupled with the resources of its close neighbor, Washington State University, just across the border in Pullman, the University of Idaho is a formidable educational force. For Arrington, the University of Idaho was an almost inevitable choice, and in fact its academic quality could hardly have been matched anywhere in the intermountain region. The university offered an amazingly broad selection of programs, from agriculture, mines, and forestry to the liberal arts and sciences. Although its graduate programs were slow to develop (it did not offer the Ph.D. until 1959), the university supported master's degrees in four areas. In short, it was an almost ideal place for a typically confused young undergraduate to shop around academically and eventually get his intellectual feet beneath him.[3]

In spite of Idaho's rising economic tide, higher education was on a secondary economic echelon, and severe budget cuts were apparent on every hand. Faculty members stretched themselves thin teaching extra courses while accepting salary and staff cuts. Students, whose budgets were already taxed by tuition, petitioned the university for subsidized housing, and the administration responded by encouraging the formation of student cooperatives—the first university in the country to do so. The three hundred members of the five cooperatives that eventually were created saved expenses by purchasing and preparing their own food and performing their own housekeeping chores. Arrington, who lived at the co-op for Mormon students at the Church of Latter-day Saints Institute of Religion, kept records showing that he subsisted for a ten-month school year on $285.38.[4]

Even raising that amount required hard work and ingenuity in capitalizing on all available resources. The Union Pacific Railroad scholarship he had won with his poultry projects and Future Farmers of America work paid only seventy-five dollars. He pieced together the other $150 from jobs in the university library, the chemical laboratory, and the economics department funded by a New Deal agency, the National Youth Administration.[5]

It was at the LDS Institute that Leonard Arrington encountered a person who would be one of the fundamentally influential persons in his life. Its director, George S. Tanner, was the genius behind the entire student cooperative movement at the university. As a descendant and a historian of the pioneers who had created the cooperative Mormon colonies along the Little Colorado River in Arizona in the late nineteenth century, Tanner was deeply steeped in the Mormon cooperative tradition. By demonstrating in a practical way how Mormon cooperative principles could work at the University of Idaho, and not just among Mormon students, Tanner was unwittingly assembling the bricks and mortar that became the thesis of *Great Basin Kingdom* and virtually all the other books in the Arrington oeuvre—namely, that Mormon cooperative principles were deeply rooted in American cultural history and could provide an effective alternative to the better-known American tradition of individualism.

Tanner's influence on the young Arrington did not stop there. Tanner was someone who we would call today a liberal Mormon intellectual. He had had the opportunity to study at the University of Chicago Divinity School, one of the finest institutions of its kind in the country, and he taught Arrington that religion and science were not incompatible, that the life of the intellect and of the spirit could coexist comfortably. From him he became aware of various translations of the Bible that opened up new and deeper meanings, and he learned of the literature of biblical scholarship and criticism. In short, Tanner opened Arrington's provincial Mormon mind to the larger world of Christianity: Tanner, he reminisced many years later, "taught me to be a Christian first and a Mormon second. That is, to put first emphasis on the Christian virtues, and second emphasis to the more unique aspects of Mormonism. There are so many Mormons who give first emphasis to the unique or distinctive doctrines and practices of Mormonism. And this is wrong, very wrong, if we are in truth restored Christianity."[6]

College is a time in which any serious student is bombarded with new ideas and new alternatives, and it is not surprising that most undergraduates change their majors more than once. Arrington was no exception. He went to college to study agriculture in order to become a better farmer. He became disillusioned with the idea, though, during his first year of agriculture courses because his professors seemed to be too concerned with the science of agriculture rather than with farming itself. The prospect of a second year of chemistry, which he had neither enjoyed nor excelled in, was the catalyst that drove him into the College of Arts and Sciences with a major in economics and minors in political science, history, and English literature. It was more than just a change of majors; it showed how much the role of the university had grown. Rather than simply acquiring a narrow, practical skill—farming—Leonard Arrington would gain a new vision through a broad liberal education.[7] Under the tutelage of Tanner and his new major professor in the economics department, Erwin Graue, Arrington's last three undergraduate years stretched his world immensely and propelled him to graduate school and a truly distinguished scholarly career.

Arrington's career ambitions were considerably facilitated by the fact that he was an excellent student, especially once he had settled in to his new home in the College of Arts and Sciences. When he graduated in 1939, he took his degree cum laude and could boast a Phi Beta Kappa key. Attainments like those open many opportunities, and he soon found himself the recipient of a Kenan Teaching Fellowship at the University of North Carolina at Chapel Hill, where he chose to pursue a doctorate in economics. Academic quality was, for Arrington, a major consideration in selecting North Carolina. Second, he was aware of a strong tradition there of southern regional studies. As a westerner, he was conscious of his own strong regional identity and thought the older tradition in the South could show him how to understand the West. Finally, he was aware of his own family roots in the Appalachian region of North Carolina and Tennessee and thought that study in the South would put him in closer touch with his own heritage.[8]

Going to North Carolina was a fortunate choice, not only academically but personally as well. For one thing, it gave him his first exposure to a racially heterogenous society. His father had worked well with racial minorities throughout his life and had taught Leonard to treat all people equally, but Idaho had nothing like the racial diversity of North Carolina. Arrington flew into his study of southern culture, reading its literature, attending musical and dramatic productions, and even working one summer on a cotton plantation. Also, it strengthened his Mormon faith by having to live, as he always had, as a member of a religious minority. There were other Mormons, at least in nearby Raleigh, where he secured a job teaching economics while still taking his own doctoral courses. In Raleigh he helped organize, and was himself elected president of, a new branch of the Mormon Church's Mutual Improvement Association. But largely he had to sustain himself in his faith, nurtured by the church literature mailed to him by his mother. Eventually, in Raleigh he met an appealing Baptist girl named Grace Fort, who was working as a hairdresser and who found it interesting to attend Mormon functions and to engage in long religious discussions with Leonard.

The entry of the United States into World War II in December 1941, disrupted everything. Patriotically wishing to help with the war effort, Arrington tried to enlist in the marines; unsuccessful, he then went to work for the North Carolina Office of Price Administration. Later, he was drafted into the army and prepared to be sent to the European theater. Quickly, he and Grace decided to get married and found a Protestant clergyman to perform the ceremony. Separated for the next three years, the couple wrote almost daily while Leonard was assigned to various posts in northern Africa and then Italy. Initially stationed in a POW camp processing Italian prisoners in North Africa, he eventually found himself utilizing his economics training in Italy, working with various economic reconstruction agencies. Ever the student, he used those experiences to learn the Italian language, in which he acquired a fair degree of fluency.

Perhaps most important among his army experiences, though, was the second of the three profound mystical experiences of his young manhood. One evening in North Africa he had just finished reading Dostoevsky's *The Brothers Karamazov*. Reflecting on the larger meaning of that great Russian novel, he concluded that "it is not theology but human hopes and conflict that concern us. Having gone through a great furnace of doubt in his life, Doesoevski came out with a great hosanna of faith. It was not so much a book about religious experience as it was a novel whose very reading was a religious experience." He sat down and wrote a long letter to his wife in which he shared those thoughts and then walked outside into the African night to reflect on what he had just read and written:

> I was still under the aura of the word-images and penetrating spirit of Dostoevski's masterful novel when suddenly I felt an exhilaration that transported me to a higher level of consciousness. The book, the writing, the mental pictures evoked by Dostoevski lifted me up into the Heavens. I felt I was absorbed into the Great Eye, the kingdom of the Heavenly One, the universe of the Holy Spirit. The experience was like listening to the finale of Beethoven's Ninth; or seeing a painting of the Madonna by Rafaello. I felt I was lifted out of the ordinary world into the beautiful world of the divine. I was sharing an experience like the beatific visions described by the mystics. That this experience would have followed the reading of a book suggested to me, as I reflected on it, that words were heavenly messengers, that I would derive pleasure in using them, and that engaging in speaking and writing was a heavenly calling. I vowed to be a teacher and a writer. I would prepare talks, articles, and books about religion, about the economy, and about people and their cares as they made their ways in life. I had fully realized the beauty and holiness of the word.[9]

Discharged in 1945, Arrington set out to continue the doctoral program that world events had disrupted and to establish himself and Grace in a marriage that had, to that point, been merely one of paper—a marriage license and a stack of love letters. Although he still had to complete a year of coursework before he would be eligible to take his doctoral exams, he realized that his most pressing responsibility was to support his wife. After applying to twelve different colleges and universities, he accepted a position in the economics department at Utah State Agricultural College in Logan (later Utah State University) at an annual salary of $3,200. Before leaving North Carolina, however, he proposed a dissertation topic on Mormon economic institutions that he could begin to research in Utah. He planned to pick up the remaining coursework at a later date.[10]

On June 22, 1946, the couple arrived in Logan to face a whole list of new beginnings. With the birth of their son James in 1948, son Carl in 1951, and daughter Susan in 1954, the family began to grow. Leonard was for the first time living in a Mormon community, where a majority were members of the church. Support from welcoming neighbors and a full spate of social and church programs, for which Mormon society is famous, no doubt helped ease some of the transitions into a new way of life. Grace, who had determined to divide her religious life between the Logan Tenth Ward, where Leonard was a member, and the Baptist church of her upbringing, soon became upset by the anti-Mormonism of the Baptist congregation and applied for baptism into the Mormon church. Noah Arrington performed the ceremony on September 15, 1946.[11]

Even with blue-ribbon graduate training and a promising dissertation topic, some eastern scholars, like Arthur H. Cole (who later steered the dissertation through the publication process), wondered how Arrington could possibly be content at what they regarded as a sagebrush institution. Cole, "a typical Harvard man, even offered to get me a job in a respectable eastern university," Leonard recalled, "so I wouldn't have to remain at that 'agricultural college out in where was it, Utah or Idaho or somewhere!' "[12] As a matter of fact, the Idaho farm boy turned academic could hardly have been happier at Utah State, and his affiliation with the university, which ended only upon his appointment as Church Historian in 1972, became one of the longest and happiest relationships of his life.

Displaying the apparently boundless energy for which he was already becoming famous, Arrington was in his office from eight to five, had an open door policy for students, went to lectures and concerts in the evenings, and attended all college functions as "a good citizen of the college." He had selected the position in Logan largely because of its proximity to the sources in Salt Lake City that he needed for his dissertation, and whenever he had a break in his teaching schedule, he took advantage of that location: "Each summer I went to SLC to do research in the LDS Church Library-Archives, leaving early Monday morning on the bus and returning Friday evening late on the bus," he recalled. "We had only one car so I left that for use by Grace." Nor did his academic work cease during his early years in Logan. "Let me explain that I was here in the capacity of a graduate student as well as a professor," he told Utah State alumni on one occasion. "I had not yet completed my Ph.D. and for two summers I signed up for research credit while I was working on my dissertation. And so I can say, quite truthfully, that I was once a student at USU—something of which I am very proud." A particularly valuable resource arrived in 1950 in the person of S. George Ellsworth, who joined the Utah State history faculty that year. Leonard was an economist by training, but as he now proposed to write economic history, he felt a need to bolster his limited history writing experience and so took a couple of Ellsworth's history seminars. Ellsworth's informal critiques and advice continued to be invaluable throughout his career.[13]

Being away from home and sojourning in cheap hotels in Salt Lake City were the least of the hardships Arrington had to endure while doing his research during those early summers in Utah. It taxed his patience and diplomacy to the utmost to breach the infamously unfriendly attitude toward researchers that prevailed in the church archives in those days under the administration of Church Historian Joseph Fielding Smith and his "loyal assistant church historian, A. William Lund."[14] Fortunately he had prepared himself by securing the encouragement and advice of Apostle John A. Widtsoe, himself an agricultural scientist with expertise in the very Mormon institutions and practices Arrington now wished to explore. Widtsoe advised him to insinuate himself gradually into the good graces of the archives administrators by asking to see only published material for a while, then theses and dissertations, then finally unpublished records. The strategy worked, and in time he gained access to almost anything he wanted. Lund's suspicion remained an annoyance, as he required that all researchers submit their notes to him at the end of the day for his censorship, but Leonard found that circumventing Lund's capricious criteria was ridiculously easy: "I made the notes on one of their Public Service typewriters and always made carbons. So I had the notes whether or not he returned them (he often did not return them), and whether or not he crossed them out (many items he did cross out, but I could see no consistent policy and thought it so arbitrary that I was sure he couldn't remember what he had approved and what he had not)." Others employed similar subterfuges, "carrying out notes in inside pockets, in their stockings and soles of their shoes, etc." In the end, "Brother Lund's system was an obstacle, an irritant, but did not impede or prevent honest and comprehensive research."[15]

Despite all the progress he was making in Logan, though, Arrington still had a year of formal coursework to complete at North Carolina before he would be allowed to proceed to his qualifying examinations and the dissertation. At what must have been considerable financial sacrifice, he took a year's leave without pay from his faculty position in 1949–50 and moved back to North Carolina. Grace and their baby James lived with her mother at her home in Raleigh (a favor the Arringtons returned many times over as they cared for Mrs. Fort in their Logan home during her old age), while Leonard spent his weekdays in a graduate dormitory in Chapel Hill. The actual coursework turned out to be easy for him because he had taught much of the material in Logan, so he devoted a good deal of time to preparing journal articles based on the research he had done for the dissertation. Apparently his faculty advisors had not previously seen a graduate student with so much energy and such an academic background: "I mentioned this [writing] to one of my professors (Frank Kottke) and he told me to quit that—to read for my writtens and orals. Well, I didn't follow his advice very well." By the time he got around to writing the dissertation, he had published seven professional articles, with no demonstrable damage to his preparation for the exams. "I did my writtens," he recalled, "with almost no special study—I had taught many courses in economics and felt I was pretty well posted on the literature. . . . As for the orals, it was the same. I had taught so much that I had verbal responses to nearly any question anyone could ask."[16]

During his last year in Chapel Hill, Arrington had the third of his mystical experiences that seemed to bear spiritual witness to his chosen destiny as a scholar of Mormon history:

> One afternoon early in 1950, sitting in a quiet alcove of the University of North Carolina library, I had what might be called my third "peak experience"—one that sealed my devotion to Latter-day Saint history. Going over my extended notes, recalling the letters, diaries, and

> personal histories of the hundreds of past church leaders and members, a feeling of ecstasy suddenly came over me—an exhilaration that transported me once again to a higher level of consciousness. . . . In an electrifying moment, the lives and beliefs of nineteenth-century Mormons had a special meaning; they were inspiring—part of the eternal plan—and it was my pleasure to understand and write about their story. Whatever my talents and abilities—and I had never pretended that they were extraordinary—an invisible higher power had now given me a commission and the experience remained, and continues to remain, with me. Regardless of frustrations and obstacles that came to me in the years that followed, I knew that God expected me to carry out a research program of his peoples' history and to make available that material to others. Whatever people might say about this mortal errand, I must persevere, and do so in an attitude of faithfulness. My experience was a holy, never-to-be-forgotten encounter—one that inspired me to live up to the promises held out for those who receive the gift of the Holy Ghost.[17]

Interpreting these three epiphanies experienced by the young Leonard Arrington is not the biographer's easiest task. The task can hardly be shirked, though, because they were profoundly important and even sacred to Arrington himself—so sacred, in fact, that he shrank from mentioning them in public and published his recollection of only the last one. One might speculate, in the first place, that a devout adherent of a religion grounded in the principle that revelation is a continuing, "latter-day" phenomenon not confined to the apostolic age would be more open to such experiences than a person of a secular or more traditional religious persuasion. Perhaps, too, such experiences were of especial importance to an insecure Idaho farm boy on the verge or in the midst of making a leap that would carry him professionally, intellectually, and even spiritually far from the secure traditions of his rural background. Those affirmations—of the validity of his place in the world, of the power and importance of language and literature, and of the grandness of the story of the Latter-day Saints—seem to have been essential spiritual and emotional milestones empowering him to make that personal and professional leap. Somehow those epiphanies seem to have kindled an interior fire that powered one of the most energetic careers in American historiography. They sustained him through discouragement and conflict with those within his own church who criticized his work. While there are notes of disappointment and even resentment in his autobiography and in his private writings late in life, they are ultimately submerged in his perennial affirmations, his optimism, and his confidence that he had done the right thing, that he had fulfilled the mission—he understood it as nothing less than that—to which he had been called.

What would the world have looked like to a young man training to be a professional economist during the late 1930s and 1940s? Certainly he would have perceived it as a place rife with problems, but he would also have learned that he was not the first economist to wrestle with those problems, and that in fact there was a rich literature and historical experience left behind by his predecessors.

One of the most enduring lessons Arrington garnered in his academic training was a deepening conviction of the dignity of the agricultural life and its validity as a field of scholarly investigation. That conviction was already lifelong and deeply rooted in his mind and emotions, but his academic work made him aware of various groups of writers, scholars, and intellectuals who held the same conviction but were able to give it an articulate expression and a scholarly base that as yet were beyond the young Idaho farm boy's abilities. By the time he left graduate school, all he had left to do was apply what he had learned to western circumstances and in particular to interpreting the Mormon economic system.

Leonard Arrington was caught up in the agrarian phase of an immense backlash against the social and economic abuses of the Industrial Revolution that had been building, first in Great Britain and then in America, almost since the revolution's beginning in the eighteenth century. In short, an agricultural revolution and an industrial revolution had fed each other, with great advances in technology, increased standard of living, and accumulation of wealth, but at the expense of the development of a vast urban proletariat whose long work days, low wages, and abysmal living conditions had generated the profits from which others had benefited.

The new industrial system was not without its critics, for as the Industrial Revolution transformed Western civilization, a bewildering variety of reformers arose on both sides of the Atlantic to protest its abuses and to suggest programs that would mitigate them. Beginning with Victorian reformers like John Ruskin, Thomas Carlyle, and Karl Marx, the backlash against industrialism grew and spread to the United States during the late nineteenth century in such forms as the Social Gospel, the settlement house movement, and the political and economic programs of the Progressive Era. Some of the reformers were very conservative, some were very radical; some were practical, others were quixotic. During his university and graduate studies, Leonard Arrington was exposed to a wide array of diagnoses of the new industrial system that he struggled to assimilate and to relate to western agriculture and to Mormonism.

The first major school of thought that he encountered at the University of Idaho was a conservative one. Changing his major from agriculture to economics meant that Arrington was placing himself under the tutelage of economics professor Erwin D. Graue. A German immigrant with a doctorate from Cornell, Graue was a proponent of the neoclassical ideas of British economist Alfred Marshall (1842–1924), a prolific scholar at Cambridge University. Marshall's ideas appeared in their most systematic form in his *Principles of Economics* (1890). Marshall was a free market theorist who believed that natural economic forces could be counted upon to control the production and distribution of goods and to regulate prices, wages, and employment in the most equitable way on their own with little or no artificial intervention by government. Marshall was a leader of a neoclassical school that differed with the earlier classical thinkers like Adam Smith, David Ricardo, and John Stuart Mill over the primacy of labor or the satisfaction of consumers' desires as the determining factor establishing the exchange value of products. The practical consequences of their theories, though, came to essentially the same thing: an almost Newtonian economic system of static relationships among primary economic forces definable by a regular system of laws.[18]

Free market theory had been considered a liberal idea in the days of Adam Smith, whose *Wealth of Nations* appeared in 1776 during the heyday of the Enlightenment. Smith and other Enlightenment rationalists had argued for the essential soundness of natural economic forces against the capricious, irrational, and sometimes ruinous state control of economies during the age of mercantilism. By Marshall's day, though, free market theory was being promoted by conservative business interests who used it to object to government regulation of prices, wages, and fair competitive practices. Often bolstered on both sides of the Atlantic by a Social Darwinism that held that economic leaders were the natural victors in the struggle for the survival of the fittest and that the poor at the other end of the spectrum were its natural casualties, the result was a callous and uncompassionate defense of the economic and political status quo.

Although Marshall remained true to his laissez-faire principles in opposing state intervention in the interests of economic and social justice, he was not himself lacking in compassion, and his book exhibits some obviously sincere agonizing over the lot of the poor in the wake of the Industrial Revolution.[19]

Marshall's hope for the amelioration of poverty and economic exploitation was not rested in individual or governmental activism. Instead, he held that inexorable technological advances were the tide that would raise all boats. Rather than widening the breach between the economic classes justified by the Social Darwinists, Marshall saw technological evolution bringing the classes together:

> The hope that poverty and ignorance may gradually be extinguished, derives indeed much support from the steady progress of the working classes during the nineteenth century. The steam-engine has relieved them of much exhausting and degrading toil; wages have risen; education has been improved and become more general; the railway and the printing-press have enabled members of the same trade in different parts of the country to communicate easily with one another, and to undertake and carry out broad and far-seeing lines of policy; while the growing demand for intelligent work has caused the artisan classes to increase so rapidly that they now outnumber those whose labour is entirely unskilled. A great part of the artisans have ceased to belong to the "lower classes" in the sense in which the term was originally used; and some of them already lead a more refined and noble life than did the majority of the upper classes even a century ago.[20]

That progress, however, was not inevitable, nor was the basic force that could bring it about, in Marshall's view, primarily economic. Development of a classless society characterized by economic justice depended, instead, "partly on the moral and political capabilities of human nature," as people chose to direct their energies to technological development and dissemination of its benefits among the populace at large.[21]

Free market theory was already under heavy attack by John Maynard Keynes and his followers by the time Marshall issued his last edition of the book in 1920. And by the time Leonard Arrington encountered Marshall in the mid-1930s, free market theory was seeming increasingly passé in the face of the massive New Deal spending in its attempts to ameliorate the effects and reverse the course of the Great Depression. Nevertheless, Marshall exerted a profound influence on Leonard Arrington.

In the first place, Marshall was an irrepressibly optimistic person whose sunny view of the future resonated with the optimism native to Arrington's Mormon faith. That faith was rooted, like Marshall's optimism, in confidence in "the moral and political capabilities of human nature." Although Arrington was much less content than Marshall to await the arrival of inevitable progress and often voted for liberal political candidates who thought that a little nudging from outside the process could help, he enthusiastically agreed with Marshall that progress was possible. Most progress, though, would not come from such outside stimuli as government programs, but would come from the daily unheralded efforts of individuals. Going back to Marshall's intellectual ancestor Adam Smith, Arrington pointed out that Smith's

> basic lesson was that no nation can be productive unless its people are individually productive. Productivity is not a function of government policy, unless government policy is simply to allow for the maximum of individual initiative and enterprise. Productivity is a function of intelligence and skill and specialization, and competition and coordination through the market. . . . The initiation of all wise and noble things, he seems to say, comes from individuals . . . and I take it as an article of faith that all the good things that are done can be traced back ultimately to individuals laboring faithfully and effectively, and sometimes the most effective contributors to the economy may be quite unaware that they are benefitting society at the same time that they are working for themselves and their families and neighbors.[22]

This kind of economic individualism was not at all inconsistent, in Arrington's eyes, with the celebrated regimentation of Mormon economic institutions and policies because all the church was doing was coordinating and directing the individual energies of its members.

Also, through his mentor Erwin Graue, Arrington learned a humanistic type of economics from Marshall in contrast to a more mechanistic, social-science economics dominated by mathematics, equations, and graphs. In his own teaching and writing, economics for Leonard Arrington, as it was for Marshall, was the study of people and of basically human relationships rather than of impersonal economic forces expressible in mathematical terms. "While there were lapses in Leonard's training under Graue, there were advantages," Arrington's biographer points out. "Graue was interested in human motives and in the psychology of economics. He taught Leonard to consider the personal drives behind the profit motive. During Leonard's graduate studies in North Carolina this approach was pretty much forgotten, but later—after the war, when he had begun teaching in Utah—he would rediscover it. He would learn during research for his dissertation that the Mormons had sometimes sacrificed economic expediency for spiritual principles, and he learned that society was not governed entirely or even primarily by love of money."[23]

One pregnant passage in Marshall's book offered a loophole in his basic skepticism of a planned economy, and it was a passage that, because of his Mormon background, Arrington could not possibly have missed. While man in his normal condition was primarily motivated by materialistic concerns, there was one case in which an altruism could be called forth to trump that materialism: "History in general, and especially the history of socialistic ventures, shows that ordinary men are seldom capable of pure ideal altruism for any considerable time together; and that the exceptions are to be found only when the masterful fervour of a small band of religious enthusiasts makes material concerns to count for nothing in comparison with the higher faith."[24] As he studied Mormon history, Arrington realized that he was studying an impressive example of just that kind of exception to the norm of materialistic motivation, in which the "masterful fervor" of the Latter-day Saints had led them to a point where "material concerns count for nothing" in their collective commitment to building their new earthly Zion. Although the young Idaho undergraduate could have had scant premonition of it at the time, it was the great theme to which Leonard Arrington would devote his distinguished career.

Later, at North Carolina, Arrington became acquainted with much more activist, even radical, diagnoses of the new industrial system than the laissez-faire passivism of Alfred Marshall. The first was progressive reform, which he encountered through the person of one of the great intellectual engines of the Progressive movement. Attending his first academic conference, the annual meeting of the American Economic Association in December 1939, Arrington arrived early at one session to get a good seat and happened to recognize Richard T. Ely, one of the seminal figures in American economic thought, then eighty-five years of age. "I . . . felt it a gift of heaven," Arrington recalled in his autobiography, "that I could talk with this short, pink-cheeked, boyish-faced man, who had influenced two generations of economists and economic policy."[25] Their conversation touched upon their mutual interest in the West and irrigation, and Ely spoke of the work ethic of the Mormons and of his admiration of their success in farming in the arid region, reminding the young graduate student that he himself had written a pioneering article about Mormon economic practices.[26] Fortunately, Arrington was familiar with the article, and later recognized that his dissertation "was merely an extension of [Ely's] pioneering work."[27]

What was it, then, that Leonard Arrington got from Ely? One of the basic theorists of the Progressive movement, Ely (1854–1943) was trained in the German seminar system of graduate education. He received a Ph.D. from the University of Heidelberg in 1879 and returned to teach at the Johns Hopkins University (1881) and at the University of Wisconsin (1892), where he was one of the architects of "the Wisconsin Idea," the reform program of Robert M. LaFollette, Jr. The Progressive economics of Ely and his Wisconsin colleague John R. Commons challenged the neoclassical theory of Alfred Marshall with the assertion that economics was the study of real-life institutions and practices rather than theories and impersonal, immutable forces and laws. It was a dynamic, activist economics that tried to get at the causes of economic dislocations and injustices and to ameliorate them through means such as government regulation, labor unions, slum clearance, and immigration restriction. The Progressive school, as one historian puts it, "found room in economics for social progress and even liberal Christian ethics; for this school, economics became, like everything else in America, purposeful."[28]

And, to the mind of the young Leonard Arrington, it seemed fully compatible with Mormonism, which held that all human institutions were malleable and that regimented group endeavor under proper leadership could create a new world order that would be nothing short of an earthly paradise. Proper leadership, indeed, was just as much an essential ingredient in Ely's Progressivism as it was in Brigham Young's Mormonism. Although Ely's economic ideas had profoundly democratic implications, he himself was no democrat; in his autobiography "he described himself as an 'aristocrat rather than a democrat,' and believed that the working classes must accept the leadership of an elite of intellect and achievement."[29] Ely had made the point explicit in his article on the Mormons that their economic success was in no way a vindication of democracy: "The agriculture pursued [by the Mormons] was irrigated agriculture, which for its success is dependent upon a compact society, well knit together. Individualism was out of the question under these conditions, and in Mormonism we find precisely the cohesive strength of religion needed at that juncture to secure economic success."[30] It is little wonder, then, that Arrington came to regard his work as merely an elaboration of Ely's ideas and to claim that Ely's Mormon article was "one of the finest ever published and still worth reading" ninety-five years after its appearance.[31]

Finally, it was perhaps inevitable that a young economist training at a southern university would come under the influence of the Agrarian movement. From its locus at Vanderbilt University in Nashville, Tennessee, the movement had burst onto the national scene with the 1930 manifesto *I'll Take My Stand: The South and the Agrarian Tradition*, an anthology of caustically critical essays by twelve prominent southern intellectuals.[32] As Arrington learned, the Nashville Agrarians were part of a long tradition of agrarian criticism. Common to that tradition was an objection to the dehumanizing forces of the factory system and the alienation of the worker from his work and a call for a return to an imagined idyllic past of small shops practicing artisan craftsmanship and small subsistence farms. The tradition found expression in the Arts and Crafts movement and the Distributist movement of Hilaire Belloc and G. K. Chesterton. "In its essentials," Chesterton's biographer summarizes, "the theory [of Distributism] was that the property of the nation, especially its land, should be distributed among the people of the nation, to replace mass-production industry by the local workshop in which the craftsman owned his roof and his tools, to re-create a yeomanry of England which had never existed in such a form except in romantic imagination, and by financial manoeuvres [*sic*] to promote the prosperity of the small shopkeeper so that the large, impersonal shop would gradually wither and perish."[33]

Obviously quixotic, the Distributist program bore every evidence of having been concocted over cognac in a smoke-filled drawing room by intellectuals whose hands had never touched a plow or a lathe. Wildly impractical though the Distributists' ideas may have been, their appeal to the "romantic imagination" was intoxicating, and the young Leonard Arrington, who read their works avidly, found in them encouragement for his belief in the fundamental soundness and dignity of rural life.[34]

The Nashville Agrarians were a more direct influence on him. When he arrived in Chapel Hill to begin his graduate work in 1939, Arrington learned that the ideas of the Agrarians had infused regionalist thinking all across the South. The South at that time was "going through a cultural renaissance," he recalled, led at North Carolina by the likes of the historian Howard Odum and the economist Milton S. Heath, who directed Arrington's graduate program. Heath "always insisted that as I became immersed in Southern studies, I should expect to return to the West and do studies of the economics and history of my native region."[35] Nor did he get from those mentors merely the idea that a study of southern regionalism could inspire a study of the regionalism of the West, for the Agrarians' "emphasis on the study of people, particularly rural people, represented an exhilarating movement away from the classical economics and sociology that had focused on the theoretical framework of the two disciplines to a concern with what was happening to people. It was a heady atmosphere for a young graduate student, former farm boy, from Idaho."[36]

The essential idea of the Agrarians was that the Industrial Revolution had introduced a consumerism that was fundamentally dehumanizing. Once the wheels of industry began to turn, they soon began producing goods in vastly greater quantities than the market could absorb, thus creating the necessity of advertising and salesmanship to create a demand for those goods. Fulfilling that demand led to a sort of wage slavery as consumers struggled to increase their incomes. The result was a vicious upward economic spiral, a road to nowhere paved by ever-increasing production and increasingly unfulfillable desire. The industrial economy, the Agrarians charged, "never proposes a specific goal; it initiates the infinite series."[37]

Agrarianism was one response of southern intellectuals to the South's defeat in the Civil War and the consequent mandate to abandon the region's perceived option, historically, to separate from the Union and establish an independent agricultural republic. Breast-beating about the "Lost Cause," those intellectuals saw, was useless; the cause was indeed lost, and southern energies should be redirected toward devising a strategy for rejoining the nation while yet retaining those traditional elements of southern life that had made it something uniquely beautiful and humane. One could be, as John Crowe Ransom saw himself, "Reconstructed But Unregenerate" in his determination to be an American, but on uniquely southern terms.[38] Arresting the national rush into that "infinite series" of production and consumption, the Agrarians realized, was hopeless, but they did hope they could call southerners to their senses and get them to recommit themselves as a region to their traditional agrarian way of life. "A farm is not a place to grow wealthy," thundered Andrew Nelson Lytle. "It is a place to grow corn."[39]

There was undeniably a romanticism about all this that appealed to the young graduate student, but to the budding economist seeking to get his intellectual feet under him, there was much to suggest a practical sense of direction as well. "The Agrarians-Distributists combined an agricultural fundamentalism in politics and economics with religious conservatism that somehow attracted me" he recalled toward the end of his career. "Not all were Southerners, not all were Catholics; but all believed in rural values and religious values. It was an approach that appealed to me. I also believed in agriculture, in rural values, in religion. My youthful experience on the farm, my work in the FFA, my Mormon heritage, and my training in economics all converged. Reading all of this, my mind was focused on my native region, the West. What could we do to prevent the wasting away that the Agrarians thought they saw occurring in the South? What could we do to preserve the values of the West that I loved[?] I hoped, one day, to get a chance to write in that vein."[40]

Upon his return to Logan from North Carolina in 1950, Leonard Arrington was confronted immediately with a pressing opportunity to write "in that vein," and he incorporated all the interpretive possibilities he had assimilated during college and graduate school. The filing cabinets of notes on Mormon economic institutions he had laboriously accumulated during those long summers in the church archives would be his foundation in that writing. It was a daunting task, and even his seemingly superhuman energy faltered at the prospect of turning it all into a doctoral dissertation while carrying out his heavy teaching responsibilities. Accordingly, he was granted yet another leave without pay from the college for a six-month period in the winter of 1951–52 to write the dissertation. One wonders what kinds of deprivations the family had to endure while no paychecks were coming in, but their faith in the breadwinner was vindicated, for at the end of the leave he produced the dissertation, "Mormon Economic Policies and Their Implementation on the Western Frontier, 1847–1900" and successfully defended it to receive his Ph.D. in 1952.

At the dissertation defense Milton S. Heath, chairman of the review committee, remarked that the committee members admired Arrington's Mormon faith, but were gratified that it had not affected his interpretation of his research. Moreover, Heath was impressed enough by the dissertation that he suggested Arrington submit it for publication under the auspices of the American Economic Association's Committee on Research in Economic History, a committee of which he was a member. Publication of one's dissertation is something all young Ph.D.s covet, especially one like Leonard Arrington who aspired to a serious scholarly career and was not content to see his first major piece of research and writing molder on a library shelf. Heath's membership on the committee would be a major asset.

Unfortunately, most dissertations are not publishable without major revision, and Arrington's was no exception. Admittedly episodic, it was a collection of eleven essays on various aspects of the Mormon economy and needed to be blended into a publishable narrative. In the end, Arrington realized that his goal was going to be nothing less than "an economic history of the Mormons, the first such work to describe the Mormon experience."[41] The goal was nothing if not ambitious, but the energetic young scholar proved himself amply capable of bringing it off. The result was *Great Basin Kingdom: An Economic History of the Latter-day Saints, 1847–1900*, one of the greatest single works ever produced on Mormon history and an acknowledged classic of western historiography that has never been out of print since its appearance in 1958.[42]

Chapter 3

Great Basin Kingdom

"A wonderful piece of research from which a splendid history could be written," was S. George Ellsworth's assessment of Leonard Arrington's dissertation.[1] It was anything but a startling evaluation, for only the rarest of doctoral dissertations are publishable as submitted without major revision. Arrington was well aware of his need for improvement as a writer and was already accustomed to relying on his colleague Ellsworth for help in that area. As he already had a publisher interested, he realized that acceptance of the dissertation would not be the end of his work on the project, and that many more labors lay ahead before he could hold his first book in his hands.[2]

That publisher was Harvard University Press, which had recently received a grant from the Rockefeller Foundation to subsidize the publication of books on economic history under the direction of the Committee on Research in Economic History of the American Economic Association. The subvention would be a godsend to a young scholar whose first book on a very large and unusual topic presented a financial risk to other potential publishers. Also, the readers assigned to the Arrington project included young scholars of great sophistication who would be able to help him improve his manuscript immensely, like Lewis Atherton, whose *Main Street on the Middle Border* would become a classic of small-town economic history, and

Edward Chase Kirkland, whose *Industry Comes of Age* would revolutionize our understanding of Gilded Age economics.[3] However, there was a snake in that garden in the form of a contract stipulation that all royalties would be returned to the fund to assist the publication of subsequent books. Even when the University of Nebraska Press issued what would become a best-selling paperback edition of the book in 1966, it did so under a contractual arrangement with Harvard that continued the royalty reimbursements. Ironically, then, Leonard Arrington began receiving royalties on the greatest book in Mormon historiography only after the University of Utah Press issued its reprint edition in 1993.[4]

Although still gaining confidence and competence as a historian, Leonard Arrington seems to have felt a sense of destiny that his research, if made coherent, persuasive, and literarily graceful, would be a major contribution to American historical literature. Getting it into that condition, though, would require a protracted period of uninterrupted thought and writing in which he would assimilate the suggestions of Ellsworth and the Harvard committee. Such an environment was simply unavailable in Logan, where the demands of the college, his students, his family, and his church responsibilities were constant distractions from his writing. Consequently, he was granted sabbatical leave from the college for the academic year 1956–57 at 60 percent of his salary. To supplement that reduced stipend and also to gain the kind of environment he needed to write the book, he won fellowships, each for half the year, at the Huntington Library in San Marino, California, and at Yale University. As things worked out, the Huntington decided to extend the fellowship for the rest of the year, and he never went to Yale. It was the first of two year-long sojourns in which he took his family to southern California where he imbibed the lively academic associations and well-stocked libraries of that region.[5]

Leonard Arrington thoroughly enjoyed a research fellowship at the Huntington Library. Private office space, enthusiastic and expert staff support, unlimited access to one of the world's great libraries and manuscript collections, and, not least, the noontime conversations with other research fellows and staff members made it a perfect environment for research and writing. Mormon manuscripts at the library, consisting mostly of items collected in southern Utah by Juanita Brooks did not prove to be a major resource for him, but the library's vast collection of books and periodicals enabled him to establish a broad context for the research he had done in the church archives and gave the book a much larger significance than the dissertation. Arrington completed one chapter a month and submitted the book in the fall of 1957 to Harvard University Press, which published it "with hardly any alterations" in 1958. From a manuscript that George Ellsworth a year before had said "was too detailed, it didn't have a central theme, and it was, to be honest, tedious and dull," Leonard Arrington had made a book that revolutionized Mormon studies and became one of the fundamental works in western American history.[6]

The thesis of *Great Basin Kingdom* is nothing less than a bold reinterpretation of U.S. history, a reinterpretation designed to situate Mormonism directly in the center of American culture rather than out on the fringes. In doing so, he had to buck a popular conception both non-Mormons and members of the LDS Church held of the Mormons as a "peculiar people," that their institutions, as their theology, represented something new on the face of the earth. "Despite their assertions of 'peculiarity,' much of what was done by the Mormons was truly American," he claims at the outset of the book. "Just as Mormonism often has been regarded as a typically American religion, so Mormon economic experience," to use the words of Thomas O'Dea, "presents a distillation, a heightening, a more explicit formulation, and a summation of American experience generally. . . . It was not only a Mormon dream, but the dream of many Americans to build on this continent a kingdom of God."[7]

What, then, was there about Mormonism that made it fundamentally American? Arrington poses two basic traditions in American culture: communitarianism and individualism. The former, of which Mormonism was a part, dates back to the Puritan Commonwealth and the Georgia Trustees of colonial times and to the communitarian movements of the Age of Jackson that directly gave birth to Mormonism: "Mormon economic policies could have sprung from nowhere but America—that fruitful, bubbling, inventive America of the 1830s. Each phase of the Mormon system was 'in the air.' A sister movement, communitarianism, drew inspiration from the same sources. The form of state action (that is, church action) envisioned by Joseph Smith was part and parcel of the Puritan democratic theory concretely expressed in the Commonwealth of Massachusetts. The policies bear remarkable similarity to those applied by the original Georgia Trustees."[8]

The other tradition was that of laissez-faire individualism, the every-man-for-himself ethos of the self-made man, which began coming to the fore around the mid-nineteenth century and burst forth in the unrestrained capitalism and exploitation of the Gilded Age. It was their commitment to the earlier tradition that made the Mormons a "peculiar people" in the American West, for it was that very West that became the theater of capitalist exploitation after the Civil War:

> The character of Mormon economic organization, as early as 1847–1849, and more certainly in the succeeding half-century, suggests the feasibility of regarding Mormon institutions as the more typically early American, and the individualistic institutions of other Westerners as the more divergent. The Mormon response to the problems imposed by the settlement of the Great Basin—a response which becomes ever clearer in succeeding decades—suggests that Mormon economic policies bore a greater resemblance to those of the ante-bellum northeast than did the economic policies of the West during the years when the

> West was won. Isolated as they were from American thought-currents after 1847, and under the necessity of continued group action to solve the many problems which plagued them, the Mormons were not affected by the growing accommodation to the private corporation, rugged individualism, Social Darwinism, and other concepts which account for the rise of laissez-faire after 1850.[9]

It was the clash between those two traditions, more than the existence of objectionable Mormon institutions like polygamy, that was at the root of the Mormon-Gentile conflict on the western frontier:

> It may yet be conceded that the well-publicized conflicts and differences between the Mormons and other Westerners and Americans were not so much a matter of plural marriage and other reprehensible peculiarities and superstitions as of the conflicting economic patterns of two generations of Americans, one of which was fashioned after the communitarian concepts of the age of Jackson, and the other of which was shaped by the dream of bonanza and the individualistic sentiments of the age of laissez-faire.[10]

Nor should Mormon communitarianism be understood as an anachronistic holdover from an earlier time, for "if the Mormon pattern was reminiscent, it was also prophetic. For it was precisely this pattern of central direction, cooperation, and long-run planning which, as the result of the failure of individuals, the success of large corporations, and the impositions of government, came to characterize national policy with respect to the West in the twentieth century."[11] In other words, as government regulation emerged in the late nineteenth and early twentieth centuries as the Progressive movement's means of restraining individualistic capitalism and later as the New Deal's means of reforming American economic institutions in the interest of the common good, Mormonism became once again a useful model. "Central planning, organized cooperation, and the partial socialization of investment implicit in Mormon theory would seem to have been a part of the democratic theory of the

Founding Fathers," Arrington observed. "Unquestionably, traditional American thought and practice sanctioned the positive use of public agencies to attain given group objectives, and this was, of course, the Mormon formula." Brigham Young was a harbinger of Franklin Roosevelt![12]

In all of this, however, one must not lose sight, as the Mormons never did, of the essentially religious basis of their institutions:

> After the settlement of the villages and the determination of property rights, the Saints were to proceed with the orderly development of local resources. This was a sacred assignment and was to be regarded as a religious as well as a secular function. . . . As explained by a leading apostle in an authoritative work, Latter-day Saints believed that the earth was under a curse and that it was to be regenerated and purified, after which war and social conflict generally would be eliminated and the earth would "yield bounteously to the husbandman." The City of God would then be realized at last.
>
> This purification would not be accomplished by any mechanistic process nor by any instantaneous cleansing by fire and/or water. It was to be performed by God's chosen; it involved subduing the earth and making it teem with living plants and animals. Man must assist God in this process of regeneration and make the earth a more fitting abode for himself and for the Redeemer of Man. The earth must be turned into a Garden of Eden where God's people would never again know want and suffering. The Kingdom of God, in other words, was to be realized by a thoroughly pragmatic mastery of the forces of nature.[13]

This essential unity of the religious and the secular, the idea of labor in the secular world being invested with a kind of sacramental quality as a working out of a religious mandate, is, as Arrington points out, something the Mormons got from the Puritans, but is also something to which they gave a uniquely Mormon institutional expression:

> Making the waste places blossom as the rose, and the earth to yield abundantly of its diverse fruits, was more than an economic necessity; it was a form of religious worship. . . . While it was a sacred duty of Latter-day Saints to purify their hearts, it was an equally sacred duty for them to

> devote labor and talent to the task of "removing the curse from the earth," and making it yield an abundance of things needed by man. Devices for converting arid wastes into green fields thus assumed an almost sacramental character; they served to promote an important spiritual end.[14]

"Converting arid wastes into green fields" as a means of "removing the curse from the earth" was indeed the heart of the Mormon plan. Like the Distributists and the Agrarians, their vision of Utopia was a rural society of small farms and villages grounded in an agrarian economy supported by small-scale industries. Rather than a decentralized political system, however, the Mormons advocated a centralized theocracy in which church and state were unified and authority flowed downward from the Prophet through the priesthood to the local level. Rather than a voluntary flight from the city and the factory back to the village and the farm, Mormon colonization of the arid West was a concerted effort, centrally planned and directed by the theocracy. As Arrington put it, it "was the directed movement of an entire new community according to the plans carefully worked out by church authorities, rather than the result of the spontaneous and independent movement of individuals."[15]

Central to the Mormon plan was the celebrated Mormon Village, an orderly community of wide streets, square blocks centered on garden plots and outbuildings and laid out according to the cardinal points of the compass, and houses set back from the streets and alternated so none faced each other. Unlike the winding lanes and the crooked streets of the quaint English villages dear to the hearts of the Distributists, the Mormon Village was a conspicuously planned utopian community. And unlike most other westerners since the prehistoric Pueblo Indians of the Southwest, the Mormons understood that community life in the arid region had to be based on equitable sharing of the limited water resources. Thus irrigation was essential to the Mormon way of life, and Arrington's description of a typical irrigation system is a picture of military regimentation that a Frederick the Great or a Napoleon might have admired: "On this cooperative nonpecuniary basis, water was diverted from a natural source into a general canal, and from that into 'laterals' and ditches which carried water to the individual plots of ground needing it. 'Corrugates' were dug next to each row to carry water to the crops. 'Waste ditches' carried the water from watered field to the next one below it."[16]

Nor was industry spurned, for even a primarily agricultural economy required supplies of clothing, tools, and building materials. Like the Distributists and Agrarians, though, the Mormons favored small, local industries in the interest of regional self-sufficiency instead of an ever-expanding factory system based on an artificial consumerism. To be sure, in Arrington's view, a premature rush to industrialize before the agricultural infrastructure could sustain it precipitated an economic crisis in Utah in the mid-1850s (exacerbated by insect infestations, harsh winters, and drought), but even though those early paper, iron, sugar beet, and other industries initially failed, the territorial self-sufficiency they sought was a sound goal.[17]

So what caused the downfall of the Mormon self-sufficient utopia? Self-sufficiency had never truly been a reality, only a goal, so the camel's nose of the national economy had always been sticking under the tent of the Mormon Zion. But in Arrington's view the Mormons proved remarkably successful over a longer period in exploiting those larger forces without being fundamentally changed by them. When the Gold Rush and the Oregon Trail brought immigrants through Utah in the 1840s, the Mormons sold them food and fresh animals, welcoming their money into the currency-starved Utah economy. When the federal government sent an army to Utah in 1857–58 to put down what it supposed was a Mormon "rebellion," the Mormon leadership negotiated a peaceful resolution and packed the soldiers off to isolated Camp Floyd west of Utah Lake. There they would have a minimal effect on Mormon society while yet providing lucrative supply contracts to the local producers and, as things turned out, a source of mules, wagons, and other supplies at cut-rate prices when they left the territory at the beginning of the Civil War. When the railroad arrived in the late 1860s, the Mormons negotiated labor contracts to help build it, used it to transport converts to Utah cheaply, and banded together in mercantile and agricultural cooperatives to assimilate outside economic forces on their own terms with minimal effects on the Mormon way of life. "The struggle for self-sufficiency which characterized the decade from 1858 to 1868 is all the more remarkable," Arrington points out, "because it was a struggle against 'normal' economic accommodation. Despite the built-in market offered by the federal army and its suppliers; despite the opening of mines and markets in neighboring Colorado, Nevada, Idaho, and Montana; and despite the contracts to construct the transcontinental telegraph line and other windfalls, Mormon leaders uncompromisingly held to self-sufficiency as the official policy of the church. They did not expect absolute economic independence, of course, but they did seek such a high degree of autarchy as to prevent closer ties with the outside world from producing changes in the essential character of their economy."[18]

Even if the impersonal economic stresses with which the Mormon economy contended during the later nineteenth century had been resisted successfully, it could not have held out forever, for consumerism, as the whole world is learning in our own day, is an all but irresistible force. "The ridicule to which the Mormons were increasingly subjected in the national press for their solidarity in establishing and supporting cooperative stores and industries," Arrington observes, "illustrates the degree to which the nation had come to embrace the apologetics for exaggerated private enterprise and uncontrolled laissez-faire in place of the traditional communitarian attitudes of antebellum democracy." Nor was external ridicule the only corrosive force against Mormonism's cooperative economy. The mercantile cooperatives, for example, succumbed to the drive for private enterprise: "The dominant tendency . . . was not the discontinuance of the cooperative as a business, but the gradual disappearance of its cooperative characteristics and its gradual replacement by private enterprise." Similarly, "With their petty restrictions on man's agency, the United Orders were neither popular nor practical, and they often produced precisely that disunity and division which they were intended to correct."[19]

As the Mormon cooperative economy was dying a natural death, the federal government administered a coup de grâce during the 1880s by stepping up its anti-bigamy legislation which limited the property holdings of the church and both disfranchised polygamists and made plural marriage punishable by prison terms. Although Mormon leaders held out valiantly for a time, the economic and social pressure eventually became too much. During the "great capitulation" of the 1890s, the Mormon Church abandoned polygamy, accepted national political parties, and even began embracing capitalism by seeking outside support for industrial development. In one of history's great turnabouts, the Mormons, who had "set down in the book of Western history the most stubbornly cross-grained chapter it contains," as historian Dale Morgan put it, within the space of only a very few years became the most patriotic and "normal" of Americans.[20]

Did the great capitulation mean, then, that the Mormon experiment in social and economic cooperation had been a failure and that it could now be consigned to a curiosity shelf in history's dusty closet while the Mormons now joined the rest of America in their individualistic pursuit of material gain? Not in the least, Arrington protested. Instead, as the Greeks had proverbially taken their Roman captors captive with the superior riches of their culture, so the Mormons showed the rest of the country the way toward rational management and exploitation of western resources. In the same sense that Brigham Young anticipated Franklin Roosevelt, so the Mormons anticipated rational central planning as realized by agencies like the Bureau of Reclamation and the Bureau of Land Management. Through cooperation, the country could achieve the greatest good for the greatest number instead of surrendering to rapacious individual aggrandizement. "As the waste involved in the short-sighted, unplanned, and ruthless exploitation of other Western frontiers became more apparent, the Mormon pattern became increasingly appreciated—became recognized as prophetic of the pattern which the entire West would ultimately adopt. . . . The design of the Kingdom, once despised as backward, is now part of the heritage which Americans are passing on to governments and peoples in many parts of the world."[21]

It is inherent to the nature, as well as a testimony to the greatness, of a pioneering work like *Great Basin Kingdom* that subsequent generations of scholars armed with sharper methodological tools, more recently discovered source materials, and the time to spend exploring in detail the subjects that the author had to present in generalities, gradually erode and reshape the original structure. Some books, in other words, are so good that they inspire the further research that leads to their own superannuation. Within that perspective, *Great Basin Kingdom* has perhaps held up better than comparable works that eventually have become like Shakespeare's "bare ruined choirs where late the sweet birds sang." In this choir, it is still the song that impresses us more than the ruins, for no other book has had the profound and continued effect on Mormon and Utah history of *Great Basin Kingdom*.

Arrington's *Great Basin Kingdom* is "great" in at least two basic ways. First, Arrington's quiet persistence in working his way into and through the archives of the Mormon Church opened our eyes to the rich depths of the sources it contained, sources that no previous scholar had been able to exploit that thoroughly. For many years one of the most valuable parts of the book was its elaborate documentation, which called attention to previously unknown sources and suggested promising paths for future research.

Second, it offered a bold new interpretation of Mormon history and its significance in the history of the nation, an interpretation that necessitated a reinterpretation of the national history as well. In that, it inspired the so-called New Mormon History with its reexamination of accepted truth in the light of research. If few subsequent works (including those of Arrington himself) have matched the interpretive creativity and empirical honesty of *Great Basin Kingdom*, there is no question that Mormon and Utah history are vastly improved by its example.

One of the fundamental difficulties in evaluating *Great Basin Kingdom* is developing a consistent definition of exactly what the problems were that the Mormons confronted and conquered. The Great Basin (and the Colorado Plateau, another major theater of Mormon colonization) is a widely varied geophysical province, parts of which present very tempting agricultural possibilities and other parts of which are as forbidding as almost any place on earth. In one passage, at least, Arrington recognized that diversity:

> The Great Basin region would seem to have been singularly uninviting to people fresh from the verdant hills and lush countryside of western Illinois. Ninety-five per cent of the land was either mountainous or desert. The horizon was broken by naked, flat-topped mountains, rugged and full of unearthly color and beauty. Between the few arable patches were vast stretches of sagebrush and bunch grass, populated with coyotes, jackrabbits, and rattlesnakes. . . . Travelers and explorers had avoided attempting to cross it; the Spaniards had refrained from settling it. Even the few Indians in the region were unbelievably primitive as regards food, clothing, and shelter. A few trappers and Mountain Men had camped, for a time, in its mountain valleys; but the entire region was, for all practical purposes, barren of civilized habitation at the time the Mormons arrived to establish their advance camp.

> As Fremont pointed out, however, the region did contain a number of valleys at the western base of the Wasatch where colonies could be planted. While these appeared to be hopelessly dry, for the most part, they could be irrigated with a magnificent array of mountain streams which flowed from the Wasatch and distending plateaus further south. The well-drained alluvial soil in the valleys was fertile, and the valley plains were sufficiently broad to support a considerable population.

The alluvial plain east of the Jordan River was characterized by "the almost complete absence of trees, a plentiful supply of potential irrigating water in the mountain creeks and streams, a number of excellent mill sites, the ample facilities for grazing, the fertility of the land as evidenced by the size of the grass and brush, the abundance of 'loathesome' large black crickets, and the large number of rattlesnakes."[22]

One wonders why it was, given that diversity of terrain, that those "people fresh from the verdant hills and lush countryside of western Illinois," would have found it "singularly uninviting." Given the existence of those "arable patches" (which in the next paragraph turn out to be fertile valley plains with "well-drained alluvial soil . . . sufficiently broad to support a considerable population"), who would have chosen to settle among the population of "coyotes, jackrabbits, and rattlesnakes"? Granted, to midwestern farmers accustomed to a climate with plentiful rainfall, the valleys would have appeared dry, but surely not "hopelessly" so, given the "magnificent array of mountain streams which flowed from the Wasatch and distending plateaus further south." Looked at historically, if the advance party of Mormons, who first entered the valley of the Great Salt Lake in July 1847, felt "hopeless" about their prospects, it must have been a fleeting feeling indeed, for they almost immediately set about planting crops and diverting City Creek to water them. Although throughout Utah history there have been defectors who, for one reason or another, have found the place inhospitable, geographer Richard Jackson, after surveying the comments of the early Mormon pioneers, concludes that "it appears that the Saints were basically quite satisfied with the general characteristics of climate, soil, grass, and healthful nature of the Wasatch Front in general."[23]

In fact, Arrington found himself caught between the myth of Mormon settlement and its reality, and he readily adjusted his description of the terrain to suit either need. The myth was that Mormon settlement was a matter of "converting arid wastes into green fields" and that the Mormons had succeeded in "colonizing and developing areas generally regarded as uninhabitable and uncultivable," areas in which "the aridity, the mountainous terrain, the severe winters, and the repeated invasions of grasshoppers and crickets militated against large agricultural production."[24]

The reality was that those fertile mountain valleys proved to be extraordinarily productive even in the face of the occasional drought, severe weather, and insect infestations that are inherent risks to Great Basin agriculture even today. To be sure, getting enough land under irrigated cultivation quickly enough to sustain the large waves of arriving Mormon immigrants made several of the early years in the valley of the Great Salt Lake a touch-and-go situation requiring food rationing. But Arrington himself reports that the harvest of 1849—only two years from the initial settlement—was sufficient to feed everyone already in the valley as well as the new immigrants of that year, and in 1850 the rationing program was ended. "A church epistle mailed in the fall of 1850," he continues, "boasted that enough grain had been raised in Deseret to sustain thirty thousand persons." As there were only some 11,000 Mormons in the West at that time, it was evident that unless that "boast" contained a really huge exaggeration, that "desolate valley" had produced an immense surplus.[25]

So the Mormon cooperative system of colonization, at least during its early years in the valley of the Great Salt Lake, met with considerable success.[26] But what kind of test was that of the validity of Mormon cooperation? With the fertile alluvial soil in the eastern reaches of the valley, well-watered by consistent and regularly spaced creeks flowing out of the mountains and the plentiful supply of the Jordan River in the valley bottom, almost any cooperative system of distributing land and marshalling water would seem likely to succeed. Yet throughout *Great Basin Kingdom* there seems to be an underlying assumption that Mormonism's theocratic regimentation was the only cooperative system that would have worked. The stark alternative, in Arrington's reading of western history, was "the waste involved in the short-sighted, unplanned, and ruthless exploitation of other Western frontiers." Forgetting his earlier thesis that Mormon cooperation was an outgrowth of a fundamental tradition of cooperation in American history, Arrington now seemed to see the Mormons as the *only* Americans capable of cooperative endeavor and the Gentile world as ridden with wasteful and rapacious individualism. "Considering the nature of the Great Basin, and the difficulties encountered in developing it," he asserted, "it is doubtful that a substantial degree of progress could have been achieved except with the aid and direction of the dominant church. . . . A group tightening-of-the-belt, facilitated by strong organization and cohesive solidarity, and attended by timely windfalls, made possible most of the investment which converted the barren wastes of the Great Basin into an oasis of beauty and strength."[27]

This idea could be called a fallacy of solipsism, because the Mormons settled the valleys of the Wasatch Front in a certain way, that is the only way it could have been done. Not only is it a betrayal of Arrington's basic thesis that the Mormon economic system represents "a distillation, a heightening, a more explicit formulation, and a summation of American experience generally," and that it was, after all "not only a Mormon dream, but the dream of many Americans to build on this continent a kingdom of God,"[28] it also ignores the fact that most great ventures in history, from the building of the Egyptian pyramids to the Panama Canal, have been cooperative and sponsored by a religion, a state, or a business corporation. Even in western history, the myth of the lone frontier scout or cowboy has to be tempered by the reality of the big corporate fur companies, the organized regimentation of the wagon trains on the Oregon Trail, the U.S. Army on the frontier, the Christian missions, the mining companies that took over the Gold Rush after the initial period of pick-and-shovel digging, and the building of the transcontinental railroad. Even the Milner Dam that provided the irrigation water by which the Snake River Valley in southern Idaho was brought under cultivation during Leonard Arrington's boyhood was an example of Gentile cooperation.

How well did the Mormon system do when applied to the really forbidding conditions elsewhere, the places where no one else wanted to settle and where, according to Arrington's claim, only Mormons could bring the desert to fruition?

Two fundamental Mormon principles affected population growth in Utah territory: the Gathering, the expectation that both foreign and domestic converts would move to Utah to join with the community of saints, and polygamy, which created large families. Together these contributed to dramatic population growth during the last half of the nineteenth century in Utah. Thus it was not long before even the impressive agricultural productivity of the Wasatch Front found itself hard pressed to feed the influx of immigrants. That, and the fact that Brigham Young sought extension of his Great Basin "kingdom" to some natural and defensible geographical limits, meant that expansion was an inherent feature of nineteenth-century Mormonism. Consequently, the Mormons before long found themselves faced with the prospect of abandoning the alluvial plains and river bottoms of the Wasatch and moving out onto the "vast stretches of sagebrush and bunch grass, populated with coyotes, jackrabbits, and rattlesnakes."[29] It was the first real test of the ability of the Mormon settlement system to bring to fruition terrain where only hunter-gatherer Indians had previously tried to live.

A few of those attempts to settle on marginal lands were outright failures, like the Elk Mountain Mission of 1855 which attempted to encroach on the Indians who were already farming the fertile bottomlands of Moab Valley where City and Pack creeks flow into the Colorado River. Refusing to move onto less promising terrain, the Mormon pioneers found themselves outnumbered and driven out by the Indians who insisted upon their prior possession. Not until the late 1870s did white settlers attempt to return to the area; and then it was individual hardscrabble farmers and stockmen who found ways to survive there, not the orderly colonization system of the Mormon Village.[30]

While Mormon settlers did establish permanent settlements in the Mormon Village pattern in other marginal areas, calling them "successes" is to stretch the term considerably. The "Cotton Mission," for example, which attempted to grow cotton along the banks of the Virgin River in modern Washington County as part of Brigham Young's plan for territorial self-sufficiency, did succeed in producing cotton, but never consistently and in quantities that would supply the whole territory. And the savage Virgin River, which repeatedly prevailed over the pioneers' primitive damming techniques, regularly washed out the farmlands during spring floods. Farther downriver, the Muddy Mission colonies were even more precarious, as floods, even more extreme summer heat, and unpalatable drinking water made life an endurance contest. Settlers there quickly abandoned any role in the cotton experiment and instead planted wheat, corn, and other crops that would help them make it on their own; building Zion might have been important, but putting food on the table was imperative, and on the Muddy Mission one could not always have both. Residents who were encouraged by enthusiastic reports from outside visitors noted that those visitors carefully timed their journeys to avoid the withering late summer heat and, as historian A. Karl Larson notes, "all the enthusiastic ebullience of the visitors did not make the Muddy any Garden of Eden to those who had to bear its heat, the malaria, and often other disadvantages. Many refused to stay there after experiencing the scorching rays of the long summer's sun." In 1867, the colony's second year, when reinforcements of 158 new settlers were "called" by church authorities to the Muddy, only two or three dozen actually went. "They came, they saw and heard," Larson says, "and left others to do the conquering; but even these too were crying for help."[31]

Nor was the San Juan Mission at the opposite, southeastern, corner of the state any more of a testimony to the efficacy of the Mormon village system. Concerned to secure that part of the territory from Gentile incursion and perhaps even federal invasion, Brigham Young was investigating the prospects of a colony there at the time of his death in 1877. Two years later, a party of pioneers from southwestern Utah was recruited by church authorities and assembled in Escalante to begin what the modern historian of the venture calls "an epic in the colonization of the great American West."[32] Epic it certainly was in terms of the endurance of the pioneers and their achievement in building a road across some of the most forbidding terrain on the continent. Calling it successful or even well-advised is, once again, stretching the language.

Explorers had previously identified two practical routes into southeastern Utah: the route through Moab Valley used by the Elk Mountain Mission and a route across the Navajo country of northern Arizona. But both of them were deemed, because of Indian resistance, too dangerous for all but very large and well-defended parties. Instead, the San Juan Mission scouted a route directly east from Escalante to the precipitous Hole in the Rock crossing of the Colorado River, then across the plateaus to the north of the San Juan River, hoping to settle along the river bottom at the mouth of Montezuma Creek. Although the pioneers succeeded, during the winter of 1879–80, in grubbing and blasting out a barely usable track to their destination, only the most starry-eyed sentimentalist (or masochist!) could have considered it a practical transportation route, and in fact it was so taxing that the party's energy gave out some eighteen miles short of Montezuma Creek, where they established the town of Bluff.

The picturesque community of Bluff is situated in a beautiful setting, but appearances camouflage the quality of farming life there. Like the Virgin River along which many of the settlers had lived in southwestern Utah, the San Juan was treacherous during its spring runoff and regularly wiped out the farms of the hard-working pioneers. Only two years into the venture, in 1882, Mormon Church authorities who visited Bluff acknowledged that the choice of the site for a colony had been a mistake and granted permission for the San Juan settlers to move up to more promising sites on the mesas to the north while still being considered faithful to their mission. Thus the communities of Grayson (Blanding) and Monticello came into existence. Even then, the greenbelt agricultural model of the Mormon village produced only a marginal existence in San Juan County until the 1890s, when Mormon cattlemen like Al and Jim Scorup demonstrated the economic superiority of cattle grazing to agriculture in that country and the economic base largely shifted from the farm to the ranch, as the individualistic cowboy in the forbidding canyons began to supersede the Mormon villager as the primary income producer.[33]

One certainly could not argue then, at least through the early history of southern Utah, that the average Mormon villager was enjoying a greater success in wresting a living from the canyon country than the cowboy, miner, or trader. On the other hand, even when one observes that the "success" of many of those Mormon settlements on marginal lands can be found only in their persistence rather than their prosperity, Arrington's thesis is not really refuted, only modified. Nor is it undermined by the realization that even that persistence is to be ascribed more to the dogged religious commitment of the settlers in the face of the most daunting deprivations than to the efficacy of the Mormon village system. If the Mormon system was not the only way marginal lands could be occupied, it was, nevertheless, *one* way, and that dogged religious commitment of the settlers was one of the essential features of the Mormon village everywhere.

Arrington's thesis is a good deal more defensible for the period before 1890 than it is when applied to the period of drought and depression between 1925 and 1939, when farm conditions really put the Mormon system to the test and the limitations of the Mormon colonization system on marginal lands finally became apparent. The changes that revealed those shortcomings were, first, a large scale shift from subsistence farming to staple farming for an outside market (which was, to be sure, a betrayal of the Mormon village ideal of self-sufficiency), and, second, a long-term phase of adverse climatological conditions that made any kind of farming impossible in all but the best regions. When agricultural prices plummeted at the same time farming conditions deteriorated in the marginal areas, the Mormon settlements in those areas were shown to have been overextended and untenable. "Environmental, sociocultural, and economic factors handicapped farmers and ranchers throughout the state," Brian Q. Cannon observes, "but most acutely in marginal agricultural areas: southern, eastern, and western Utah. Haphazardly extended beyond its environmental and economic limits, agriculture there began to flounder on its wobbly framework."[34]

Some of the factors in that agricultural disaster, Professor Cannon continues, "stemmed only partially from human land use: in a dialectical relationship society and nature had forged them." Insect pests, drought, and poor soil are beyond human control. Larger economic forces, too, conspired against the farmers' interest: "Among those problems were low farm prices, falling livestock and land values, and low production levels. Relatively high farm operating costs, mortgage payments, taxes, and irrigation and drainage expenses combined to further reduce farmers' and ranchers' earnings. . . . But regardless of their origins, the problems mandated sociocultural adjustments, including changes in agricultural practices and characteristics." Among those factors humans could have controlled, however, were "ill-advised dry farming, small farm size, and lack of range rights. Others were poor range management, improper drainage, ineffective irrigation networks, and overextended water resources." Social problems, too, fell under the realm of human control: "a population-land imbalance, insufficient or inadequate social institutions, poor housing conditions, and migration. . . . All of these practices pointed to the need for land use adjustment." Cannon suggests, finally, that Mormonism itself may have exacerbated some of those problems: "Mormons' large family size contributed to population pressure and kept the size of irrigable farms small, while Mormons' insularity and conservatism may help to explain why they had fallen behind Colorado and California in terms of irrigation and engineering technology by the twentieth century."[35]

Utah folklore has it that the Mormons were so deft in their management of nature that (no doubt with some divine help as well) they were able to make water flow uphill. Unfortunately, during the agricultural depression of the interwar years, they found themselves incapable of making water flow at all, nor could they control any of the other natural dislocations that were driving farmers into the poorhouse. But how about the human adaptations Professor Cannon enumerates? Whatever their skill in managing nature, the Mormons had excelled even more impressively in managing people, and it had been the church, after all, aided by pressure from population growth and encouraged by generally favorable climatological conditions, that had sent those farmers out onto that marginal land in the first place. Surely Mormon cooperation, the mechanism by which the Great Basin had been exploited, would now come to the aid of those victimized by the Depression, at least to the extent that humanly controllable factors were involved.

To some extent, the church did act, forming the Church Welfare Plan in 1936 under the leadership of President Heber J. Grant.[36] In spite of that program's successes, its benefits were to be seen only in the future, and in terms of the present disaster it was closing the barn door after the horse was gone. Instead, church members, at least, if not church leadership—and the state government as well—simply turned their empty pockets inside out and opened the door to federal aid: by the time the Depression came to an end in the early 1940s, only eight of the forty-eight states had received more New Deal aid than Utah.[37] Why? According to Professor Cannon, it was a case of persistence of Mormon paternalism and religious commitment: "In their efforts to eradicate these [agricultural] problems, New Deal reformers faced two common attitudes: expectation of government aid and religiously motivated tenacity to even submarginal land."[38]

The religious tenacity, as we have already noted, is a fundamental theme in Mormon history and in fact was the very glue that held the Mormon cooperative system together. Mormon colonies were missions to which people were divinely called, not volitional opportunities, and it was that sense of divine mission that sustained them through some of the most amazing deprivations in western history. Less easy to explain is how the Mormons, so accustomed to the pursuit of self-sufficiency and to the expectation of succor from the church during hard times, should so suddenly (so it seems) have transferred those expectations to the federal government. Great capitulation indeed!

Great Basin Kingdom, of course, contains only an embryonic answer to that question, ending as it does in 1900, well before the post–World War I agricultural collapse. In a later article, though, on the drought of 1934, Arrington attempts to bridge that gap: "Important ingredients [in minimizing the suffering of Utahns from the drought] were the expeditious responses of [Governor Henry H.] Blood, the effective organization put together by [Utah Federal Emergency Relief Administration Director] Robert Hinckley, and the cooperative spirit of the people. One national FERA troubleshooter expressed it succinctly: 'It was a great pleasure to finally fall into a state where there was no bitterness, no quarrelling, and all that goes with it.'" That same cooperative spirit, Arrington continues, "permeated the people of the state who, in the spirit of their pioneer ancestors, subdued self-interest in the cause of meeting the dual crisis of depression and drought." Why, though, did they regard it as natural to approach government rather than the church as the agent of that cooperative spirit? Because "above all, they [the Mormon pioneers] established a principle that happily is still with us—that federal and state governments, as agents of the people, have a responsibility to provide relief from disaster and, insofar as possible, maintain the economic health of the nation and its constituent parts."[39]

In other words, whether by the act of joining the Union or some other process of osmosis by means of which Mormon cooperative values have seeped throughout American culture as a whole, Mormonism has somehow redeemed America. Their "errand into the wilderness," unlike that of the New England Puritans, has succeeded, and succeeded to such an extent that even the federal government, once excoriated by the Mormons as their persecutor and invader, can now be looked to with confidence as the agent of broadcasting Mormon institutions and values: "As the waste involved in the short-sighted, unplanned, and ruthless exploitation of other Western frontiers became more apparent, the Mormon pattern became increasingly appreciated—became recognized as prophetic of the pattern which the entire West would ultimately adopt. . . . The design of the Kingdom, once despised as backward, is now part of the heritage which Americans are passing on to governments and peoples in many parts of the world."[40]

A skeptic would wonder how this process of redemption had taken place—whose cultural telescope had been so closely focused on the Mormon experiment and who had been so profoundly impressed by its success that it had become the basis of a whole philosophy of the welfare state? One wonders who, besides Leonard Arrington, had ever seen any Mormon roots beneath the New Deal. The only Mormon to have exerted any major influence on Franklin D. Roosevelt was Marriner S. Eccles of Ogden, and he was a banker—the architect of the Banking Act of 1935 and long-time chairman of the Federal Reserve Board. How central was banking to the Mormon village? Eccles's concern was the rejuvenation of American capitalism, not American agriculture. And the success of Mormon cooperation in dealing with the Great Depression had not been any inspiration to the New Dealers: what the Mormons had done was to hold out with irrational tenacity on untenable farmland until the New Deal cavalry had come charging over the hill. The Mormon village system had been a particular way of settling on marginal land, and in the final analysis it had not fared much better nor much worse than any other system; when the chips were down, all American farmers found themselves in a similar fix.

Nor was it Mormonism, by a long ways, that had first suggested that governments have an obligation to look after their people in times of economic hardship, for that had been a fundamental political axiom from ancient times: witness the pharaoh, at Joseph's instigation, reserving the surplus grain from the seven fat years to feed the Egyptians during the seven lean ones. Of course not every government throughout history had acted upon or even acknowledged that obligation, and even in the United States the prevailing philosophy of economic leaders like Alexander Hamilton and Henry Clay had seen government's role as a promoter more of capitalism and industrial development than of the economic welfare of the common people. During the late nineteenth century, responding to the social and economic abuses of the unrestrained Industrial Revolution, the Progressive movement began calling once again for deployment of government resources in the interest of the exploited classes at the bottom of the social and economic pyramid. And with the exception of Richard T. Ely and few others, the Progressives did so with little or no reference to the Mormon example. It is perhaps much better to return to Arrington's original thesis, that cooperation was a fundamental theme in the larger history of American culture and that both the Mormons and the New Dealers had grown independently from that root.

As indicated previously, part of the greatness of *Great Basin Kingdom* lies in the very boldness of its thesis, which entails not only a reinterpretation of Mormon history, but a reinterpretation of American history itself. Unfortunately, though, Arrington goes too far and claims too much for his material, for what he proposes is nothing short of a theology of irrigation, in the proposition that organized irrigation can effect a rejuvenation of human nature itself and, through that, a rejuvenation of an entire culture. Donald Worster points this out: "Morality, it would seem, as well as prosperity, was somehow produced by the technique of water control and management and the social relations it required. People learned to put aside their selfishness and greed, found themselves arriving at a more organic sense of community, felt more brotherly toward their neighbors than they had done back east where they had depended on rainfall to water their crops. At this point in the history of the American West," Worster concludes, "we leave the land of factual, objective, verifiable description, the land of economic statistics and crop reports, and enter the more spacious, intriguing land of myth."[41]

Even if we can find a way to regard such agencies as the Bureau of Reclamation and the Bureau of Land Management as Mormonism writ large, we have to question Arrington's belief that they have produced the kind of moral improvement that Mormonism seeks. As Dean May points out, that kind of "faith in the irrigation ditch as an agent of social regeneration seems in retrospect naïve and simplistic," and as Worster observes, much modern reclamation has seemed more to produce a wider scope for individualistic greed and environmental destruction than a new ethic of self-denial and cooperation: "Few among us confidently believe today, as our ancestors did, that producing more wealth of every kind is the highest way to serve God; indeed, that old materialism often looks nowadays like the quickest way to decadence and impiety."[42]

One has to wonder, too, just where we should look for evidence of this redemptive effect of Mormonism. While Arrington could claim, on the one hand, that Mormon cooperative values had so infused the larger culture that they were now emanating from the national government in its social welfare programs, at the same time he could see in his native Twin Falls community a particularly bad example of Gentile perversity in defeating Mormon attempts to build a better school system. While still working on *Great Basin Kingdom* in 1957, Arrington complained to BYU President Ernest Wilkinson that "whatever the degree of one's impatience with the state of things in Mormon valleys, he cannot help but note the contrast with a place like Twin Falls, where, even after their high school was condemned, six years and two bond elections were required to get a new high school built; where the only positive community improvement program is being fostered by the Mormon minority (a former bishop is now secretary of the Chamber of Commerce); and where a large proportion of the people find nothing better to do than get drunk on Saturday nights."[43] Magic Valley was obviously experiencing decline rather than progress, as measured against the day when Arrington had been a student in that very high school and boasted of the superior education he had received from his Gentile teachers.[44]

Finally, one of the hoariest myths perpetuated by *Great Basin Kingdom* is the myth of the Mormon village, the basic mechanism of Mormon settlement and the basic means by which the Mormon religion exerted its social and economic regimentation. Even today, a traveler who visits a rural Mormon community will be struck, as were the nineteenth-century travelers who saw the Mormon village in its purest form, by the obvious external manifestations of Mormon organization. The large square blocks, the wide streets oriented to the cardinal directions, the houses set back from the streets—all echo the Lombardy poplar borders, the orderly irrigation canals, and the "inside-out" granaries on the farm plots outside of town that are characteristically "Mormon." Unfortunately, that obvious physical orderliness has until quite recently tempted historians, sociologists, and economists to see the Mormon settlement process as much more uniform than it actually was and on that basis to make unjustifiably invidious comparisons with non-Mormon communities that are then treated as haphazard, ephemeral, and comparatively uncivilized.

The classic study that exerted a major influence on Arrington's thought—not only in *Great Basin Kingdom* but also in *Building the City of God*, his 1976 study of Mormon communalism written with Feramorz Y. Fox and Dean L. May—was Lowry Nelson's *The Mormon Village*.[45] "It must be kept in mind," Nelson admonishes, "that the City of Zion was essentially a Utopia. It was a community designed for the dwelling place of the Saviour, and of human beings perfected after the order of the Christian tradition; i.e., free from greed, selfishness, and vanity. It was the master passion of the Mormons to build this perfect city in preparation for the millennium which was imminent." Thus an ideal pattern was created from which deviation could not be tolerated. This essentially static view persisted through the 1970s when Richard V. Francaviglia extended it from the town to the larger landscape of Mormon settlement areas as well in the form of a mythical ideal he called Canaanville, an imaginary town embodying the common features of many actual Mormon villages he had studied. "Canaanville exists in the mind as a vision of one of hundreds of small Mormon towns in the West. The town is hardly, however, the result of imagination; rather, it is a carefully generalized concept which emerged from detailed studies of Mormon towns. The description of Canaanville is a description of many a Mormon town." Although he acknowledged that "the Mormon landscape . . . is an entity which is changing," it nevertheless "exists in various degrees. . . . The Mormon landscape stands as a unique entity, a conscious transformation of the geography of America."[46] The Mormon village, then, had become to scholars an archetype, a static rather than a dynamic phenomenon that was essentially the same wherever it was applied. It appears in that form in *Great Basin Kingdom*, illustrated by the "Diagrammatic Sketch of a Typical Mormon Valley."

Recent scholarship has sharply challenged the idea of the Mormon village, and thus the Mormon settlement process, as static and uniform. Much less research has been directed to challenging the uniqueness of the Mormon village in western settlement and the concomitant notion of its civilized superiority over comparable Gentile settlements.

Wayne Wahlquist, for one, casts doubt on Nelson's assumption of "a uniformity in town plats that did not exist, and . . . wonders if there was not more cultural diversity from village to village than he recognized." For Wahlquist, Francaviglia's definition of a "Mormon lanscape," is grounded in such fuzzy criteria that we are left wondering how many "Mormon" features make a town a "Mormon town," particularly in the light of the fact that most, if not all, of the communities he studied contained a significant quotient of Gentile residents. "Since it is highly unlikely that any settlement is 100 percent Mormon or 100 percent non-Mormon," Wahlquist protests, "the reader wonders exactly what constitutes a Mormon, part-Mormon, or non-Mormon town. Without more explicit information, [Francaviglia's] whole series of maps is of doubtful value." As a specific example, Wahlquist challenges Francaviglia's interpretation of the existence of uniform building materials in a particular town as evidence of central religious direction: "No evidence has been found in diaries of early pioneers that indicates people chose their building material because of any religious compulsion or even direct instruction or suggestion of Brigham Young. For the most part, they chose the building material that was most readily available."[47]

Nor does Wahlquist accept the myth of the settlement process itself as uniformly organized and centrally directed, at least in the Mormon Core area of settlement along the Wasatch Front. While Utah Valley was settled in such a centrally organized way, Davis and Weber counties to the north were "nondirected settlements founded by individuals acting on their own." With fewer than 10 percent of the families settling along the Wasatch Front doing so as a result of direct church orders, it is not surprising, then, that when those same families moved away from the Wasatch into what one might call "frontier" settlements, they "did so as a matter of personal choice rather than in response to a church 'call.'" As a general impression, "the frequency of individual choice in selecting the home community and the lack of persistence [mobility, he points out, in those frontier communities was high] stand in sharp contrast to the commonly held notion that families were told where to settle by LDS church leaders and that people stayed and made a go of it no matter how tough things became."[48]

Local studies of specific Mormon communities and comparative studies of Mormon and non-Mormon communities in similar environments have confirmed neither the uniform application of the compact Mormon village nor its superiority to less uniform Gentile settlement patterns in taming inhospitable regions. In his study of Mormon settlement in Sanpete County, Utah, Lowell Bennion finds a high degree of incidence of the compact Mormon village design only during the earliest years of settlement when conflict between whites and Indians was frequent and severe. By the late 1860s when the Indian menace had gone away, new settlements were commonly built in a dispersed manner and even the older towns began to disperse as well. Bennion even finds that Brigham Young himself encouraged such dispersion because of the greater convenience of settling along stream courses.[49]

Another geographer, Marshall E. Bowen, in his meticulous and innovative reconstruction of the history of two clusters of settlements, Mormon and Gentile, in the arid lands to the north and south of Wells, Nevada, in the early twentieth century, echoes the findings of an earlier comparative study of Mormon and Gentile settlements in Colorado by Evon Vogt and Thomas O'Dea. Those scholars show that the social cohesion of the Mormon communities in both cases gave them a distinct advantage in braving the rigors of dry land agriculture.[50] Incontestably, the positive community spirit promoted by common worship services, social activities, and the ready support of neighbors in difficult times was a significant psychological boost to the Mormons. In the end, though, as Bowen's findings indicate, such things were social palliatives rather than economic salvation, for neither Mormon nor Gentile communities held out for more than about fifteen years. They all collapsed at about the same time and for the same reasons: too many jackrabbits and too little water conspired with the disastrous climatological conditions and depressed farm prices after World War I to make marginal land agriculture unprofitable.

Both Bennion and Bowen encourage further local and comparative studies, and even casual glances at other instances of Mormon and Gentile towns suggest how fruitful such studies could be. For example, two neighboring southern Utah communities, the Gentile mining town of Silver Reef and the Mormon farm community of St. George, suggest a very different and much more complex picture of the proverbial contrast between the Wild West disorderliness of the Gentile town and the sober civilization of the Mormon one. Arrington's narrative in *Great Basin Kingdom* of the history of St. George and the Cotton Mission of the 1860s suggests some of that complexity, but the contrast is even less stark than he and the other Mormon historians of the area have indicated.

Nels Anderson, for example, one of the originators of the invidious contrast, refers to Silver Reef as a "shack town" because of its frame structures built on stone foundations, as opposed to the orderly rows of neat stone houses in St. George.[51] But one wonders, in the first place, why the Reefites, realizing that the economic base of their community was an extractive industry (silver mining) that would soon peter out, should have been expected to build for the ages? And when one examines plat maps of the two towns, it is very difficult to tell which is which, for the streets of Silver Reef, three blocks wide by eight blocks long, were laid out close to the cardinal directions and bore such prosaic names as Main, East, and West streets, much like a typical Mormon village.[52]

In terms of civilized amenities, Silver Reef during its brief existence (roughly 1875–85) was far ahead of St. George in several important areas. The Roman Catholic priest (later bishop) Fr. Lawrence Scanlan, for example, built a church in Silver Reef in the late 1870s (the first Utah Catholic church outside the Wasatch Front), and established a school in its basement staffed by nuns from the Holy Cross order. (Silver Reef had a public school as well.) Later, he built a hospital across the street, once again staffed by nurses from the same order and a trained medical doctor, Dr. J. T. Affleck, and supported by taxation of the mine owners—perhaps the first public health care system in the territory. St. George at the same time had no hospital, and medical care was provided by various naturopathic practitioners of the herbal medicine and folk cures developed by Samuel Thompson (1796–1843). It was only after Silver Reef was abandoned in the mid-1880s that St. George acquired its first doctor—the selfsame Dr. Affleck, who moved over from Silver Reef. St. George schools were staffed—when they existed at all—by various volunteer teachers who often had little more education than their students.[53]

Even the economy of St. George proved almost as ephemeral as that of Silver Reef. As Arrington points out, the Cotton Mission did succeed in growing cotton, but it was never profitably manufactured or even produced in quantities that vindicated the venture. Despite heavy monetary subsidies from wealthier Mormons in northern Utah, the cotton experiment expired within a decade.[54] Unlike the miners at Silver Reef, of course, the Mormons at St. George had farming to fall back on.

Ironically, one of the most profitable resources of the Cotton Mission was the manufacture of wine to be sold, in large part, in Silver Reef. Infamous for its poor quality, it was, according to the trader Don Maguire who visited Silver Reef twice during its heyday in 1878–79, "a villainous stuff, containing about as much of the juice of the yellowjacket and wasps as it does of the grape. . . . So rascally is the nature of this drink that people of Arizona and Nevada claim that a man who drinks a quart of it will get up in the night and steal his own clothes."[55] Leonard Arrington, while acknowledging the terrible quality of the wine, points out that it was a major economic resource for struggling Washington County and calculates that Dixie wineries were producing about three thousand gallons a year at the end of the 1870s.[56] One could say, in fact, that the Silver Reef Gentiles provided a market for Mormon agriculture that made the Mormon village economy much more profitable—and thus successful—than it would have been otherwise. One Mormon historian of Washington County, Marietta M. Mariger, goes so far as to assert that Silver Reef "saved a colony" (the Cotton Mission) by bringing the capital, the freighting, and the markets that enabled the Mormon colonists to develop economic diversity that pulled them out of the agricultural poverty in which they had seemed to be stuck. Eventually, of course, the railroad network that spread throughout the territory and linked those rural settlements to a larger economy guaranteed the success and sustainability of the Mormon village system.[57]

The overall quality of life in any community is to some degree in the eye of the beholder, but the facts examined here indicate that St. George was not exactly the agrarian utopia some Mormon historians have tried to make it out to be, nor was Silver Reef the hellhole they have portrayed. Don Maguire, once again, thought the balance leaned rather heavily the other way: Silver Reef, he said, was "so neat, so clean, so thrifty . . . that I was reluctant to leave it. I knew that its thoroughly civilized and American-like expression would contrast favorably with the Mormon towns of southern Utah, and that it would be like passing through a foreign land until we reached the Colorado River."[58]

Post-Arrington research and reflection has tended toward a blurring of the vivid distinctions he drew between Mormon and Gentile institutions and even values, though most of his distinctions have to be drawn by inference rather than direct comparison. In view of the immense advancement of understanding of Mormon history and institutions that *Great Basin Kingdom* brought us, it seems most ungrateful to expect that Arrington would have sharpened that understanding further by offering such comparisons and contrasts. And yet that is exactly what we need in order to appreciate the Mormon experience fully, for *Great Basin Kingdom* is a duet with one part missing. Fortunately, while many scholars seem to have thrown up their hands and chosen to regard the book as the last word on Mormon history, others have found its thesis clear, compelling, and yet challenging. The latter group has tried to test, to amplify, and to modify Arrington's thesis in the interest of developing a more precise understanding of Mormon history and its exact place in the larger context of western history. Consequently, the primary voice in that duet is being more clearly articulated while the counterpart of the other voice is becoming audible as well.

Some of what we would now regard as shortcomings of *Great Basin Kingdom* must be ascribed to the shortcomings of the secondary literature with which Arrington had to work in the 1950s. As we have seen, the concept of the Mormon village as the primary institution of Mormon colonization, for example, was at that time static, uniform, and universal. Unless he had had the time to test that literature through studies of the settlement patterns in specific local communities—which of course he did not—there is no way he could have appreciated the large variations that in fact existed.

Lacking the empirical studies that would have revealed such

complications, Arrington tended to exaggerate the degree to which Mormon cooperation existed and the accomplishments it achieved; at the same time, he failed to appreciate the potential of Gentile cooperation under political, corporate, or voluntaristic direction, which was manifest in many historical examples. Thus he tends to overvalue the Mormon achievement in settling the fertile and well-watered Wasatch Front where almost any type of cooperation would have succeeded. At the same time, he overestimates the success of Mormon colonization in marginal areas where in fact the Mormons were able to hold on to a precarious existence only through their dogged religious commitment rather than through any superiority of their economic and social institutions. Even then they succeeded only under near-ideal weather conditions; when things turned bad (one could almost say "returned to normal") both Mormon and Gentile settlements went under.

Likewise the literature on the "Gentile" settlement of the West perhaps exaggerated the Wild West elements in western history at the expense of the more sober and less colorful elements. There is no question that trapper rendezvous, cattle towns, and mining camps, which were populated by young, single men with few restraints on their materialistic and libidinous drives, could be infamously uncivilized places. However, it is also true that that phase of western settlement passed fairly quickly, yielding almost everywhere to families and stable institutions of civilization. And the eye of the beholder is a vital factor as well: while Mormon righteousness could be offended by the saloons, gambling emporia, and other "conveniences for sinners" in the mining town, it was all too easy to ignore the schools, the hospital, the opera house, the newspaper, and other conveniences for the civilized.

There is much that is easy to admire about the Mormon experience, both in the pages of *Great Basin Kingdom* and in the larger literature of Mormon history: the initial migration of the Mormon people from the Midwest under the creative, if autocratic, leadership of Brigham Young; the organization of the handcart companies of the 1850s and the church trains of the 1860s; the cooperative movement following the coming of the railroad that enabled the Mormons to assimilate the products, both material and cultural, of the outside world at their own rate; and the dedication of the rank and file to their church and its leaders, manifested in their acceptance of calls to colonize some truly forbidding regions—these and many other aspects of Mormon history call forth the ready admiration of Mormon and Gentile alike. Arrington should have rested from his labors after making those points and describing in such rich detail how those accomplishments came about. But in overstating the unique efficacy of Mormon institutions and in attempting to make a larger theological point of them—that irrigation made a better person, and that Mormonism had redeemed a selfish and materialistic nation by pointing the way to the welfare state—Arrington was simply overreaching anything his material could support. As Donald Worster points out, claims like those put us into the misty realm of mythology. The reality, expertly narrated in *Great Basin Kingdom*, is captivating, inspiring, and significant enough.

Chapter 4

Church Historian

Ironically, when *Great Basin Kingdom* was published in 1958, Leonard Arrington was lecturing in Italy on a Fulbright teaching fellowship. Consequently, he did not see a copy of his magnum opus until his return home in 1959, nor was he more than dimly aware of the enthusiasm with which the book had been greeted by reviewers.

His entire family accompanied him to Italy, and the year abroad turned out to be a wonderful cultural experience for all. The children, ranging in age from ten to four, began learning the Italian language, while Grace enjoyed the museums, concerts, and shopping. Leonard delivered lectures in his wartime Italian, first writing them out in English, then translating them with the help of a graduate student who polished his grammar and style.

Upon his return to Logan for the 1959–60 academic year, Arrington found himself the center of scholarly celebration for having written a book that almost everyone recognized as an instant classic, a book that found an immediate place in the classroom and that set the standards for scholarship in Mormon history for the next generation. Even the great western historian Dale L. Morgan, who wrote the only review that one could call negative (he scored Arrington for slighting the pre-Utah period of Mormon history and for neglecting the Gentile influence on Mormon economic history), nevertheless had high praise for the book: "I cannot imagine that anyone seriously interested in

Leonard Arrington and his first wife, Grace, with their three children.
Special Collections and Archives, Merrill Library, Utah State University.

Mormon history," he wrote, "whether as reader or practicing scholar, will be able to do without it, for *Great Basin Kingdom* is a massive ordering of data about the Mormons."[1] Although the path ahead was not even dimly visible in 1959, the reputation Arrington gained through the success of his first and greatest book would eventually lead to his appointment as official historian of the Church of Jesus Christ of Latter-day Saints.

In the meantime, though, Arrington threw himself with his characteristic energy back into his teaching, his church involvements, and his scholarship.[2] In the latter arena, in order to help finance the writing of more history, he began arranging contracts with various patrons to write what became a succession of biographies of Mormon historical figures, including pioneers Charles Coulson Rich and Edwin D. Woolley, the entrepreneur David Eccles, and Utah governor William Spry, among others. To enable him to undertake those projects while carrying out his grueling teaching and church responsibilities, Arrington began the practice of subcontracting much of the research and writing to graduate students and other assistants—a practice that would continue, as some of the projects themselves continued, during his tenure as Church Historian. Generally the money for the project was transferred through a university trust fund, out of which both Arrington and his assistants were paid. The books appeared under the authorship of Arrington alone, but the assistants' work was both honestly and gratefully acknowledged. Those and Arrington's other biographies will be discussed more fully in the following chapter. None of those projects, however, had the power to propel his scholarly career in the creative, original direction toward which his great first book had pointed. How could he follow up on *Great Basin Kingdom*?

Extending his study in the form of a sequel that would cover Mormon economic history in the twentieth century might have been an obvious answer. As quickly as that idea came up, though, he recoiled from it. "I do not think it is practical," he wrote to fellow historian Rodman Paul, who was a western manuscripts scout for Alfred A. Knopf, "to write a history of the Mormons since 1900 as a kind of sequel to Great Basin Kingdom. Before this can be done, many monographs must be written—histories of individual enterprises, missions, organizations, businesses, etc. The records of all of these are scattered and I do not think that one person could obtain access to all of them nor do I think it would be possible to research all of this from the primary materials in less than four or five years. Instead, what we need is a series of individual studies—dissertations, theses, and so on. Then a masterful synthesizer can come in to put the story together."[3] *Great Basin Kingdom*, of course, had occupied him for a lot more than "four or five years," so it was clearly not just the time required that intimidated him; rather, he had a vivid memory of the arduous labor involved in creating such a synthesis largely from scratch and saw the immense advantages of recruiting others to help with that groundwork.

This interpretation is borne out by the nature of alternative projects he proposed that were equally ambitious in scope but could be based in larger part on secondary literature. One such idea came forth when he was approached by Merrill Jensen about a position at the University of Wisconsin. Responding to Jensen's concern that Mormon history might be too narrow a specialization for the history department at Wisconsin, Arrington pointed out that "my interests do run beyond the field of Mormon studies; in fact, my Great Basin Kingdom, as you probably noted, was basically an attempt to see beyond the Mormon story into the economic development of the West. I have felt that as I broadened my research, I should like to do next an economic history of the West—meaning the area west of Kansas, let us say; perhaps the trans-Mississippi west."[4] Such a project would probably take longer than "four or five years," but enough spadework had been done already that it would not have to be planted entirely in virgin soil. Another of Arrington's ideas embraced Mormon history exclusively but in a more general scope: "The consensus of my colleagues," he wrote to Rodman Paul, "is that I should attempt a one volume history of the Mormons from 1830 to 1970, which would be geared to possible use in university classes in the American West, American Civilization, etc. This would be a 'new type' history, rephased [*sic*] in matter. It would give more emphasis to the activities of the Mormons, than of developments within the Mormon church. It would include political, economic, social, and cultural developments, as well as theological and intellectual. It would minimize such matters as organizational changes, changes in doctrine, and the well-warned [*sic*] conflicts between Mormon officials and the Federal Government. It would represent an attempt to see Mormon developments from the standpoint of the average pioneer or member."[5] In its embryonic form, this is the book that became *The Mormon Experience*, written with Davis Bitton in 1979. It was the idea for this book that led to the creation of the History Division in the Church Historical Department, over which Arrington would preside as Church Historian.[6]

Arrington's initial plans, which he had discussed with fellow Mormon historians at least as early as 1966, did not extend to the idea of a whole new department within the church, but rather for granting a select group of scholars open access to the church archives, the same kind of access he had enjoyed while working on *Great Basin Kindgom*. That access would lead to the writing of a series of ground-breaking monographs that would support the kind of general syntheses that Arrington shrank from creating on his own. He and S. Lyman Tyler, director of libraries at Brigham Young University, hoped that the series could be published with the aid of subventions from that university. He breathlessly described the idea to Thomas G. Alexander, a fellow Mormon historian with an energy and a spacious vision almost equal to his own:

> Incidentally, Lyman Tyler and I have been trying to work out a plan whereby "senior scholars"—i.e., L.D.S. historians with Ph.D.s—such as yourself, Jim Allen, etc., etc.—could have access to all the documents in the Church Historian's Office, and work without restriction. We are making some headway with this and hope to be able to announce the plan during the winter. It will include only a limited number of people—only a dozen people, perhaps, in whom the church has confidence; and for that reason it will have to remain confidential. I talked to Jim Allen about it at Portland, and if you will ask him he will tell you all that I know about it.[7]

Keeping the project secret, one speculates, would save church officials from having to explain what would inevitably be perceived by excluded scholars as a capricious policy, though as a private institution the Mormon Church has every right to pursue whatever archival policies it wishes, even capricious ones.

The steps by which Arrington's research plans led to a restructuring of the church's historical department and his appointment as Church Historian are well documented in his autobiography and need only a general summary here. The central figure, besides Arrington, was Apostle N. Eldon Tanner, a Canadian businessman and politician who had been appointed Second Counselor to LDS President David O. McKay in 1963. Tanner had at least two appealing attributes to Mormon historians: he was interested in history and thought it was an important avenue to establishing an institutional memory and identity, and he was committed to professionalism, believing that specialists understood their fields better than anyone else and should be left alone to do their job. Elder Tanner began meeting with Lyman Tyler shortly after his appointment to learn what historians could do for the church and what their concerns were about access to the materials they needed to do their job. Arrington began attending their meetings in 1966. In 1967 he wrote Elder Tanner to inform him of Alfred A. Knopf's interest (expressed through Rodman Paul) in publishing a general history of the Mormons, and he asked for unlimited access to the church archives to research the project. On January 17 the church's governing body, the First Presidency, approved the project and officially opened the archives to Arrington.

When President McKay died at the beginning of 1970, his successor was the former Church Historian Joseph Fielding Smith. This meant that the historian's position was now vacant. Traditionally, the Church Historian was a member of the Quorum of the Twelve, and Elder Howard W. Hunter, although he was not a professional historian, was chosen for the position. However, Elder Hunter, who was a friend and former stake president of Arrington's, "took his appointment seriously," as Arrington recalled.[8] On August 24, 1970, he formed a committee of prominent Mormon historians to discuss a reorganization and professionalization that led to creation of the History Division within the church's Historical Department. Among the committee's recommendations were the establishment of a professional advisory board, the appointment of a professional historian as Elder Hunter's assistant, the funding of fellowship grants for research by outside historians, and the writing of a new multivolume history of the church to celebrate its sesquicentennial anniversary in 1980.[9]

From a historian's point of view, one of Elder Hunter's most endearing qualities was his realistic understanding of his background and abilities. Realizing he was no historian, and excited by the prospect of having a true professional in charge of his department, he happily relinquished that responsibility as part of the proposed reorganization. On January 5, 1972, Apostle Tanner called Arrington to a meeting to discuss the reorganization, and to his surprise Arrington found himself being offered the position of Church Historian. Eventually three divisions were created out of the Historical Department: the History Division under Arrington's direction; the Archives Division under Earl Olson; and the Library Division under Don Schmidt. (In 1974 an Arts and Sites Division was added under the directorship of Florence Jacobsen.) Initially the entire Historical Department was entrusted to Elder Alvin Dyer as managing director. One half of Arrington's position was to be funded by the church and the other half by an appointment to a newly created endowed chair at Brigham Young University (BYU). Similarly, Arrington was allowed to appoint two assistants, James B. Allen and Davis Bitton, whose positions were also half funded by their academic institutions, BYU and the University of Utah, respectively.

Reorganization of the Historical Department was a happy day for Leonard Arrington, a happy day for Mormon history, and in fact a happy day for history generally, for it signaled a new openness and a new professionalization that stood in contrast to the often suspicious demeanor and capricious policies of Joseph Fielding Smith and Will Lund, manager of the archives' search room. Arrington's papers reveal that it was an especially welcome opportunity for him, for he had for some time been looking for a chance to strike out in a new scholarly direction. Although in later years he was always effusive in his recollections of his long affiliation with Utah State University (USU), after twenty years on its faculty he had begun to feel that he had reached an end to his usefulness there and that his ties to the institution were becoming restrictive instead of productive. The university had allowed Arrington a leave of absence to finish his doctoral coursework; the Huntington fellowship to write *Great Basin Kingdom*; the Fulbright fellowship in Italy; and the sabbatical replacement for John W. Caughey at UCLA. Nevertheless, the grueling teaching schedule (together with his church duties which, to be sure, were not the fault of the university) kept him from being able to consider research projects on the scale of *Great Basin Kingdom*.

As early as 1959, while on his Fulbright fellowship in Italy, Arrington was making plans to leave Logan and, as we have seen, was seriously entertaining a move to Wisconsin, among other places. "We are probably committed to return to Utah State during the coming year—at least morally committed," he wrote to Merrill Jensen, "and I suspect it would be a psychological mistake for me and the family to make a move this year. However, we shall be interested in other offers for the following year. We have reached the point in Logan where we shall have to build a

Davis Bitton (*left*) with Leonard Arrington.
Bitton was Assistant Church Historian
and coauthor with Arrington of *The Mormon Experience.*
Special Collections and Archives, Merrill Library, Utah State University.

new house in another year. We shall make the break with Utah State next year (that is, for the year 1960 and beyond) or never. Frankly, I don't see much future there unless something develops during the next year. They have no sizeable graduate program, and there are few majors to work with even at the undergraduate level. I have chances to go to Brigham Young University and the University of Utah, where opportunities would be better. We may also decide to investigate the possibilities at Berkeley, Stanford, and U.C.L.A. We have always been interested in California, but have never volunteered."[10]

By 1971 those constricting opportunities at USU had almost convinced Arrington to accept the chair endowed at BYU by Utah cattleman Charles Redd (whose biography he would later write), a chair which Redd had funded with the contingency that it be given to Arrington. In a despondent diary entry he gave several reasons drawing him to that decision. As an economics professor he felt he had no future at USU: enrollment in his classes was very low, and he suspected that the students he did have had been sent there by other professors who just wanted to protect his job. In twenty-five years he had directed only three master's programs in economic history (though he had directed many more in economics). Also, he felt alienated from his own field because of its shift to econometrics, which he never understood and did not find interesting. He saw his life as a teacher of economics and economic history coming to an end. The USU library was limited in size, and the acquisitions staff did not seem interested in supporting him. And finally, he offered the perennial complaint of the humanist: "We seem to be more interested in pushing athletics and engineering than regional western history."[11] There was a push as well as a pull behind Arrington's move to Salt Lake City.

As mentioned earlier, a basic motive behind the reorganization leading to Arrington's appointment as Church Historian seems to have been a trend toward professionalization. As Davis Bitton speculates, "Apparently it was part of a recognition in many of the Church departments that experts should take over specialized functions, leaving the General Authorities free to exercise their role as spiritual leaders and as traveling ambassadors rather than being bogged down in departmental responsibilities. One can guess, too," Bitton continues, "that at least some previous Church Historians recognized that they simply did not have the training or the credentials to be historians. They had administered as well as they could, given the many demands on their time, but here was an opportunity for a recognized historian to show what could be done."[12] The historian Douglas Alder sees the new professionalization as a belated response to Fawn Brodie's unflattering 1945 biography of the Mormon prophet Joseph Smith, *"No Man Knows My History,"* which initially triggered fears among the church hierarchy of additional attacks if unsympathetic scholars were allowed access to the church archives. "It took many years after the appearance of the Brodie book," he speculates, "for the councils in the Church to come to the decision that perhaps it would be wise to invite the scholars inside the organization and allow them to write the history in a professional manner rather than to insist that they remain outside the official structure."[13]

Practically speaking, the duties of Arrington and his staff (following Bitton's recollections once again) were twofold: one was to present church history to a popular audience through the publication of articles in church magazines and through informal speaking engagements, or "firesides," and similar venues; the other was to take the lead in producing scholarly books and articles that would be so thoroughly researched and objectively interpreted that they would serve as models for other scholars based on the theory "that a little judicious pump-priming would yield positive long-range results—respect for the Church, its history, and leaders who were willing to support thorough scholarship."[14]

Davis Bitton and James B. Allen, whom Arrington chose as coequal assistant Church Historians, were both senior scholars with solid academic backgrounds and impeccable credentials as faithful church members. Bitton, who had earned a Princeton doctorate in early modern European history, modestly recalls that he "often wondered at the chain of circumstances that

The History Division staff during the 1970s.
Leonard Arrington is at the top left.
Special Collections and Archives, Merrill Library, Utah State University.

brought me to serving on Leonard's team," and that he "started dabbling in Mormon history" only during an early teaching position at the University of Texas.[15] In fact, no one who knew Bitton could ever have considered him a "dabbler" in anything, for he was a powerful intellect, a proverbially graceful writer, a popular though demanding teacher, and a scholar of the highest order. Already at the time of his appointment he had been "dabbling" in the compilation of his *Guide to Mormon Diaries and Autobiographies*, which became the indispensable reference source for research in Mormon history after its publication in 1977.[16] Allen, a Logan native, held a Ph.D. in American history from the University of Southern California. A professor at BYU, he had already published widely on Mormon history, including the collection *Mormonism in American Culture* edited with Marvin Hill, and many articles in Mormon magazines and western scholarly journals. Allen was also president of the Mormon History Association at the time.[17] Arrington never had cause to regret those two appointments. "If I have ever had a personal revelation, it was the revelation to choose both of you as Assistant Church Historians," he wrote them in a thank-you note on the fifth anniversary of the founding of the History Division. "It was something which came to me almost immediately after my appointment, and rereading of my diary entries of the time suggests that I had the feeling at the time that it was an inspiration."[18]

Supporting those three historians was a staff of research historians, oral history experts, editors, and secretaries that, by Bitton's calculation reached a maximum size of seventeen. That number, however, is a bit understated because so many people worked part-time or for a limited period, and many others passed through on summer research fellowships. The History Division included a large number of people working in diverse capacities during its decade of existence. The quality of those people was extremely high, for Arrington was able to choose among a group of "younger, well-trained, and eager young scholars," most of whom had just completed or were still finishing degrees from institutions in the Ivy League and the University of California system, as well as Utah universities.[19]

To my knowledge, all those who were involved in the History Division look back on its inception as a time of unparalleled opportunity and limitless possibilities in which the doors would be thrown open, the windows would admit fresh breezes, and Mormon scholarship would come into its own at last. "The euphoria of being part of something like the [History] Division in 1972 is hard to convey," Bitton remembers. "It seemed like a heaven-sent opportunity. Our leaders were behind us, liked us, encouraged us. We had available one of the great collections of primary source material in the world. There was much that needed to be done." Not surprisingly, for good churchmen, a prayer of thanksgiving was natural and appropriate. "Upon learning that the appointments had been made and accepted, something for which I had fasted and prayed," Arrington remembered, "I called Dean Jessee into the office and Dean, Jim, Davis, and I knelt in prayer to express our thanks and to ask blessings upon our endeavors as we entered into our work. . . . I arose from the prayer with a certainty that the Lord was cognizant of and approved our appointments and would bless us in our endeavors. I have always felt that my assignment . . . was a special endowment from on high."[20]

The high seriousness of the religious ecstasy did not preclude insertion of some earthly humor into the celebration. Ever one to love a good laugh, even when at his own expense, Arrington many years later recited a bit of doggerel sent him by one of his friends who thought it good to deflate any lofty pretensions that the concurrent professorial appointment at BYU might have encouraged:

> Professor Arrington, he's honored. "Given a chair."
> It's not his head they're honoring. And that's fair.
> Use your best part, Professor. Rest it there![21]

Events of the following decade would bring new delights and at the same time severely test Arrington's humility and sense of humor. "Do you think we can survive our own candor?" the historian Laurel Thatcher Ulrich wrote him in 1982 after the great experiment was all over.[22] By that point an unambiguous answer was probably impossible.

But that was all in the future. In the present, it was time to roll up the sleeves and get to work. Without perhaps fully realizing it, Arrington had already been developing the basic philosophy that would hold the History Division together and give it its ethos. It was deeply rooted in the Mormon cooperation so elaborately delineated in *Great Basin Kingdom*. As early as 1969, when he was planning his general history of the Mormons, Arrington told a friend that this history, unlike much of *Great Basin Kingdom*, would include a focus on art, drama, literature, and other cultural aspects of the Mormon experience. "I have been toying with a manner in which to approach this," he wrote to a friend, "and would like to use the same notion of building the kingdom that I used in *Great Basin Kingdom*. Do you know of any reference in a scripture—Book of Mormon, Doctrine and Covenants, Bible, etc., wherein a reference is made to building the kingdom in any other sense than the physical sense of constructing buildings, cultivating crops, and so on? In other words, can you think of any scripture that would suggest that painting a portrait, sculpturing a hero, writing a novel, or some other cultural contribution would represent one means of building the kingdom?"[23] Now, with a scriptural sanction or not, Arrington had the chance to create a *cultural* cooperative: instead of building orderly Mormon villages, dams, and irrigation systems, these new pioneers would regiment their energies toward the writing of history.

The History Division's administrative organization already suggested this: From the First Presidency down to the local ward, the Mormon system was led by a bishop or president with two counselors. Although the same titles was not used, the leadership of the division, with Arrington as Church Historian and Bitton and Allen as assistants, certainly followed the same pattern. "Jim, Davis, and I made up a unified and imaginative 'troika' in administering the History Division. . . . We also built our faith as we engaged in this honorable calling."[24]

Under their leadership, the junior historians and staff were not allowed to work willy-nilly on individually defined projects. "Projects were not picked at random," Bitton recalled. "They were cleared in meetings with [the head of the Historical Department]. . . . In meetings between Leonard, Jim, and me, and in larger meetings with the whole staff, we discussed needed projects and thought in terms of priorities. Those that seemed strongest were carried by Leonard to meetings of the heads of the different divisions of the Historical Department and on up the ladder. Individuals either volunteered or were assigned to work on given projects."[25]

With this communal ethos, individuals were often shifted from one project to another as needed to move specific projects along in accordance with the division's priorities. Generally, the final publication appeared under the byline of the principal author or authors while other contributors were acknowledged in a footnote or acknowledgments section. But getting adequate credit for one's contribution seemed less important than finishing and publishing the work. Much of the work was published in Leonard Arrington's name, for he had the biggest reputation and anything under his byline would be readily accepted by publishers and widely read. But authorship was sometimes shifted among other staff members to suit a particular outlet and maximize the number of publications they could produce. Writing to Wendell J. Ashton of the church's Office of Public Communications, for example, Arrington said, "You asked us to do a review of [Donna Hill's] *Joseph Smith: The First Mormon.* This has been done and we are running it under the name of Davis Bitton, who has a University of Utah connection. We think it might be advisable to have a review appear under his name since my name appeared on the William Wise [*Massacre at Mountain Meadows*] book previously. There is a strong possibility that my review of the Wise book and this review by Davis of the Hill book will be published in BYU *Studies.* I assume you have no objection." To non-Mormon scholars with more individualistic bents, that blending of egos toward a common purpose seems quite amazing, but one must always remember that the division staff regarded their work as a church commission; they were building Zion in a way for which they were uniquely capable. Bitton once again: "When one remembers that all of this was assumed to be not only professionally meritorious but also a fulfillment of a commission from the Church, . . . it is perhaps understandable that we often had the strong feeling that God was in his heaven and all was right with the world. . . . Good cheer, encouragement, interest, pride in the accomplishments of any individual in the group were strong features of the History Division. It was a heady atmosphere."[26]

It was a good thing, perhaps, that emotions were running high, for the Division had set an ambitious program for itself, including simultaneous initiatives on several fronts that would need a deep reservoir of enthusiasm to carry out. In addition to writing articles for popular Mormon periodicals, a series of edited primary documents would be written for Deseret Book to be published in what would be called the Mormon Heritage Series. Biographies of important church leaders like Brigham Young and Eliza R. Snow were to be written, as were histories of various church organizations. Finally, two new general histories of the church were to be written, one for Mormons and one for non-Mormons, the first was to be published by Deseret Book and the other was already being discussed by Arrington with Alfred A. Knopf.[27]

The ambitions of the division extended, also, far beyond writing their own books and articles. An essential project of the division from its very inception was the commissioning of a multivolume history of the church to be published in celebration of its sesquicentennial anniversary in 1980 and written largely by scholars outside the History Division staff.[28] An oral history program was carried out by William Hartley, Gordon Irving, and Gary Shumway. Eventually a summer research fellowships

Leonard Arrington as Church Historian. *Special Collections and Archives, Merrill Library, Utah State University.*

program offering grants of $1,000 for outside scholars wishing to use the church archives to write Mormon history was created. These and similar projects were costly, and the church budget did not include funding that would come close to sustaining them all. Consequently, bringing in outside money to help make ends meet was necessary. The oral history program, extremely expensive because of travel, transcribing, and editing interviews, received a major grant from the descendants of James H. Moyle. Eugene England, Sr., made another substantial donation to support individual projects deemed worthy by Arrington. Finally, a special Mormon History Trust Fund was created from individual donations and also from royalties and honoraria contributed by division staff members in the interest of supporting additional projects.[29]

Some rough weather during the division's first year of existence rocked the boat, but it remained upright and on course. One event was the death of President Joseph Fielding Smith. Although as Church Historian he had kept the moat around the church archives full of water and alligators and had written the rigidly orthodox *Essentials of Church History* used in the Church Education System, in his brief tenure as president of the church he had welcomed the opening of the archives and encouraged the new History Division in its proposed writing projects. Fortunately his successor, Harold B. Lee, also backed the division. When Lee died after only a year and a half in office, he was succeeded by Spencer W. Kimball, also a friend of the historians. Further down the hierarchy, Elder Alvin Dyer, who succeeded Elder Howard W. Hunter as administrator of the Historical Department and was universally recognized as a firm backer of the program, suffered a stroke and was forced to resign. Fortunately once again, his replacement, Elder Joseph Anderson, was also perceived as a friend of the historians, so their work went on under the conviction that they had the backing of the church authorities.[30]

It did not last. During the next ten years, the History Division staff and other scholars who enjoyed the new open access to the archives produced a truly astounding quantity of publications, most of which were of a very high quality in thoroughness of research, soundness of interpretation, and gracefulness of writing, but they did so in the face of diminishing support from church authorities, lack of enthusiasm from their publishers, and mounting criticism from conservative readers.[31] Opposition from the most conservative members of the Quorum of the Twelve, like elders Ezra Taft Benson, Mark E. Peterson, and Boyd K. Packer, was perhaps to be expected, but the historians had not expected that their immediate supervisors, Elder Joseph Anderson and his successor Elder G. Homer Durham, would fail to defend them. Nor had they anticipated spies within their own department who would compile dossiers on what they regarded as heretical or disloyal statements to be passed along to the Twelve and ultimately to the offender's bishop or stake president. That the historians maintained such a high level of energy, enthusiasm, and productivity within that increasingly hostile environment is just as praiseworthy as the doggedly faithful perseverance of those earlier Mormon pioneers who fulfilled their callings to the Muddy or the San Juan Missions.

"From the beginning, we detected some negative rumblings," Bitton remembered.[32] One of the earliest was a brief caution offered by Elder Thomas S. Monson during a dinner celebrating Deseret Book's agreement to publish both the Mormon Heritage and the sesquicentennial series. "Measure twice and cut once," Elder Monson admonished the historians. But no one realized how closely their measurements were going to be scrutinized.[33]

A much louder rumble sounded during a meeting Arrington had with the First Presidency on January 30, 1973. Two proposals he and Elder Joseph Anderson presented were met with a less than enthusiastic reception. One was for an annual award for a student research paper and the other was for creation of a Friends of Church History organization to publicize the holdings of the archives and the work of the History Division staff. President Harold B. Lee bristled at the prospect of student researchers investigating sensitive topics like polygamy and suggested that topics should be cleared by the First Presidency ahead of time as they had been doing with BYU thesis topics. "He said," Arrington recorded in his diary, "that there is a philosophy that we ought to be critical in our writings so as to make accommodations to the Jack Mormons and non-Mormons and dissenters. This has been the policy of the editors of *Dialogue*." Although

President N. Eldon Tanner interjected, with Lee's approval, that the intention was not censorship of the papers themselves but rather that some topics should simply be eschewed, it appeared to Arrington as a type of intervention in the policies of the History Division that he had be given to understand would not occur. Nor were the officials immediately interested in the Friends idea, for they decided to table it pending further discussion among themselves. They also tabled the matter of payment for the authors of the sesquicentennial series. Rather than the enthusiastic support and laissez-faire policy regarding the internal running of the History Division that the historians had been led to expect, Arrington came away with the feeling that his proposals had hit a tight bottleneck: "The net result of the meeting is that I don't seem to be getting very rapid approval on any of my projects and those that are approved are hedged with a number of restrictions that will make it difficult for us to do a proper professional job."[34]

Conflict burst into the open in 1974 when History Division staff historian D. Michael Quinn published an article in *Ensign*, a popular church magazine, on the origins of the office of presiding bishop (the chief financial officer of the church). At one point in the article Quinn suggested that, contrary to popular understanding, Edward Partridge had not been the first incumbent. Although Quinn, a researcher of great care and Herculean energy, had his facts right, his assertion was taken by some conservative readers as an insult to Partridge's memory. Unfortunately, space considerations in the magazine had necessitated an abridgment that prevented presentation of Quinn's full documentation. The flap that ensued resulted in President Spencer W. Kimball of the First Presidency suggesting that Arrington submit an apology to the readers. In the end, the best Arrington thought he could do was to send a note to Jay Todd, the publisher, regretting that the format in which the article had been run was unfortunate and that the article should be considered "exploratory" and not an official church position. Arrington decided not to push the issue further "on the theory that any confrontation would result in a directive that we would have to clear all of our articles with somebody, and I want to avoid that at all cost."[35]

There was a background to that comment, for there had been a debate since the creation of the History Division over whether their writings were subject to what was called "correlation." The Correlation Committee, created in 1960 under the general directorship of Elder Harold B. Lee, was part of a movement to tighten and enhance the authority of the priesthood in the family and the ward and the authority of the central church administration in general. Writers, editors, and publishers were required to submit all writings that were to be used in the Church Educational System to the committee for approval. Mormon orthodoxy has never had a tightly defined body of normative doctrines as, for example, the Roman Catholic Church has in the writings of St. Thomas Aquinas. That, plus the fact that all General Authorities are entitled to make doctrinal pronouncements on behalf of the church, risks the possibility of a variety of people saying a variety of things that may not be consistent. The Correlation Committee's goal, in part, was to ensure consistency insofar as possible.[36]

Correlation may have been a good or even a necessary thing for the church at large and its publication program in particular; certainly it has been a major force in shaping contemporary Mormonism. But for the historians it was lethal. In the first place, they perceived correlation to be nothing short of censorship, and censorship, to boot, by persons who were in no position to know the facts as well as the historians. Accepting that was impossible. Nor was it possible to accept Earl Olsen's recommendation that all new facts and interpretations generated by the History Division be submitted for approval to the Quorum of the Twelve.

Arrington bristled at the suggestion, in the first place because of its unwieldiness, for thousands of new discoveries were emerging each year. Besides, he pointed out, scholarship is simply not democratic. "I do not think we could determine the truth of what had happened in history by having the Quorum of the Twelve vote on it," he retorted. "You do not determine historical truth by counting noses."[37] Therefore, as Douglas Alder added, "In order to implement this venture into serious research, the historians argued that they could not accept the assignment if their writing was to be censored. That is a very unkind word for Correlation review, but any limitation of free inquiry in the scholarly world is perceived as censorship. Traditionally in all disciplines, scholars have demanded that their work must stand the examination of other scholars but only *after* publication. In no way can scholarship be committed to a party line or to a review procedure that would prevent the stating of facts as facts."[38]

Moreover, clearance by the Correlation Committee would mean that the historians were making official pronouncements on behalf of the church. Orthodoxy and consistency in religious doctrine might be a good thing, but historiography is an organic entity that has to be allowed to grow and change as new documents, methods, and insights become available to the historian. As Davis Bitton argued, the History Division was engaged in a different type of writing from those who were producing materials for religious instruction: "The research and publication program of the History Division was not part of any system of classes, [and] it was not presuming to make statements about the current doctrinal positions." Therefore they were able to persuade the General Authorities to allow the three senior historians, Arrington, Bitton, and Allen, to constitute themselves as a "reading committee" for the division's writings. Eventually, though the historians felt compelled to submit some of their major works, like Arrington and Bitton's *The Mormon Experi-*

ence, to officials like Elders G. Homer Durham and Boyd K. Packer for their comments, they were able to sidestep the Correlation Committee. Summing up the experience, Bitton observes that the self-censorship procedure worked rather well and that "some of the specific matters in our publications that later turned out to be irritants did not do so because of our historical or doctrinal inaccuracy."[39]

What kinds of things, then, *were* irritants? It did not take long for the historians to find out, for their very first publication, Dean C. Jessee's edited collection of *Letters of Brigham Young to His Sons*, provoked the first criticisms.[40] Although, by Arrington's characterization, the book showed the great Mormon leader "to be both a deeply religious man and also a sensitive, loving, and understanding father" dedicated to the principles of "the importance of acquiring practical knowledge and skills, the obligation to be of service to others, and the need for total dedication to the kingdom of God"—the antithesis of the iron-fisted autocrat of anti-Mormon mythology whose word meant life or death—the fine-toothed combs of some readers located facts they found objectionable. One of those was Elder Boyd K. Packer, who, instead of discussing his reservations with the historians, instead sent a four-page letter directly to the First Presidency in which he objected, among other things, to revelations of litigation over Brigham Young's will by disgruntled family members and that Brigham Young, Jr., had used tobacco. Though Packer's letter concluded on a complimentary note, it warned that he expected a sanitized version of Mormon history and even raised once again the threat of requiring the historians' work to be sent through correlation. The First Presidency suddenly sprang the letter on the Quorum of the Twelve at a meeting on November 14, 1974, at which one of the historians' supporters, Elder Bruce McConkie, was absent, and the other, Elder Howard Hunter, was unaware of the letter and unprepared to respond. Although no disciplinary action resulted and the historians felt they still had the confidence of their backers among the Twelve, they had learned from what quarter their opposition was going to come, what the nature of at least some of that opposition was going to be, and, most ominously, that they could not expect the courtesy of an opportunity to defend their work directly.[41]

Those rumblings of discontent only grew louder with the 1976 publication of *The Story of the Latter-day Saints* by Division staff members James Allen and Glen Leonard.[42] In the master publication plan of the History Division, the Allen-Leonard volume was to be one of two general histories of Mormonism, this one for a Mormon audience and the other, which became Arrington and Bitton's *The Mormon Experience*, for a general readership. The immediate goal of the Allen-Leonard book was to provide a modern, professionally researched and written replacement for Joseph Fielding Smith's *Essentials of Church History*, an old warhorse of 1921 used in the Church Educational System. Smith's book had many deficiencies: besides being sadly outdated, it was narrow in focus, defensive in tone, and intellectually provincial.

The appearance of *The Story of the Latter-day Saints* was an occasion of much justifiable rejoicing in the History Division. It was pro-Mormon in its interpretation, and though it gave little consideration of the secular views of Joseph Smith and not much coverage of the less admirable episodes in Mormon history, it was exhaustively researched and contained an immense bibliography, was written in a lively, appealing style, and was as objective as one could reasonably expect for a volume written and published within the church. Thirty years later, one can still confidently recommend it as a solid survey of Mormon history.

Once again, though, the book ran into rough weather in the offices of the Quorum of the Twelve. Leading the attack this time was Elder Ezra Taft Benson, the rock-ribbed right-winger who many regarded as a superannuated holdover from the McCarthy era. As secretary of agriculture in the Eisenhower administration, he had backed measures favoring agribusiness over the small farmer and after his return to Utah promoted the John Birch Society. Now, to the consternation of liberal-minded Mormons, he was president of the Quorum of the Twelve, poised to ascend to the presidency of the church whenever the frail health of President Spencer W. Kimball should fail.

Without mentioning the book by name, Benson attacked it obliquely in two speeches at Brigham Young University, complaining in the first instance about those who would "humanize" church leaders and downplay the role of revelation in church history in favor of influences from the cultural environment. He also bristled at the use of terms like "communitarian" to characterize the regimentation of Mormon society and economics and institutions like the United Order of Enoch; "communitarian" was too close to "communist" for the old right-winger.[43] Once again neither Arrington nor the authors of the book were invited to explain their interpretations and terminology directly to their attacker. Eventually Arrington was summoned abruptly to a meeting of the First Presidency, though given no inkling of the purpose of the meeting nor any indication of how to prepare for it. Elders Hunter and McConkie were also invited to the meeting but given no more information than Arrington. To their dismay, Elders Benson and Petersen showed up and promptly unleashed a litany of attacks on the book and "grave warnings" against those who would write such a thing. Fortunately Arrington retained his composure and responded effectively to each objection, pointing out, among other things, that the book had been written by faithful Latter-day Saints and that it had been well received by its intended audience as an informative and faith-promoting volume.

Although there was no hope of pleasing Benson and Petersen, presidents Kimball and Tanner emerged from the hour and forty-five minute meeting apparently reassured that the History Division was accomplishing its purpose of reinterpreting Mormon history in the light of new sources and professional standards and that the church had nothing to fear from the historians. Arrington did agree to Kimball's request that he allow some designated representative of the Twelve to review future book manuscripts. For his own part, when President Kimball got around to reading *The Story of the Latter-day Saints* for himself, he found it "a great work and could not comprehend why anyone would think otherwise," according to a report passed on to Arrington from Marvin J. Ashton, head of Deseret Book's board.[44]

But even though that attack ended well, by 1977 all was not well. A sea change in attitude, policy, and administration on the part of the church hierarchy was revealed that constricted, then ultimately abolished the History Division. For one thing, a University of Utah undergraduate wrote and circulated a research paper in which he chronicled with alarm what he regarded as a new secularism in the History Division, citing heterodox statements purportedly gleaned from interviews with Mormon scholars, and even linking this "New Mormon History" with Jerald and Sandra Tanner, the apostates who made a business of publishing documents (sometimes purloined from the church archives) damaging to the church. Circulated among the Twelve by Elder Mark E. Petersen who obtained his copy from the student, the alarm generated by the paper led to restrictions on publication by faithful Mormons in what were perceived as the dissident magazines *Sunstone* and *Dialogue: A Journal of Mormon Thought* and what amounted to the blacklisting of writers like Carol Lynn Pearson, Claudia Bushman, and Scott Kenney.[45]

On April 29, 1977, the History Division staff was summoned to a meeting with President N. Eldon Tanner in which he announced the release of Joseph Anderson as director of the church's Historical Department and his replacement by Elder G. Homer Durham. Arrington greeted the change initially with enthusiasm: "We are very pleased with the choice," he wrote to his children. "[Durham] has been a good supporter, lo these many years." And later, "we are thrilled to have him. He will be professional help as well as providing good ecclesiastical interference and administration. We are grateful for him. He has agreed to read all our manuscripts from both the professional and ecclesiastical point of view, and this will help me share the responsibility somewhat. This lifts a psychological burden."[46] One can understand the enthusiasm. Although Joseph Anderson may not quite have been "a fog who could be hoodwinked," as Carl Arrington characterized him, he had been a benign director who had not given the division the aggressive support the historians needed in their relationships with the Twelve and the First Presidency. As Arrington had complained as early as 1973, "We submit programs to Elder Anderson, he submits them on to Elder Hunter, he submits them on to the Quorum, and so on. And nothing ever gets done."[47]

Durham, for sure, would be a different story. A son-in-law of Mormon Apostle John A. Widtsoe, Durham was a cultivated person with a deep love and knowledge of music, a political science scholar with a doctorate from UCLA, and an educational administrator who had served as president of Arizona State University and as Utah's first commissioner of higher education. He was also something of a historian, who had written a monthly column on the subject for many years in the church publication *Improvement Era* and had edited several volumes of historical documents. As one might expect, Durham brought a very different administrative style to the Historical Department from Anderson's benign neglect. Durham "wanted to *run* the department," according to Arrington, "to set goals and objectives and means of attaining them. For our own and the church's good, we were expected to obediently acquiesce." Depending on the nature of those "goals and objectives," Durham's activism was not necessarily a bad thing. "Stimulating and resourceful as he was, we supposed that he would enthusiastically support our staff and programs. . . . We were hardly prepared for the extent of his cutbacks."[48] Before long, it became apparent to the History Division staff that Durham had been appointed to attenuate and eventually to dismantle their entire program.

The reigns tightened almost immediately. Arrington submitted a detailed report on the projects currently underway or planned by each member of the staff, and Durham held interviews with each person to discuss those projects. Durham began requiring that every manuscript generated by the History Division had to be submitted to him for editorial emendations and approval before publication. And he attempted to take over the Mormon History Trust Fund, that repository of monies that the division administrators had used to support research projects by non-staff members. In the latter move, Arrington stuck to his guns and kept Durham from integrating that money with the general department budget, thus removing Arrington from control of it. Most ominously, Durham refused to hire replacements for several staff members who had left the division, and in fact he served as a one-man placement agency for any who wanted to leave and work for another church institution or agency.[49] Finally, Arrington himself was informed by the First Presidency in February 1978 that he was being relieved of his title of Church Historian, which would be given to Durham himself, and appointed director of the History Division.[50]

Not surprising, perhaps, the division's most ambitious project, the multivolume sesquicentennial series, was dropped. Although Durham and President Gordon B. Hinckley had decided at the time of Durham's appointment that they would drop the project, it was not until 1979, when it became apparent that all sixteen volumes would not be ready by 1980 and the publisher, Deseret Book, decided that the project was "not realistic," that it was officially abandoned. Though it had been the flagship program, in many ways, from the beginning, Arrington took its abandonment philosophically. By allowing the individual authors to seek their own publishers, they had been freed from Deseret Book's tight editorial policy and also from the production bottleneck that made it possible for them to issue only three new books per year. Also, the authors would now receive royalties instead of the flat fee they had been required to accept under the original arrangement.[51]

The final step in dismantling the History Division came on June 29, 1980, when Arrington was called to a meeting with Durham and Jeffrey Holland, president of Brigham Young University. In their search for a way to honor President Joseph Fielding Smith, he was told, they had decided to create a research institute at BYU in his name and transfer whatever was left of the History Division personnel and projects to that campus. For the time being, the staff was physically to remain in their present quarters, but they would be relocated eventually. Durham justified the decision to Arrington by asserting that it was a way of saving the writing of church history from the increasing hostility among the First Presidency and the Twelve. By getting the historians out of church headquarters and its hostile administration and into a university environment, they might feel safer and even more welcome. Arrington was not so sure: "Elder Durham tried to give the impression that this was something that was desired and established by the General Authorities of the Church and BYU. My frank opinion . . . is that he himself is the master arranger of all this business and that he was not compelled to do it or even requested to do it, but that it was his way of placing the History Division under a university rubric, which is where he has believed all along it should be."[52] Although Arrington clearly understood that this decision meant that history would be sidetracked and marginalized as an official church program, he decided to meet it graciously and cheerfully and required his staff to adopt a similar demeanor. Privately, though, abolition of the great enterprise over which he had so optimistically and energetically presided for the past decade sent him into a tailspin of depression and indecision: "The only thought in my mind is whether to take up the options that I have to go to the U of Utah or USU instead of running down to BYU in 1982. Or, maybe going up to a little two-and-a-half-acre plot on the family farm in Twin Falls and pitching hay and showing chickens."[53]

Thus the sesquicentennial year would witness not the publication of the much-anticipated sixteen-volume history that would be the vindication of objective, professionally written history under the aegis of the church itself, but rather the dismantling of the History Division and the banishment of its remnants to BYU. Lavina Fielding Anderson recalls that "the staff, shocked but hardly surprised, made no organized response as they had done to earlier pronouncements. The dreadful logic that had created the Institute was all too apparent." And Arrington went to great lengths to put a cheerful face on the decision and to permit himself no expression of discontent around which the staff could rally in making such an organized protest. "As others began to react," she concludes, "Leonard's determined cheerfulness gave those who were indignant or angry or frightened no foothold. And for those who saw positive aspects, he added reinforcement."[54] Burning bridges was not Leonard Arrington's style. On the chance that Durham was indeed telling the truth and that the "Move South" (reminiscent of Brigham Young's evacuation of Salt Lake Valley in 1858 in the face of an invading army) was indeed a tactical diversion designed to shield the historians from the likelihood that the hostile Ezra Taft Benson would become president of the church, Arrington had little choice but to play along and to do so cheerfully. Traffic between Salt Lake City and Provo runs in both directions and leaving that bridge standing might be to leave the way back home open. "I interpreted our move to BYU as a way to preserve our scholarly integrity," Arrington asserted. "As several persons told us, the Church didn't want to be in the position of 'approving' or 'disapproving' what we write. Under university administration, we could continue our scholarly work in an atmosphere of academic freedom. We did so, and I feel sure that we did our research and writing in a responsible manner, both as to the scholarship and as to the probity."[55]

The move itself took two years, and it was carried out in an increasingly hostile environment in the Church Office Building; as Anderson puts it, the church's "refusal to accommodate or cooperate that extended even to personal pettiness and revealed what could only be interpreted as paranoia about Leonard's physical or psychic presence."[56] By the end of the two-year period, the historians felt the pressure rising: "They've now removed our privilege to park in the Church Plaza," Arrington wrote on April 28, 1982, "but I've made an appeal to allow it until August. [Church Archivist] Earl Olson is sure anxious to get rid of us." Several months later he recorded an even greater insult: "It is a commentary on the way they treated us that we had tried several times to get them to carpet our floor, with a flat turndown every time. 'We can't afford it.' But the very afternoon after we left they were in our area cutting out carpet to put on the floor. I'm going to let out that little bit of information to someone so it won't be lost on posterity. A final indignity."[57] Three years later, when Arrington and Thomas G. Alexander met with Utah governor Norman H. Bangerter to discuss the process by which a new director of the Utah State Historical Society might be chosen, he was pleasantly surprised at the governor's cooperativeness in contrast with the church people

Arrington had had to deal with during the move: "I couldn't help but recall the contrast. The church people didn't listen, were stiff rather than friendly, and, in the case of Elder Durham, at least, were arrogant and unyielding.[58]

In the end, rather than returning to Utah State University or accepting an appointment at the University of Utah (or returning to his Idaho farm), Arrington accepted the directorship of the Joseph Fielding Smith Institute. But it was little more than a nominal appointment, for he retained his home in Salt Lake City and traveled to BYU only when necessary for a meeting or a class. The decade of the 1980s was increasingly occupied by work on his biography of Brigham Young, and he received permission to do that work at home where he would have minimal interruptions and would be close to the church archives.

Leonard Arrington's misfortunes during that time were not all professional, for on March 10, 1982, his wife of thirty-nine years died of heart disease. Grace Fort Arrington's life had encompassed a great deal: a quick courtship and marriage under wartime duress, years of separation from her new husband during the war, setting up a household in Logan, Utah, which must have seemed the end of the world to a North Carolina girl, and eventual conversion to what must have struck a Southern Baptist as the strange religion of Mormonism. But resilience was obviously an essential part of her character, for she was a true companion to her hard-driving husband and loving mother of their three children.

Her death was perhaps the only event that had the power to switch off that immense engine of scholarly production that was Leonard Arrington. Although the biography of Brigham Young was all but finished, he set it aside during long months of mourning and was not able to return to it until the fall.

Famously gregarious by nature and inept (perhaps willfully so) at domestic tasks, Arrington was not designed for a solitary life. As his scholarly work resumed, so did his social life, and in the hope of remarrying he began dating a series of women. (Curious to the outsider, but vividly indicative of the closeness of his relationships with his children, Arrington recounted his dates in elaborate detail in his weekly letters to the children.) After about a year of such dating, he began a courtship with Harriet Horne, granddaughter of the activist and educator Alice Merrill Horne and daughter of a prominent gynecologist in Salt Lake City. They found much in common; not only had they been previously married and had grown children, but coincidentally Harriet had once (1950–53) been president of the Relief Society in the Twin Falls ward over which Leonard's father was bishop. The two were married in the Salt Lake Temple on November 19, 1983. Whatever slings and arrows might come his way during the move to BYU and the barrage of attacks from church leaders who should have been his friends, he would not have to face them alone.[59]

Unfortunately, the move to BYU did not shield the historians from attacks by conservative church leaders, as they had hoped. While the move was still underway, Elder Boyd K. Packer went on the attack with an address to employees of the Church Educational System on August 22, 1981, in which he admonished historians to subordinate their commitment to the full truth to their obligation to promote the faith. "Some things that are true are not very useful," he urged. "Those who have carefully purged their work of any religious faith in the name of academic freedom or so-called honesty ought not expect to be accommodated in their researches or to be paid by the Church to do it."[60] Although Packer's comments were directed to teachers of religion and not to historians specifically, historians could see how easily they could come under his indictments as well. Even though no one in the History Division had "purged their work of any religious faith"—quite the contrary, for all of them were

Leonard Arrington and his second wife Harriett.
The ice sculpture commemorates his background as a chicken rancher.
Special Collections and Archives, Merrill Library, Utah State University.

believing, practicing Mormons—it was clear that Elder Packer saw an inherent conflict between faith and reason. From there, things only got worse as attacks from Packer and other conservatives intensified, leading ultimately to the resignation of former History Division staffer D. Michael Quinn from the BYU faculty in 1988 and his eventual excommunication along with five other "dissident" scholars that September, including fellow Division staffer Lavina Fielding Anderson.[61]

Looking back on his decade at the helm of the History Division, Leonard Arrington had good reason to be proud. Although the big sesquicentennial project had failed as an integrated effort, several volumes were published. Dozens of books and articles had poured out of the division offices, and staff members were conspicuous as spokespersons for church history at firesides and other speaking engagements. Pioneering works in women's history had been nurtured by the division. Numerous staff members and summer fellows who had cut their professional teeth under the sponsorship of the division went on to distinguished careers.

But why had their work not been more fully embraced within the church? "Maybe we brought some of [the hostility] on ourselves," Davis Bitton speculates, for "it is not hard to understand that employees who had come up the ladder at a time when [academic] training was not a prerequisite would feel threatened by university hotshots with their Ph.D. degrees and their claims to know how things should be done. . . . Although I think we were not guilty of looking down on those who were faithful workers in their different roles."[62] Certainly the offenses were unintentional, but, as Bitton speculated, one can easily imagine how older church employees might have felt invaded when that pack of young, ambitious, and enthusiastic historians burst into the Church Office Building with all their energy and big ideas and started overturning the hoary myths of Mormon history.

A Mormonism that wished to achieve the intellectual maturity obviously sought during the administrations of presidents Lee and Kimball would eventually have to learn to accept nuance and even ambiguity in its understanding of truth. In that, the historians were clearly on the right side. Perhaps the hostility they evoked grew from the fact that they demanded too much of a good thing too fast, like a starving person who gobbles a sumptuous dinner.

One certainly cannot say the total experience of the History Division was catastrophic in any sense, for the flood of new publications has enriched Mormon historical understanding immeasurably. "Our History Division," Arrington concluded, "was a little like the Zion's Camp episode of the 1830s [in which Joseph Smith had led a military expedition to relieve the persecuted Saints in Missouri, but never engaged in battle]: It did not succeed in its ostensible objective, but it may have identified a corps of leaders and provided valuable experience out of which great things developed. . . . I have faith that this work will continue to have the blessing of the Lord." For his part, Davis Bitton looked forward to meeting President Lee in the afterlife and saying to him, "It was not an easy assignment, for there was no way of pleasing everybody. But we worked hard. We did our best. Thank you for your confidence."[63]

Roland Rich Woolley, lawyer to Hollywood
celebrities, who financed three of Arrington's biographies.
Special Collections and Archives, Merrill Library, Utah State University.

Chapter 5

Arrington and Roland Rich Woolley

Although he was an economist by training and an economic historian by trade, in his career Leonard Arrington completed a series of biographies of Mormon leaders, from early pioneers like Charles Coulson Rich and Edwin D. Woolley to business entrepreneurs like David Eccles and Harold Silver to Utah governor William Spry and the great prophet and colonizer Brigham Young. One of his earliest books was a biography (William Spry) and his last book was a biography (Madelyn Silver). This fact should not be surprising, for as we have seen, Arrington saw economics as one of the humanities, not as one of the social sciences; to him, economics—and later history—was about people, not impersonal forces that can be expressed statistically. Although he saw Mormon history as the story of cooperative effort, it was in fact the history of many individuals voluntarily putting their shoulders to the wheel to realize a common goal.

Unfortunately, Arrington's biographies, as acknowledged even by his close colleague and collaborator Davis Bitton, "are not what he does best, tending to be competent, thorough, valuable, but not brilliant, not inspired."[1] Perhaps this could be expected as the biographies were largely commissioned by family members who wanted the best sides of the subjects brought to the fore. In addition, almost all of them were written in part or entirely by research assistants with varying degrees of interpretive and literary skills. Though, the most limiting factors in Arrington's biographies were, in the first placc, his compulsion toward hagiography, which kept him from honestly facing his subjects' shortcomings and demanding that he keep them solidly among the Mormon faithful, and even more damaging, a psychological naïveté that kept him from plumbing the depths of their motives. The same sunny optimism, the love of people, the vibrant faith in human nature that made Leonard Arrington such a generous and supportive colleague and friend were the very qualities that held him back as a biographer, for he was reluctant to see anything but the best in his subjects, reluctant to hold them strictly to account when their actions were clearly less than admirable, and unable to entertain the possibility that ulterior or interior motives might have been driving their exterior lives.[2] And of course the fact that all of his biographies except *Brigham Young* were "vanity" books, commissioned to celebrate the achievements of a family member, inevitably means that they are long on praise and short on criticism.

As noted above, most of these books were written entirely or in large part by one or more assistants, yet in most cases Leonard Arrington's name appears alone on the title page. In American academia there is a long and inglorious tradition of professors purloining the work of their graduate students with minimal or no attribution. The graduate student (so the justification goes) gets the experience, while the professor gets the publication. One could argue that Arrington's practice was only a part of that larger tradition.

My argument, however, is that Arrington's relationship with his research assistants was essentially different from that dubious tradition. In the first place, as noted in the previous chapter, there was a cooperative ethos among the History Division staff that enabled individual historians to subordinate their egos and contribute their labors to the common goal of producing history. While most of Arrington's research assistants worked directly for him instead of the History Division, one can see in their relationships with him the same kind of self-effacing cooperative spirit. Many of them were secretaries or students who lacked the skill to produce books on their own and were happy to be contributing to his. Arrington paid them well for the most part and acknowledged their contributions effusively in the book. I have been unable to find even one complaint from a researcher about the way they had been treated. Finally, in cases where the researcher had done most or virtually all of the work, Arrington listed that person as a collaborator;[3] in fact, Arrington's research assistants received more credit for their work than those who had worked in the "history factory" of Hubert Howe Bancroft in San Francisco in the late nineteenth century—the closest historical analogy to Arrington's "factory." While Arrington's practice might not pass muster among liberal advocates of strict academic freedom and honesty, it did have its own ethic that was understood and agreed upon by him and his assistants and cannot in any reasonable sense be considered exploitation.

Arrington's greatest benefactor was Roland Rich Woolley, who paid for three of his first four biographies. Woolley's family heritage was solidly Mormon: he was a direct descendant of the Mormon pioneers Charles C. Rich and Edwin D. Woolley (and thus a relative of Spencer W. Kimball, who became president of the Church in 1978). He married a daughter of Utah governor William Spry. As well connected as he was in his Utah home, though, Woolley decided, after completing law school, to seek his fortune on California's Golden Shore, where the rapidly burgeoning population of retirees, movie stars, and millionaires in Los Angeles during the 1920s seemed to offer lucrative opportunities for an ambitious lawyer.[4]

Woolley's instinct paid off handsomely. One of his first clients was the flamboyant evangelist and faith healer Aimee Semple McPherson, a national celebrity: "No movie star in Hollywood shone with the brilliance of Aimee Semple McPherson," asserts her biographer.[5] In May 1926, McPherson had disappeared during a beach outing and was presumed to have drowned. A month later she emerged from the Mexican desert claiming she had been abducted and held for ransom until she devised a way to escape.[6] When a grand jury investigation turned up no credible evidence supporting her story, McPherson was bound over to trial for corrupting public morals and obstructing justice. Woolley, who had little or no trial experience at the time, surprisingly emerged as the head of the defense team. His strategy was simply to insist that McPherson tenaciously stick to her story while the prosecution's witnesses repeatedly changed theirs, and the case against her unraveled to the point where the district attorney had to request a dismissal.[7] Although hardly a triumph for McPherson, the case brought Woolley's skill as a trial lawyer into the spotlight. He was subsequently retained by a succession of celebrity clients including Olivia de Haviland, John and Lionel Barrymore, and Leo Carrillo.

Woolley's practice brought him a huge fortune, and as age began to catch up with him in the late 1960s, he starting looking for ways to spend some of it on culturally worthwhile projects. The first was a commissioned biography of his father-in-law, Governor William Spry. Spry was certainly worthy of a biography, for his was a success story dear to the American Dream. The son of an English tailor and seamstress who had converted to Mormonism and emigrated to Utah in the 1870s, Spry rose from stable boy to prominent politician. He became a part of Reed Smoot's Republican Party machine called the "Federal Bunch." During his two terms as governor (1909–17), Spry advocated reclamation projects, development of Utah's mining industry, improvement of the school system, and construction of a state capitol and an armory. Although his party and his church supported Prohibition, Spry followed Smoot in advocating a local option policy to avoid Mormon-Gentile conflict that might damage the ability of the two groups to affect more important measures. His courageous veto of a Prohibition bill in 1915 ruined his chances at a third term. Even more controversial was his refusal in that same year to grant a stay of execution to the labor radical Joe Hill. Despite pleas for clemency from President Woodrow Wilson and the Swedish ambassador, Spry allowed the execution.[8]

To write the biography, Woolley hired a popular writer in California named William L. Roper. Unfortunately, the manuscript Roper created was not satisfactory to Woolley, largely because it lacked professionalism and did not project the gravitas he thought his wife's father deserved. Reed Mitchell, of the *Deseret News*, read and critiqued the Roper manuscript. At that point Reed Stout, another California lawyer and history buff with a pioneer Mormon background, suggested Leonard Arrington, whose *Great Basin Kingdom* he had read and admired.[9]

In the perspective of subsequent events, it is probably not proper to say that Arrington acted unwisely in accepting the Woolley commission, for two later books that were much better than the Spry biography would result from Woolley's funding. Nevertheless, Arrington came into the project too late, after the mold was already set by Roper's manuscript. In addition to Roper, Arrington had to contend with Reed Stout, Dennis McCarthy (another lawyer who was a sort of agent for Woolley in Salt Lake City), and the Utah State Historical Society and the University of Utah Press, who agreed to publish the book collaboratively. And of course there was the imperious Woolley, who was determined to see the great achievements of his wife's father memorialized and who had clear ideas on just what those achievements were. While the resulting book was a useful addition to Utah history, if fell far short of what it might have been if Arrington had been given a free hand.

Cutting the length of the manuscript was probably the worst suggestion Arrington accepted, because the cut was not done proportionately. The Joe Hill episode, important though it was, occupies 87 of the book's 225 pages. Mitchell's assertion in his critique that that was the "heart" of the book expressed his political ideology (clearly reflecting Woolley's conservative politics). They felt that the suppression of labor radicalism by the execution of one of its proponents was the most important achievement of Spry's governorship. The authors clearly contend that Spry had done the right thing and that justice had been served in both the trial and the execution: "Judged on the basis of what is now known about Hillstrom's [Joe Hill's] background and on an impartial analysis of the entire case, it would appear that Governor Spry's assessment of the case was reasonable."[10]

Such a politically charged conclusion is certainly open to debate. The obsessive focus on the Hill case takes attention away from the issues in which Spry's character as a "man of firmness" produced some really far-reaching benefits for Utah, such as his courageous insistence on "local option" instead of Prohibition in the face of opposition from both his party and his church, which was one way of diminishing the Mormon-Gentile antagonism, and his strong commitment to reclamation.

The "folksy" tone Mitchell noted in the Roper manuscript was not changed in the published book. Although it defeats the seriousness of tone Woolley wanted in the portrayal of his father-in-law, it was apparently retained because Woolley wanted Spry's life to serve as an example to America's youth of the rags-to-riches potential in the American Dream, and thus the story was presented in prose that young people presumably could digest. This is also apparent in the dedication of the book: "Dedicated to the Youth of America. May they be inspired by the integrity, patriotism, and courageous public service of Governor William Spry."[11] Most of the folksiness appears in manufactured dialogue that the authors put into the mouths of their characters and said was based on adaptation from "sound primary sources."[12]

Equally dubious is the basic thesis of the book, that Spry pulled himself up from humble beginnings to the highest office in state government: "That a penniless immigrant boy should have risen to become chief executive of his adopted state demonstrates, once again, the spirit of freedom and opportunity in contemporary America."[13] While it is true that Spry was a hard worker in pursuit of his ambitions and was not afraid to work at humble jobs, it is also true, as the facts of the biography indicate, that he came from a comfortable middle-class background and that he had help from powerful patrons in his rise to power.

Reviewing the book in the *Pacific Historical Review*, Jan Shipps thought it fell far short of adequacy: "Ideally a biography should make a significant addition to our store of knowledge about a person's life, or deepen our understanding of the time in which he lived, or both. This study, unfortunately, does neither."[14] Such a judgment seems a bit harsh, for the authors do succeed in bringing together the basic facts of Spry's life and career, and one does emerge at the end of the book with a comprehensive understanding of his contribution to Utah history. Nevertheless, the book should be ranked toward the bottom of the list of books Arrington wrote or was involved with. Presented at the outset with a seriously flawed manuscript and hampered by interference from Woolley and his agents, Arrington simply had the deck stacked against him. The other two projects funded by Woolley would fare much better.

While the Spry biography was still under preparation, Woolley negotiated an agreement with Arrington to produce a biography of his grandfather, Mormon apostle and pioneer Charles C. Rich, eventually published in 1974 by Brigham Young University Press.[15] Perhaps mindful of the fact that too many cooks had had spoons in the broth during the making of the Spry book, the agreement this time put Arrington in charge of both research and writing. Woolley agreed to help locate source materials, but even though he reserved "the right to make corrections and suggest alterations in the text," Arrington was charged with the responsibility of producing a biography that is "'professional'—objective, scholarly and interesting." Woolley also stipulated "that the biography be told 'as it was,' and that it shall be a work of truth and integrity."[16] Although some scholars would blanch at the clause allowing Woolley's editorial hand, in fact the arrangement proved to be amicable, for Arrington produced a manuscript that Woolley found entirely acceptable. "Mr. Woolley did not attempt to suggest a favorable treatment, nor did he even read the manuscript through before it was published, and he insisted that I talk about Rich's warts and all," Arrington wrote to Dennis Lythgoe in response to his allegation that Arrington's laudatory interpretation had been imposed by Woolley.[17]

Financially, Woolley agreed to pay Arrington five thousand dollars in five installments. The money was paid directly to him, rather than through some kind of trust fund at Utah State University. This meant that Arrington had complete control over disbursal of the money, but he would also have to write the book on his own time, with no reduction in his university responsibilities. Those responsibilities, as we have seen, were heavy, so if the project were to be completed within a reasonable period, much of the work was going to have to be farmed out to research assistants. In recruiting those assistants, Arrington followed an ad hoc process similar to that by which Falstaff raised his army from out of the hedgerows, enlisting anyone who had some time and needed some money. It was a motley bunch with widely varied backgrounds, from professional historians (Ronald G. Watt, Richard Jensen, and F. Ross Peterson) to former students (Richard Daines) to sec-

Charles C. Rich, Mormon pioneer of San Bernadino, California, and Bear Lake on the Utah-Idaho border, was the subject of Arrington's 1974 biography. *Used by permission of Utah State Historical Society.* *All rights reserved.*

retaries (JoAnn Bair and Chris Rigby).[18] Fortunately, his regiment functioned better than Falstaff's, and each member produced their contributions on time and competently.

As the subject of a biography (of course the choice was Woolley's, not Arrington's), Charles C. Rich offered both strengths and weaknesses. As an early (1832) convert to Mormonism who lived until 1881, he had witnessed or experienced most of the defining episodes in early Mormon history, from the Zion's Camp expedition of 1834 in Missouri to the murder of Joseph Smith in Illinois to the crossing of the plains and the establishment of far-flung Mormon colonies in San Bernardino. A polygamist and an apostle, Rich was third in line of succession to the church presidency at the time of his death. Rich was a walking embodiment of Mormon history.

Unfortunately, his personality was not nearly as interesting as his resumé. Arrington makes much of the parallels between the early lives of Rich and Abraham Lincoln, who were both born in 1809 in Kentucky, moved to Indiana, and eventually located in Illinois. Both were tall and strong, and both married relatively late.[19] The comparison makes an interesting literary device, but it is superficial, for Rich had none of the eloquence nor the complex interior life of his famous contemporary: "Laconic in his manner, modest and deferential, Charles Rich was great because he was intelligent, practical, and understanding. . . . He was not articulate nor clever with words; from his diaries, journals, and letters one can only sense the deepness of his feeling." Thus Rich's biography is a tale of externals: "Charles Rich's story is the story of Mormonism—its faith, its attempts to establish a Christian society, its conflicts with neighbors and the United States government, its failures and its successes."[20]

Such a personality makes for a frustrating biography. "The primary reason for the inadequate portrayal of Charles C. Rich is as you suggested earlier, the lack of materials," Arrington wrote to Dennis Lythgoe, "His diary entries are short and there is no introspective matter. Moreover there are not effusive accounts by people who associated with him."[21] Thus Rich's thoughts and motives regarding even the most life-changing events are obscure. Hosea Stout, who was Rich's friend before either of them became Mormons (Rich would later convert Stout), remembered him before his conversion as "an uncommon civil steady, honest young man but made no pretensions to religion & I soon had a great regard and attachment for him." So why did he convert? Although Arrington points out that religious revivals were common in the Illinois of Rich's youth, no motivation for or change in attitude after his conversion is described other than possible attendance at religious revivals and the conversion of a friend of theirs, Morris Phelps. Rich's own explanation gives only the method by which he examined Mormonism, with no indication of what appealed to him in the new religion and changed him from a religiously apathetic person to the zealous convert.[22]

Rich's biography, then, became the story of an almost faceless archetype of the faithful Mormon: "Charles Rich was unwaveringly loyal to his church—its encounters and its programs. Baptized a member of The Church of Jesus Christ of Latter-day Saints in 1832, Rich was unhesitatingly obedient to its many calls and assignments."[23] Not surprising, then, reviewers had few flattering words for such a bland biography of a bland person. Robert Flanders, writing in the *Journal of American History*, indicated that "*Charles C. Rich* is a not-very-penetrating biography which asks few new questions and provides few new answers." Rodman Paul, in *BYU Studies*, says that "in his bibliographical essay Arrington speaks of his book as a 'history' of Rich, instead of using a more personal term such as 'biography' or 'life.' The distinction is important, for the reader is brought tantalizingly close to Rich's personality without ever feeling that he truly knows the man. The details of Rich's life are here, but the very fullness of those details makes one long for the additional insights that could have been provided by interpretive analysis and by a more deliberate attempt to reconcile conflicting evidence." Arrington himself admitted that "the book would have been better if I could have looked into the mind and soul of this fascinating leader of a heroic era."[24]

On the other hand, Lavina Fielding Anderson, referring to "high praise among [uncited] reviewers," laments the short life given the book by its publisher: "It was disappointing, then, after this fine beginning, to see BYU Press's inadequate marketing system virtually drop the book and then ruthlessly remainder the copies within a few months—hardly standard operating procedure for an academic press."[25] Despite Flanders's complaint of the lack of originality in *Charles C. Rich*, JoAnn Bair's chapters on the colonization of San Bernardino, based on the researches of Eugene Campbell and Joseph Wood, and Ross Peterson's narrative of the Bear Lake colonization are useful accounts of far-flung Mormon settlements that might otherwise have waited a long time before finding their historians.

Arrington's last Woolley-funded book was a biography of the lawyer's other grandfather, Mormon pioneer Edwin D. Woolley.[26] It is unclear whether the initiative for the book began with Arrington or Woolley, but Arrington had become interested in the subject in 1973 while doing research on pioneer wards and discovering an extraordinary richness of records of Salt Lake City's Thirteenth Ward. Located in a nine-block area of what is presently downtown, with boundaries reaching from South Temple to Third South, and Main Street to Third East, the elaborateness of the ward's documentary record was largely the work of its longtime bishop, Edwin D. Woolley, who served in that capacity from 1854 to 1881. A skillful businessman who had run general stores in Nauvoo, Illinois, and in Winter Quarters, Nebraska, as well as the Tithing Store and later his own business after his immigration to Salt Lake City in 1848, Woolley served as a close financial advisor to Brigham Young and brought the meticulous record keeping he had developed in those roles to his administration as bishop.

In addition to his long service as bishop of one of Salt Lake City's most prosperous and prominent wards, Woolley's life offered other attractions to a biographer. An 1837 convert from the Quaker faith, Woolley, like Charles C. Rich, had lived through a great deal of early Mormon history including the Kirtland and Nauvoo phases and the trek across the plains. As an economic historian, Arrington found in Woolley an important source on the church's financial affairs. And unlike Rich, Woolley's letters and other personal documents, though not large in extent, were articulate and frank regarding his personal life. Finally, Woolley's life afforded an opportunity to study the role played by what Arrington called the "middle wagon" people in Mormon history—those were neither the top echelon leaders like Brigham Young and Charles C. Rich, nor the impoverished masses who converted in Britain and Scandinavia and flooded into Utah in the 1850s.[27]

By the summer of 1974 Arrington was already at work on a biography funded by Roland Rich Woolley. Although he was now Church Historian instead of a college professor, and thus free from the academic responsibilities that limited his research and writing time, Arrington had learned the efficiency of turning over projects with outside funding to research assistants. The first of those to work on the Woolley project was his son Carl, who spent the summer doing research on Woolley. By August, though, Carl left the project to pursue his own writing career, and Arrington began casting about for someone new. He could see two possibilities; one, as he wrote to Woolley, was to give "a fellowship of say $2,000 to some student working on a Ph.D. at the University of Utah or BYU. He would commit himself to work on the project halftime during the school year. I think in that period he could finish all of the research and preliminary writing." Alternatively, he could "employ somebody fulltime on the project for the next few months. . . . There are some well-educated and well-qualified wives in Salt Lake City who might not want to take a permanent job but might be willing to take a job for a few months like this one."[28] Rebecca Cornwall was one such wife, and when he offered her a contract in September 1974, it began perhaps the most fortunate collaboration of his professional life with the exception of his work with Davis Bitton.

The terms of the contract were that Cornwall would be assigned a desk in the archives search room for her exclusive use. She would work an average of twenty hours per week (rather than the full time Arrington had hoped) for $3.15 per hour up to a total stipend of $2,000. Arrington was given full editorial rights over her drafts and agreed to pay her up to ten percent of any royalties earned, the rest going to the Mormon History Trust Fund.

Finally, it was agreed that she would produce an average of one chapter every three weeks.[29] For her part, Cornwall was delighted with the terms; upon first being approached with the proposal, she wrote, "You said not to get excited but of course I am, although if your offer does not come through I keep telling myself the other things I had planned for the winter would be just as exciting. . . . I am delighted that you've considered me."[30]

Cornwall, whose background was in creative writing and who eventually left Arrington's employ to pursue a career as a writer of fiction, brought a literary verve to the projects on which she worked that few others in the History Division—and certainly not Arrington himself—could equal. In addition to writing the Woolley biography and the unpublished biography of Arrington up to his appointment as Church Historian, her skill was so great that Arrington used her as a speechwriter and editor on other History Division projects, despite the fact that she was never a Division staff member and worked only on a contract basis directly for Arrington. As he acknowledged, it was a great relationship: "I have been working with Mrs. Cornwall on each chapter, both before she writes her draft, and then going over it carefully after she finishes it. So we are working together well," he wrote to Woolley, and his thanks to her for helping him on an important speech were heartfelt: "I just wanted to tell you in writing how much I appreciated all your work in connection with the BYU Commencement talk. It went over very well and most of the credit is due to your efforts."[31]

In the end, Arrington's contribution to the project was minimal, apparently consisting of little more than working out the general outline of the chapters and some editing of the drafts; in actual fact, the book was Cornwall's. Realizing that fact almost immediately as the writing got under way, Arrington's sense of fairness prompted him to ask Woolley to allow him to put her name on the title page instead of in the acknowledgments: "She is such a fine writer that it will not be necessary for me to make extensive changes in her work. This will not only lesson [*sic*] the burden on me but it will mean a fine biography in finished form."[32]

But Woolley would have none of it. No matter how good Cornwall was as a researcher and writer, Woolley wanted the prestige of Arrington's name—and his name alone—on the title page. His rejection of Arrington's suggestion was patronizing:

> Let's keep Becky in her position as your researcher not as co-author. The book is to be the product of Dr. Leonard J. Arrington. Every great writer and author has to have assistance and I am delighted to know that she is giving you such fine assistance, but let's keep her in her proper perspective as your researcher. At the right time I certainly will be willing, if the excellent effort continues, to give her an extra bonus. But let's not spoil her. You can give her honorable mention in your preface just as you will give honorable mention in your preface to Preston Parkinson [who had provided source material] for his fine cooperation. But let's not let the tail wag the dog.

A few days later he added, "Naturally people want to ride on your coat tails as much as they can. But let's keep them as best we can where they belong."[33]

In his relationship with Roland Rich Woolley, Leonard Arrington did not make final decisions. Arrington got credit for a book for which he had served as little more than an editor and advisor, and Becky Cornwall was relegated to the acknowledgments section. And the best Arrington could do there was to protest that their authorial relationship "has been tantamount to collaboration."[34] That was all Cornwall or Arrington could do, because Woolley was simply holding them to the terms of their contract. Cornwall never complained, and in fact kept working for Arrington. His name appeared alone on the title page of the best of all the Arrington biographies.

Of the several outstanding virtues of *From Quaker to Latter-day Saint*, perhaps the most conspicuous is its literary grace, which is apparent virtually anywhere one opens the book and for which Cornwall alone is to be credited. Leonard Arrington was a good writer, but one would hardly consider him a prose stylist. "For the most part his sentences march across his pages like the orderly field rows of the Arrington farmlands bordering the Snake River," historian Richard Etulain says. "Carefully linking his sentences, paragraphs, and chapter subsections with judiciously chosen transitions and straightforward syntax and diction, Arrington suffuses his writings with a well-ordered, evenhanded tone, inspiring confidence in readers."[35] Fair enough; Arrington certainly possessed a clear, serviceable prose style. But the appearance of Cornwall's eloquent style under Arrington's name alongside the stalwart declarative sentences of *Charles C. Rich*, written by less-able assistants, or even those of *Great Basin Kingdom* would lift the eyebrows of any skeptical college professor with suspicions of plagiarism.

Like the Rich biography, the story of Woolley's life is a microcosm of early Mormon and Utah history, though the greater abundance of documents allows a greater abundance of detail. Also, Cornwall did not feel confined to the hard facts of Woolley's immediate experience and instead wandered far and wide to paint the larger picture of the environment in which he lived. Of those instances, Arrington was most fond of her narrative of the 1848 crossing of the plains. "I am particularly proud of . . . the chapter on crossing the plains [which] I believe to be one of the best accounts in a chapter of what it was really like," he wrote to BYU president Ernest L. Wilkinson, noting in addition that it had drawn high praise from General Authority S. Dilworth Young, a Woolley descendant, who "congratulated me on the particularly fine job of that."[36] But other readers could just as easily identify other favorites—the California cattle drive, the development of church financial institutions and policies, or the life and governance of the Thirteenth Ward.

As much as Cornwall's literary grace, though, what sets the Woolley book apart from the other Arrington biographies is her sense of psychology and her courageous willingness to venture into the realm of informed speculation by filling in patterns perhaps only suggested by the sources in order to propose a consistent matrix of motivation.

Intriguing in its exploration of the social and psychological dimensions of religious conversion, rich in historical and descriptive detail, and written in a graceful, metaphorical prose, *From Quaker to Latter-day Saint* is everything one could want in a biography, Mormon or otherwise. The Woolley family was pleased with the book: Roland Rich Woolley was happy that his historian had produced another volume of family history with his funds; Elder S. Dilworth Young, as we have seen, was delighted with the book; and at a press conference Arrington and Woolley presented a copy to a smiling President Spencer W. Kimball. It is not known whether President Kimball's busy schedule allowed reading of such a massive volume, but his wife Camilla certainly read it and went out of her way to tell Arrington how much she had enjoyed it, especially the humor. "So I guess I passed the inspection of the prophet's family," Arrington wrote, with a sigh of relief. The *Church News* not only covered the presentation ceremony but even ran a review of the book, though to Arrington's chagrin it was drawn entirely from the dust jacket copy and the table of contents and bore no evidence that the reviewer had actually read the book. Even the humblest foot soldiers of Zion loved the book, as Arrington told in a humorous tale of self-deprecation: on a tour of the Deseret Book warehouse where the books were prepared for shipping to retail outlets, one of the workers told Arrington that they all loved the book; "It was the perfect size for packing."[37]

Regrettably, all of that good will reaching even to the Prophet himself could not calm the troubled waters at church headquarters that eventually swamped the History Division, for the Woolley book appeared in the same year (1976) as Allen and Leonard's *Story of the Latter-day Saints* and Arrington, Fox, and May's *Building the City of God*, both of which provoked irremediable consternation among the conservative General Authorities. The following April, as we have seen, G. Homer Durham replaced Joseph Anderson as head of the Historical Department, and the end of the History Division had begun.

Chapter 6

The Later Biographies

During the same period in which Leonard Arrington, Rebecca Cornwall, and the other research assistants were working on the Charles C. Rich and Edwin D. Woolley biographies, Arrington accepted a commission from the wealthy Eccles family to write a biography of David Eccles, Utah's first millionaire. A pioneer entrepreneur in such things as timber, railroads, sugar, and land development, Eccles was perhaps the most important single figure in the transformation of the Utah economy from agriculture to capitalism and industry in the late nineteenth and early twentieth centuries.[1] One can imagine that the Eccles commission appealed to Arrington for at least two reasons: not only was it another lucrative subsidy for historical writing, it also provided a tempting opportunity for Arrington to stick his toe into the troubled waters of twentieth-century Mormon economic history. As we have seen, he had refrained from launching into a sequel to *Great Basin Kingdom* because he could find in the twentieth century none of the grand yet simple themes that had shaped his interpretation of developments before 1900.

Apparently unwittingly, in accepting the Eccles commission Arrington had stepped into the midst of a long-standing family feud that, in an amazing turn of developments, actually worked to the immense improvement of his biography. David Eccles had been a polygamist. His largest family, by his first wife

Bertha Jensen, lived in Ogden, while his smaller second family, by his second wife Ellen Stoddard, lived in Logan.[2] The commission had been offered by means of a grant to Utah State University by Mrs. Nora (Nonie) Harrison, a daughter from the Logan branch of the family, while Arrington was still a professor there, and he was given an expense account and a reduced teaching load to write the book. With that money, Arrington hired his former secretary JoAnn Bair, who had worked on the Rich biography, to do the research and prepare chapter drafts, and George Daines, a former student, to research each of the Eccles businesses and to prepare the short histories that appear in the appendices.

Unfortunately, no one in the Logan branch had enough Eccles material to sustain the writing of the biography. Those materials were in possession of Mrs. Cleone Eccles, widow of David's son Royal, of the Ogden branch. Royal Eccles had long collected materials on his father's life with the idea of writing his own biography, an idea unfulfilled at his death. Although Mrs. Eccles was willing to make her husband's material available for Arrington's use, she made it clear that she was not interested in the kind of objective biography that Mrs. Harrison understood she was funding; rather, she wanted a laudatory exercise in hagiography.[3] Caught in the middle, Arrington had to exercise his best diplomatic skills. In the end, he negotiated a "Memorandum of Understanding" with Mrs. Harrison in which he accepted her stipulation "that the biography be 'professional'—objective, scholarly, and interesting." Although Mrs. Harrison reserved the right to "make corrections and suggest alternations [*sic*]" to the manuscript, she further stipulated that "the biography be told 'as it was,' and that it shall be a work of truth and integrity." For her part, Mrs. Eccles, "in consideration of the wealth of material collected and prepared by the late Royal Eccles," was granted by Mrs. Harrison the right "to make corrections and make alterations in the text, and that due acknowledgments shall be made of the important contributions of Mr. and Mrs. Royal Eccles."[4] Although the memorandum went a long way toward clearing a path upon which Arrington could work, no historian would want to be caught in that kind of crossfire, and it is perhaps no surprise that Arrington's manuscript pleased neither side.

Shortly after he became Church Historian, Arrington and his assistants completed the manuscript and submitted it to Mrs. Harrison, who was not pleased by its lack of objectivity. Mrs. Harrison and her husband Dick lived in California and one of their neighbors was the great western writer Wallace Stegner, who himself had grown up in Utah and who had written a variety of personal, historical, and fictional works about his home state.[5] Apparently after broaching the idea with Stegner, the Harrisons got Arrington to ask him to review the manuscript for a stipend of $1,000 to be paid from the Harrison fund at Utah State University, and Stegner accepted.[6]

Stegner's detailed fifteen-page critique of the manuscript was, as Arrington put it, nothing short of "a miniature manual on how to write a good biography."[7] As one would expect from a novelist, most of Stegner's suggestions are literary, instructing Arrington in ways to enliven the facts of his narrative by employing novelistic techniques like the cliffhanger chapter ending, the flashback, inserting speculative details using the subjunctive, and heightening the dramatic effect of Eccles's business ventures by narrating them chronologically as they developed, rather than following each to its own individual conclusion. Becky Cornwall already knew most of those devices and was employing them on the Woolley biography, but they were unfamiliar to JoAnn Bair, who wrote most of the Rich and Eccles books, and whose style was therefore much more pedestrian. To implement Stegner's ideas, Arrington put his editor Maureen Ursenbach Beecher to work on the Eccles project. The result was an immense improvement in the book's style, but Arrington's delegation of the work meant that he himself did not learn Stegner's lessons very well for his subsequent projects.

Stegner also made substantive suggestions, mostly to give the book more bite by indicating how close Eccles operated to the edge of both morality and legality. Of Eccles himself, Stegner was under no illusions. "Am I cockeyed in thinking that Eccles was one of the biggest land pirates, timber pirates, coal pirates, railroad pirates, in the West?" he asked historian Fawn Brodie. "You'd never know it from Arrington's biography, and I am . . . about to suggest that he wipe off the whitewash and do the buzzard for what he was: a hell of an acute buccaneer whose conscience stopped at the edge of the family, or at the farthest, of the Church, and did not extend into business enterprises where the public lands, the laws of the United States, or other irritating irrelevancies were involved. Arrington, from what I know of him, is a perfectly nice guy; but if anybody ever wrote a Faith-promoting, Saint's-Life, exemplum of a biography, he did."[8] On the other hand, as he indicated to Arrington, Stegner was aware of the Eccles family pressures that put limitations on how far he could go in exploring Eccles's dark side:

> What I say will be necessarily bound by the instructions given you by the family, and the inhibitions imposed on you by the family. I understand that there were some—the Geddes matter, for instance—and though I don't think biography should have to be written within such limitations, if they exist, they exist, and you have no choice but to write your book within them or give it up entirely. So, when I here and there suggest that David Eccles ought to be studied and judged as a tycoon who more than once bent the law (especially in the acquisition of timberland), and behaved pretty much as all tycoons of his period behaved, you will understand that I am expressing my opinion; maybe you can't follow my suggestions even if you want to.[9]

More than once Stegner points out the flatness of Arrington's interpretation, or rather lack of interpretation:

> I miss the historian's judging and commenting voice. . . . Your perspective is fairly consistent from within your documentary materials—the diaries, letters, reminiscences, business records, and interviews. You do not comment on them, judge them, or quite sufficiently relate them to outside events and circumstances. Now and then I kept wishing for a guiding voice through this, the voice of the historian able to see the family and David Eccles in the context of a longer time and a larger West. You report faithfully; you seldom judge or comment. I think you should.

Nor did Stegner neglect to give examples of what that kind of "guiding voice" might say. The ambitious young David Eccles, for one thing, in his exploitation of natural resources, "chose to attack them alone, Gentile fashion, and not in concert with his church (which might, as you say, have inhibited his actions). . . . He was an operator, not a co-operator." And Stegner felt that the ruthlessness with which Eccles prosecuted his ambitions ought to be brought out: "Eccles is fascinating, like a ditching machine. He digs through lawn, shrubs, roots, rocks, and part of the fascination is watching his foot-by-foot, inevitable progress, and the neat trench he leaves behind him."[10]

As Arrington saw, David Eccles represented a new type of Mormonism and a new type of Mormon who stood at the transition point between the old cooperative, agrarian model whose financial component never transcended the ken of the small shopkeeper Edwin D. Woolley, and the twentieth-century model grounded in capital, investment, and industry. But the ethical price paid by that transition scarcely comes out at all in the book, notwithstanding the fact that Eccles's greed and lack of regard for legal or ethical considerations in pursuit of his ambitions were proverbial, as illustrated in an apocryphal anecdote Arrington dared not include in the biography: Eccles's death was caused by a heart attack he sustained while rushing up South Temple Street in Salt Lake City to catch the last train back to Ogden. As Arrington privately told the humorous anecdote, two bystanders

David Eccles.
Arrington's biography of the "pioneer western industrialist" embroiled him in a controversy between two of the polygamist's families. *Used by permission of Utah State Historical Society.* *All rights reserved.*

saw him collapse and ran over to render assistance. "One said to the other, 'Do you know who this is?' The other replied, 'I'm not sure but I think it's David Eccles.' The other said, 'Oh, is that so? Let's find out for sure.' So he reached in his pocket and pulled out a nickel and waved it in front of David Eccles's eyes. No response. The man then declared with finality, 'No, it can't be David Eccles. There's no glint there.'"[11]

Eccles, as Stegner pointed out, should be grouped with the Robber Barons of the late nineteenth century, those ambitious and ruthless capitalists and exploiters of labor, consumer, and resources who built modern American industry and finance. No doubt under pressure from the Eccles family, Arrington soft-pedaled instances of unscrupulous or illegal practices when he had to deal with them at all. As Lee Scamehorn observed in a review of the book, "Arrington implies Eccles, through his lumbering enterprises [Scamehorn's example], engaged in fraudulent practices to obtain titles to timber lands. If, indeed, this was the case, the author should be more explicit. . . . Arrington recognizes the existence of those practices, suggesting that they resulted from 'unreasonable and shortsighted' federal regulations governing public timber lands (p. 93). Blame for the plundering of natural resources, the author seems to say, rests not with individuals and corporations, but with faulty public policies!"[12]

Glossed over in the biography, David Eccles's business practices can only be adequately discovered through detailed study of each of his individual enterprises—a literature which has been slow to develop and which is in no way accomplished by the appendix of short histories compiled by Arrington's student George Daines. One study which *is* adequate, Craig Torbenson's history of the Promontory-Curlew Land Company, one of Eccles's last ventures, suggests the complete picture will not be a pretty one.[13]

None of this, however, troubled Arrington in any major way, and the general tenor of the biography is the rags-to-riches story of a penniless Scottish immigrant whose financial genius benefited all: "Within his Church and the vast western area, predominantly Mormon, [David Eccles] was known, but even more, among non-Mormons he was respected as a loyal Latter-day Saint who functioned successfully among Gentile businessmen; he pioneered the secularization of business in the Mormon cultural setting. To the opening and industrialization of the vast intermountain and northwest he contributed his vision, his energy, his prudent management. The West, vast and growing when David Eccles found it, was even fuller of promise when he departed it." In the end, Arrington reminisced, "I was delighted to do the biography of David Eccles. He was an excellent example of the American success story."[14]

When Arrington became Church Historian in 1972, there were two galling lapses in Mormon biographical literature, for the then-standard biographies of the two greatest leaders in Mormon history were both unflattering in tone and written by authors outside the church. The standard biography of Joseph Smith was the hostile *No Man Knows My History*, by the apostate Fawn Brodie. Equally unacceptable to Latter-day Saint readers was the 1969 biography of Brigham Young, *The Lion of the Lord*, by the non-Mormon Stanley P. Hirshson. Both books had been published by Alfred A. Knopf and had won a wide national circulation for a largely negative interpretation of the origins and early history of the Mormon Church.[15] In time (1977) a better researched and interpretively more favorable life of Joseph Smith appeared in Donna Hill's *Joseph Smith: The First Mormon*, but a favorable biography of Brigham Young was still lacking.[16]

Hirshson's book, while inadequate in most ways, was actually not as bad as Arrington liked to assert, for he saw no value in the book at all. With great pleasure, he reported that the 1970 annual meeting of the Mormon History Association had voted it "The Greatest Missed Opportunity of the Year." With no reference to the book's interpretation, Arrington judged that "the Hirshson book is a poor excuse for an authentic biography, and the reason it's so poorly done is that the author spent not even one day in the hundreds of boxes of Brigham Young materials in the Church archives here in Salt Lake City."[17] During that visit to the church archives, Arrington said, Hirshson "learned two things: First, that there was an enormous body of material that . . . would take him years to go through; second, that he could not see everything that was there." Thereupon Hirshson "went back to New York using as his source the articles about Brigham that had been published in New York newspapers. The statements in these biased reports were almost never checked against documentary sources, and so Hirshson's portrait of Brigham was that of a liar and a scoundrel. Little was said about Young's genuine accomplishments as a leader."[18] Hirshson told a different story. By his account, he was rebuffed at the church archives, given "no help or encouragement," and led to believe that "the widely circulated stories of secret materials in the possession of the Mormon church are, if not false, exaggerations."[19] Arrington's autobiography pretty much corroborates Hirshson's report, for he says the vast bulk of the Young papers were discovered by History Division staff member D. Michael Quinn in an uncataloged state in the basement of the Church Office Building.[20] While Hirshson undoubtedly should have pressed harder for access to such Young materials as were available, he can hardly be held culpable for not using records of which even the archivists were unaware and who, even if they had known about them, properly would have denied access due to their unprocessed state. Hirshson consulted more than New York newspapers, doing primary research in the manuscript collections of the Utah State Historical Society, the Bancroft Library, and other repositories in addition to examining the *Journal of Discourses* and other published Mormon sources.

All of that notwithstanding, however, the discovery of the Young papers rendered the Hirshson biography even less adequate than it had been, and necessitated a new look at the great Mormon colonizer. Who would be willing to undertake such a project? Arrington's papers during the early years of the History Division contain feelers from a number of scholars, no doubt with varying degrees of seriousness: James Allen, Klaus Hansen, Richard Bushman, and Arrington's favorite, Jack Adamson of the University of Utah English department. Although inactive in the church, Adamson was steeped in its culture and was an original thinker and powerful writer. Unfortunately, Adamson's unexpected death from a heart attack in 1975 removed him from the contenders.[21]

Ultimately it was Arrington himself who decided to undertake the biography. He had wanted to do it from the beginning, but as he wrote in 1973, when he was still occupied with setting up the History Division, "my administrative duties are so onerous that I cannot see any possibility of getting to it in the next two or three years." In the end, it was none other than Mormon president Spencer W. Kimball who persuaded him to begin the book and even suggested the course he should take in writing and publishing it:

> He considered it shameful that most libraries in the United States and Great Britain had only anti-Mormon material on their shelves, and he wanted something written that libraries would buy and that would convey an accurate picture of our great prophet. To be sure that the book would be given national recognition he suggested it be published by Alfred A. Knopf, the most respected press in America. He also asked me to have the book read in manuscript by non-Mormon historians as well as by LDS historians so that we could be sure the book would be written so as to appeal to non-Mormon readers as well as LDS readers. I told him I would do my best. President Kimball also suggested that I undertake the project on a private basis so that no one could blame the Church itself for any inaccuracies or misinterpretations. I followed this counsel and paid all the expenses privately connected with its research and writing.[22]

To the degree that Arrington "followed this counsel," it proved to be good advice. Knopf, "the most respected press in America," certainly provided a national circulation for the book,[23] and Arrington did insulate the church from blame for "any inaccuracies or misinterpretations" by paying his research assistants out of his own pocket and doing the writing on his own time. (Concomitantly, it insulated Arrington from meddling by church officials, perhaps also a consideration in President Kimball's mind.) There is no indication, however, either in Arrington's papers or in the book's acknowledgments, that he ever solicited critiques from any non-Mormon readers, and that omission renders the book vulnerable to the cogent criticism that it is too much of a corrective to the hostile historiography it was written, in part, to counter. What one most misses in the book, in short, is the editorial touch of another Wallace Stegner.

Although the Young biography might not have been Arrington's best, it certainly represented the culmination of the communitarian approach to history writing he had pioneered back in the USU days and developed during the History Division and Smith Institute phases of his career. Not only did Arrington reenlist the services of Richard Jensen and Ron Watt from the days of the Charles C. Rich biography, Becky Cornwall from the Woolley project, and Maureen Ursenbach Beecher from the Eccles book, but he also drew heavily on research, writing, and editing from his associates in the History Division and the Smith Institute: Ronald Walker, Ronald Esplin, William Hartley, Dean Jessee, and others. The acknowledgments section, in fact, is a virtual roster of his team members through all those years.[24]

The book's greatest virtue is in the depth to which it draws upon the collective expertise of that pool of great scholars, who immersed themselves in the newly available Brigham Young papers that were discovered and processed by the church archives during the previous decade. It was an expertise that even Leonard Arrington, for all of his lifelong familiarity with the sources and traditions of Mormon history and culture, could not have hoped to develop by himself. And of course no previous biography had come anywhere close to that depth of documentation.

But the shortcomings of the book were almost as conspicuous as its virtues. For one thing, like all the previous Arrington biographies, except the Woolley, it is almost entirely innocent of psychology. The story of Young's conversion to Mormonism, for example, a central event in the life of the great religious leader, is grounded almost entirely in later family reminiscences and sermons recorded in the *Journal of Discourses*. Valuable as those sources are (we could wish for similar documents from the hand of C. C. Rich), they are later formulations that may or may not accurately represent the actual experience. It is true that, unlike Joseph Smith, Brigham Young was no writer and not much given to the kind of introspection the biographer wants, and thus there are few if any contemporary sources that open windows to his interior life. That would seem to be all the more reason to view his later reconstructions of the event, which created a particular image for public approval, with a jaundiced eye and look for ways to read between the lines and probe to see if a different image might emerge. Evidence of such probing would at least assure the reader that the biographer has attempted to get beneath surface appearances, even if nothing is found there.

On Brigham's later life in the church, as an apostle and eventually as president, Arrington often seems to soften his image as a dictator and perpetrator of violence. On the Danites, for example, the fearsome enforcers much beloved of anti-Mormon mythology, Arrington points out that their creation in Missouri was unauthorized and their existence brief. When they cropped up again in Utah, he likens them to "Minute Men who were prepared to leave at a moment's notice to pursue Indian or white raiders in order to recoup stolen cattle or horses." On the verbal ferocity Young would unleash upon his enemies from the Tabernacle pulpit, Arrington claims that his bark was worse than his bite and quotes Young to the effect that "I have never hurt any person any other way except with this unruly member, my tongue." His intemperate rhetoric, which even Arrington admits could reach ghoulish proportions, was in reality "only a cover for Brigham's basically nonviolent feelings, for he was basically a nonviolent person." Nor did the Lion of the Lord possess anything like absolute authority over his own people: "The assumption that Brigham was a dictator whose will was law does not hold up against evidence of his frustration in establishing the United Order."[25]

These and many other examples in which Arrington shows

Brigham Young to have been a wise and compassionate leader, though one of implacable determination, and a loving family man are most welcome as correctives to the hostile and simplistic generalizations of anti-Mormon literature. They also go a long way to support his thesis that Brigham Young was a more complicated person than previously appreciated. "Some of the fascination with Brigham is that one can know a great deal about him yet never fully understand," he concludes; "his personality was full of ambiguities and complexities."[26]

And yet, much of Arrington's emphasis on Brigham's softer nature is disingenuous. It is true that the United Order enjoyed only a very limited success both in duration and extent, not only in its thoroughgoing collectivism, as at Orderville, but even in the corporate capitalism of its centralized businesses. But that is a poor gauge of Brigham's authority, for he had placed himself in the path of a tidal wave of individualism and free enterprise that swept everything before it in the late nineteenth century. By the end of the following century, much larger and much more authoritarian regimes like those in the Soviet Union and China would find even themselves yielding before the same forces. And how could writers like Arrington and his associates ever have claimed that words—especially the violent thunderings of which Brigham was capable—had no effect on the actions of those who heard them? One could as cogently claim that the words of Hitler and Churchill had no effect on their countrymen before and during World War II and that those of Winston Churchill had no effect on its resolution.

It is, in fact, in Arrington's downplaying of Mormon violence and Brigham Young's role in it, especially his involvement in its most egregious manifestation, the Mountain Meadows Massacre, that one finds the book most disappointing. Probably the most bitterly debated episode in Brigham Young's life has been the Mountain Meadows Massacre, and if a reader could reasonably expect one thing of a new biography, it would surely be new research and insights into that deplorable event. *Brigham Young: American Moses* presents absolutely nothing original in either research or interpretation of this event. If Hirshson's Brigham Young biography was the "Greatest Missed Opportunity" of 1969, then Arrington's revisiting of the Mountain Meadows Massacre was the greatest missed opportunity of 1985.

Before 1950, when Juanita Brooks's now classic *The Mountain Meadows Massacre* appeared, Mormon historiography had dealt with the massacre as an aberrant act of violence largely provoked by the emigrants themselves. Most of the killing, so the story went, had been done by Indians, though a few Mormons had been dragged into participation under threats from the Indians and from the fanatic John D. Lee, who was executed for his role in the massacre in 1877. For the most part, Brooks continued to blame the emigrants for their own demise, but she also pointed out that other southern Utah Mormon leaders were as culpable as Lee, and that in fact a large force of Mormons had been involved in the killing. Their involvement, though, could be explained (if not excused) as an aberrant event carried out in a hysterical state of mind created by fanatical preachers during the Mormon Reformation. Brooks exonerated Brigham Young who, she said, had no foreknowledge of the massacre and in fact had issued orders to let the emigrants pass peacefully—orders that had not reached the scene in time to prevent the massacre.[27]

Although Brooks's book initially outraged conservative Mormons and caused her to be largely ostracized in her own community, it was immediately accepted as the standard work by western historians generally, and over the years it even gained acceptance within the Mormon community as basically fair-minded and the least devastating means by which the Saints could come to grips with their history's darkest shadow. When Arrington came to write his biography of Brigham Young, he

Although Arrington's 1985 biography of Brigham Young was less critical than it might have been, it was the first biography to be based on full access to the Young Papers. *Image of front cover used by permission of Alfred A. Knopf, a division of Random House, Inc.*

followed Brooks's facts and interpretation in almost every detail, despite the fact that the intervening thirty years had brought to light new sources and that Brook's interpretation was beginning to look a bit shopworn. Over ensuing years, younger scholars with the energy to probe the sources more deeply and with less inclination to protect the image of Brigham Young as a gentle father figure have constructed a very different picture.[28] They point out, among other things, that the emigrants probably had little or no role in provoking the incident, that the Indians also played only a minor role, that the violent rhetoric of Brigham Young, who had instigated the Mormon Reformation, was a major factor in whipping up the hysteria that swept the territory in 1856–57, that he had at least tacitly approved the massacre, and that he had actively covered it up after the fact. Every element in this reinterpretation was available to Arrington in the 1980s if only he had been interested in looking deeper into the sources and thinking deeper about their meaning, but Hirshson's shadow hung so heavily over him that he simply was not interested in giving due consideration to Brigham's dark side.

Nor was he interested in looking deeply into polygamy, another of Mormon history's skeleton-filled closets. As Stephen J. Stein observed in his review of the book, "Arrington presents Young as a model husband and father" for the emulation of twentieth-century Mormon men, but ignores the "heavy official obligations" and "his almost constant travels" that "undercut severely his capacity to be the ideal husband of many wives and the caring father of many children." Furthermore, as Stein points out, the rise of feminism and of women's history during the 1960s (movements Arrington ironically supported, as Stein does not note), compels the Brigham Young biographer to address polygamy from the women's side as well, as Arrington does not. Questions nowadays focus on issues like rivalry among the wives, the nature of their sexual relations with their husband, and the issues raised by Ann Eliza Webb's divorce suit; yet Arrington the feminist largely ignores them.[29]

Brigham Young: American Moses is by far the most extensive biography of the great Mormon leader yet to appear. Arrington's communitarian approach to writing history paid handsome dividends, for he was able to assign research associates to aspects of Young's life for which no secondary literature yet existed, thus in effect creating a monographic literature and synthesizing it at the same time. It would have been difficult for one person to accomplish such a feat alone and impossible for him to complete it at all without sacrificing every other project in which he was involved. Nevertheless, the work cannot be considered definitive, for in his concern to create a more positive image of Brigham Young than one finds in Hirshson and the anti-Mormon literature, Arrington neglected to balance it with an equally frank examination of the dark side. Brigham Young was too complex to deserve anything less.

After Brigham Young, Arrington returned to a series of "vanity" biographies similar to the ones he had written for the Woolley and Eccles families: the Silver family supported the writing of the lives of Harold Silver, an inventor and engineer whose devices facilitated the production of sugar from sugar beets, among other things; his wife Madelyn, a teacher and aspiring writer whose career was cut short by death just as it was beginning; and the grasping livestock baron Charles Redd, a David Eccles of the canyon country who, incidentally, had put up the money for the endowed chair held by Arrington at BYU and the Center for Western Studies at the same institution.[30] Also, at the time of his death in 1999, Arrington was collaborating with his second wife Harriet on a biography of her grandmother, Alice Merrill Horne, an early-twentieth-century poet, feminist, promoter of the arts, and member of the Utah House of Representatives.

Once completed, the Horne biography will be a major contribution to Utah women's history, for Horne was a powerful personality whose career and example made a significant difference in the status of Utah women and the arts. Of the others, the Harold Silver biography is significant because it represents a return on Arrington's part to the kind of economic history in which he had been trained in graduate school, a history not of statistics and impersonal forces and trends, but a history propelled by creative individuals. "History is made by people—by men and women—not by input-output ratios, investment opportunities, foreign exchange balances, or other quantitative measures of economic health," Arrington pointed out in the preface.[31]

The Madelyn Silver biography was also significant in that it at least identified a major theme in the experience of Utah women even if it failed to exploit its potential: how, within the role restrictions of Mormon culture, does a creative woman balance her family obligations with her literary impulses? Silver's "private diary furnishes evidence that she was frequently haunted by the feeling that her call to wifehood, motherhood, church and community activity deprived her of full expression of her literary talent, which she had dreamed of developing in poetry, short stories, and plays," Arrington notes. "She found a substitute in teaching literature and religion, and in using poetry and short stories to illustrate her class presentations and lectures. Was the alternative satisfying? Did the joys of wifehood, motherhood and sisterhood counterbalance or only postpone Madelyn's yearning to write? As she strove to meet outside expectations, did she fail to grow richer and deeper? Was she unsuccessful in developing a fuller self?"[32]

Her diaries also reveal a deep feministic orientation—indeed, an almost cynical feeling that Mormon culture had become inherently inimical to the needs of creative women. At the basis of her dissatisfaction was a historical interpretation: "Historically, Mormon (and Utah) women had equal access with males to the church's (and territory's) institutions of higher learning, the right to file for divorce on grounds of incompatibility, the virtual guarantee of such divorce petitions, the right to own property, the right to engage in any business enterprise, official encouragement to be trained as bookkeepers and take care of the family's finances if husbands were inefficient, and official instruction to seek medical treatment from other women doctors rather than males." In time, though, church authorities had taken all that away: "During Madelyn's lifetime; that is, from the 1920s onward, Mormon women experienced an erosion of their autonomy and status, both social and ecclesiastical. Church authorities who helped bring this about were unaware of or chose to ignore early Mormon teachings and examples of female autonomy," she felt.[33]

Madelyn Silver, then, might have made an ideal subject for a biography if she had lived long enough to explore her potential, for she was an intelligent, articulate woman with an awareness of history and of her own circumstance, caught between her inner artistic impulses and her personal and cultural obligations to her family. Although she taught and wrote during her child-rearing years, she had placed her hopes on shifting her energies toward a literary career once the children were gone. Tragically, she died within weeks of her last son's entering college, so her potential remains largely unknown.

In retrospect, Leonard Arrington left an ambiguous legacy as a biographer. On the one hand, he brought to his work in Mormon history a sense that people were the basic vehicles of the historical process, and thus that the study of individual lives could elucidate that process. On the other hand, Mormon biographical literature, which in his day was largely hagiography, has only partly emerged into serious critical study because of his efforts. So much of his work was family funded, and thus encumbered with interpretive restrictions, that he was hampered in turning Mormon biography into a critical enterprise. And, with his felt obligation to keep all his subjects safely within the fold of the faithful, his optimism that ignored or undervalued the darker sides of their personalities, and his lack of psychological insight, Arrington deprived his biographies of the critical edge needed to bring Mormon historiography to a new level of intellectual maturity. Finally, Arrington allowed most of his subjects to be chosen for him, and those choices were not always the ones that would offer the best vantage points on the development of Mormon history. The Woolley biography, enhanced by the intellect and literary skill of Becky Cornwall, was a fortunate exception. The David Eccles book was also a fortunate choice, but despite Wallace Stegner's prodding, it unfortunately did not receive the critical eye which that shady career deserved. It is also unfortunate that funding could not have been found to enable him to divert his attentions from Madelyn Silver to Alice Merrill Horne, whose long and well-documented career would have allowed a more adequate exploration of some of the same themes.

Chapter 7

The Later Histories

The nineteenth and twentieth centuries in Mormon history seem almost like two different worlds. Just as America emerged from what the historian Henry Steele Commager calls "the watershed of the nineties," so Mormon history experienced its own watershed at the same time, symbolized most conspicuously by President Wilford Woodruff's 1890 Manifesto that abandoned polygamy. But the Mormon watershed included much more than the Manifesto, important though it was. At the same time, other developments like the reorientation of Utah political parties along national lines instead of church affiliation and the diversification of the economy to include capitalism and industry as well as agriculture constituted a larger movement that historian Gustive Larson calls "the Americanization of Utah." That movement culminated, in some ways, with Utah's achievement of statehood in 1896, but its social, economic, and political ramifications dominated Utah history throughout the twentieth century.[1]

From unity to multiplicity: as Henry Adams saw, it was the great theme in the history of Western civilization itself in its transition from the medieval to the modern, and Mormon history, as it faced the twentieth century, became a microcosm of that theme.[2] From theocracy to democracy; from communitarianism to individualism; from agriculture to capitalism; from church sponsorship and control to church investment; from home industry to the factory; from self-sufficiency to world economy—how could Mormonism retain its uniqueness and remain faithful to the vision of Joseph Smith and Brigham Young when those changes were pulling it into a vastly different world? Mormon historians are still laboring to survey in all its dimensions the process by which the church accomplished that feat.

Leonard Arrington saw that theme clearly and also saw clearly the challenges it presented to the historian. *Great Basin Kingdom*, for all its richness of detail, was at bottom a very simple book, for it narrated the single theme of the application of Mormon cooperative institutions to the task of settling the arid West. To be sure, the latter chapters dealt with the intrusion into the Mormon kingdom of outside social and economic forces largely through the arrival of the railroad, but they showed the Mormons blunting the effects of that intrusion and assimilating those alien forces on their own terms and in ways that left their culture essentially intact.

Having sketched, then, nineteenth-century culture in its essential features (at least its economic ones, with considerable attention to their social and political ramifications), the obvious next step was to move into the next century and show how that culture became permutated into the Mormon world as it is today. But, as we have seen, Arrington paused at the brink of that prospect and called for reinforcements before he plunged in. As he wrote to fellow historian Rodman Paul, he thought it premature to attempt a history of Mormonism in the twentieth century until a proper foundation had been created in monographic studies of many narrower topics.[3] At the same time, though, he came to realize that even his treatment of nineteenth-century institutions, especially the economic aspects of communalism, was not as full as it might be. This chapter is the story, in part, of Arrington's own efforts to create that monographic substructure and then his attempt, with Davis Bitton, to put it all together in an integrated narrative.

His first venture into twentieth-century Mormon economic history was his history of the Utah-Idaho Sugar Company (U and I Sugar) commissioned by the company in July 1965 and hastily completed by the following April in order to meet the company's desired release date for the book in October 1966.[4] Unlike the other book projects begun during his days as professor at Utah State University, this one was written with very little assistance from others and it was completed before he left for Salt Lake City to become Church Historian.

As one would expect, given the haste of its composition, *Beet Sugar in the West* is a relatively slight book—only 173 printed pages excepting appendixes and documentation. Nevertheless it boasts some impressive attributes, not the least of which is Arrington's conspicuous enthusiasm for what many historians would consider an arid topic. When offered the opportunity to write the book, Arrington says in the preface, "I jumped at the chance." But that was not just empty flattery of a corporate benefactor, as he points out, for he himself had grown up on a farm that grew sugar beets (among other things) "and knew first-hand many of the problems which had confronted the industry." Finally, he was encouraged in the project by the university, an agricultural college which had " 'grown up' with the industry and . . . contributed much to its advancement." As an indication of his personal interest and involvement in the subject, he dedicated the book to his father, "N. W. Arrington, Sugarbeet Grower Extraordinary."[5]

Arrington had freedom to choose the themes to be developed and the interpretations to be followed, for he had been granted "assurances that the company would make available all its historical documents and records, and that I would be given complete freedom in interpreting the history in an honest and straightforward manner." Given that freedom, Arrington naturally turned the book into the kind of humanistic treatment of economics in which he had been trained and to which he naturally inclined, and attempted to put that western company into its national context, rather than "dwell exclusively on the unique experiences and contributions of the firm, and emphasize company personalities and statistics." Arrington indicated that he "tried to choose themes that put U and I policies, problems, and achievements in their industrial and national perspective . . . and thus to integrate local and national history with reference to the beet sugar industry."[6] It was a promising manifesto for a pioneering venture into recent Mormon history. Although U and I Sugar was not always an exclusively Mormon company, the kind of breadth of perspective Arrington brought to its history is even today an attractive model, like *Great Basin Kingdom*, for a Mormon history interpreted in the larger context of American and world history.

As one would expect from an old Idaho sugar beet farmer, Arrington described the problems and techniques of sugar beet cultivation with an infectious zest and an unfeigned admiration for the farmers who have been able to master its rigors: "Sugarbeets are a relatively temperamental crop; they require special care and intensive cultivation. The soil must be well-prepared; good stands depend upon proper planting, irrigation, and cultivation; and, until the mechanization of recent years, the heavy labor required at thinning, weeding, and harvest-time has tended to discourage all but the hardiest farmers."[7] Perhaps surprisingly, though, for a man who found himself technologically challenged by the operation of a can opener, Arrington describes the chemical and mechanical intricacies of extracting the sugar from the beet with an equal zest and in an intimate detail that requires the reader's close attention.[8]

Most impressive, though, is Arrington's thesis that the sugar beet industry was the enterprise that propelled the Mormon economy into the twentieth century by grafting capitalism and industrialization onto the traditional agricultural base. Although sugar beets had been grown and processed profitably elsewhere, when transplanted to Utah and Idaho they took root not only in the well-watered soils of the Great and Columbia basins, but, even more important, in the society and culture of the Mormon people who found themselves uniquely prepared to turn the lowly vegetable into an international economic force.

Initially told that intensive watering through irrigation was bad for sugar beets and that only the smaller beets contained a high enough sugar percentage to be profitable, Mormon farmers had had enough experience with irrigated agriculture to recognize that both ideas were myths and that in fact well-watered fields could produce immense tonnages of large beets with high sugar content. Moreover, Mormon social regimentation had already given them the means of marshaling even relatively meager water resources in the interest of large-scale agriculture, while the large infusions of cash from sugar beet sales enabled them to consider even larger reclamation projects than their subsistence agriculture of the nineteenth century had permitted. Most impressive, in Arrington's view, was the great sugar beet irrigation project developed in the Bear River Valley of northern Utah, which reclaimed some 54,000 acres through the building of 140 miles of canals and provided support for 25,000 people. Once again, as in *Great Basin Kingdom*, Arrington allowed his enthusiasm for irrigation to assume theological proportions: "Once the abode of jackrabbit and beaver, Bear River Valley and its giant water project were finally redeemed by the sugarbeet."[9]

Even considered exclusively in its agricultural dimension, sugar beet cultivation represented a major shift in the Mormon economy, from subsistence to staple farming and from consumption to cash. Throughout history, the line between subsistence and staple agriculture has never been rigid, for subsistence farmers—those who farm mostly to produce their own food—have always produced a certain surplus for a cash income, and producers of staple crops like the cotton planters have also grown a major part of their own food on garden plots. Certainly the line was blurred in nineteenth-century Utah even during the pioneer period (1847–69) as Mormon farmers fed not only themselves but also sold food and animals to the gold rush miners and other overland travelers and to the soldiers at Camp Floyd, and they even exchanged agricultural products for industrial goods via the large "church trains" that transported emigrants to Utah before the completion of the railroad. And of course the railroad accelerated that shift by providing easy access for Utah farm products to the national market. Nevertheless, the rapid shift toward sugar beet cultivation from the 1890s until World War I represented a major reorientation of Mormon agriculture.

The larger significance of sugar beets, though, is not just in their agricultural importance; rather, they represented a shift as well into capitalism and industry, for the Mormons decided from the beginning not just to market the raw beets but to manufacture their own sugar as well. That decision required not only the importation of machinery and technological knowledge but also the means of generating capital and a labor force. As Arrington pointed out, during the days before the mechanization of sugar beet farming, it was a very labor-intensive enterprise in which all its essential operations were done by hand. The factories required a labor force as well, to feed beets into the machines and operate them and to package and transport the sugar. Labor, however, turned out to be the easiest challenge to meet, for large Mormon families provided a work force of young farmers willing and experienced in field work, and even the adult farmers were available for factory jobs when the harvest was done and welcomed the work to keep them busy through the winter.

Generating the capital required for the purchase of machinery, the erection of factories, and the construction of irrigation projects was a different matter, and one that required not only a new role for the Mormon Church, but also generation of capital through the cultivation of outside investors. During the nineteenth century most industrial ventures in Utah were small in scale and local in scope and the church created and ran them directly, financing them by tithing funds. The sugar beet industry, however, required far greater financial resources than tithing could provide. Thus the church came to assume a new role as an investor and an encourager of investment, and although church leaders and individual Mormon entrepreneurs controlled the corporate boards, they had to do so cognizant of the interests and the approval of the stockholders, many of whom were non-Mormons, in mind.

Thus, in Arrington's interpretation, the sugar beet industry redeemed not only an agricultural region like the Bear River Valley but in fact it redeemed the very economy of Mormonism itself, grafting onto its nineteenth-century base a twentieth-century superstructure and integrating the two into a whole that allowed it to retain its essential uniqueness while yet moving into the modern world. While Mormon farmers continued to employ traditional irrigated agriculture accomplished by the labor of large families and coordinated by church organization, they added an industrial component to it, processing their own farm products and financing it all with capital invested by Mormon businessmen and outside, non-Mormon, sources. Moreover, like the great "trusts" that were dominating the American economy at the end of the nineteenth century, Mormon control of the sugar beet industry concentrated immense financial power through both horizontal and vertical integration. As one history of the United States explains, "combination had a great many advantages. . . . Where combination was along horizontal lines—the combination, for example, of all manufacturers of typewriters—it was easy to control production and price. Where combination was along vertical lines—the control, by one corporation, of all the elements of raw materials, transportation, manufacture, marketing, and finance of a single product, like the Ford car—it gave a degree of independence and of power that no isolated industry could expect to enjoy."[10] The sugar beet industry offered both types of combination and began the large shift in the Mormon economy and culture that has made it the financial power that it is today.

Arrington does not indicate where the Mormons learned the techniques of combination, whether it was an indigenous development or modeled upon the examples of other combinations of the day like the oil or steel trusts. One could imagine that it was both, for corporate combination was simply "in the air" nationwide, and yet the Mormon cooperative experience in both agriculture and business meant that they had few lessons to learn from scratch. Furthermore, U and I Sugar gained direct experience in the operations of a trust after 1902 when its directors sold a controlling interest in the corporation to the Sugar Trust itself, Henry Havemeyer's American Sugar Refining, which consolidated its control of the American sugar industry at that time by buying up most of the independent producers. In Arrington's interpretation, it was a mutually beneficial merger: Havemeyer gained the virtual monopoly he sought, while the Mormons gained the capital and technological expertise they needed to expand their operations throughout the West. Additionally fortunate for U and I was the fact that Havemeyer was a relatively enlightened Robber Baron who was more interested in profits than power; he recognized the efficiency of the Mormon administration of the company and allowed "the same management to remain in control, with full local autonomy."[11] When antitrust actions on the eve of World War I forced Havemeyer to divest himself of some of his sugar interests, the Mormons were able to buy back the stock they had sold him and resume full ownership. Thus the canny Mormon sugar beet entrepreneurs found a long enough spoon to gain a full meal at the devil's table while not being devoured themselves.

U and I's expansion into other parts of the West outside Mormon Country almost inevitably required a certain secularization and professionalization in its administration in which "appointments and advancements no longer bore a churchly cast; policies no longer contained ecclesiastical overtones." Investors, too, were scattered throughout the nation, though the Mormon Church retained some 47 percent of the stock. Moreover, Arrington points out, the secularization of U and I was never complete, for the company maintained a communitarian ethos deeply rooted in its Mormon heritage: "Its historic ties with the church have infused a concept of stewardship that is both rare and praiseworthy. There is a strong sense of obligation to the community, to growers, to labor, and to the consumer [that is lacking in purely secular enterprises]."[12]

In Arrington's view it was that communitarian spirit that defined the very uniqueness and genius of Mormonism. As we have seen, the thesis of *Great Basin Kingdom* was that communitarianism was one of the fundamental strains in American culture, and that one of the basic functions of Mormonism in American history had been to keep alive that sense of social obligation as the culture at large descended into a cycle of individualism and exploitation with little concern for the common good. Although he had given as much space as possible in his magnum opus to Mormon communitarian institutions, he recognized the need for much more detailed and systematic study of them. In 1964 he began pursuing various avenues by which that study might be accomplished and the communal aspects of Mormon history be made more widely known.

He proposed that Deseret Book publish an anthology of eight journal articles he had written on Mormon communitarian institutions. Although the articles (which were never in fact published as an anthology) went beyond what he had been able to do in *Great Basin Kingdom*, they "would represent, at best, a selection of readings on the subject," he admitted to fellow historian Richard Poll. "They would offer, under one cover, to church members some readings that are not generally available, and might be stimulating in counteracting the individualistic overtones that have come to dominate the current scene."[13] He also encouraged one of Poll's graduate students, Arch Egbert, to follow through on his proposed dissertation topic on the history of the United Order of Enoch, adding the additional incentive, which also never came about, of offering to turn over to Egbert all of his own notes on the Order.[14]

Lastly, he approached Everett Cooley, director of the Utah State Historical Society, about publishing under the Society's auspices an edited version of Feramorz Fox's lengthy study of Mormon communitarianism. Fox, president of LDS Business College, had completed the 426-page page study in 1937, but presumably the financial strains of the Great Depression had made it impossible for a publisher to consider a book of that length on what was probably seen as an esoteric subject. Arrington had discovered the typescript in 1946 while working on his dissertation and was immediately impressed with its potential to elucidate a neglected aspect of Mormon history that had been, in fact, the church's unique contribution. "Somehow, we need to remind citizens of the state of [t]his heritage of cooperation and collectivism and idealism," he urged Cooley. "People like [Ernest] Wilkinson and [J. Bracken] Lee and others have caused us to virtually forget this aspect of our past. It is one of the few well-documented movements of this type in American history which was not influenced directly by 'foreigners.' That is, no direct influence from Rapp, Owen, and others. A native American collectivism, and therefore significant in reasserting the American tradition of experimentation. A collectivism not tarred by the Marxist brush!"[15]

Thus was the genesis of *Building the City of God: Community and Cooperation among the Mormons*, Fox's manuscript which Arrington and Dean L. May, a Brown University Ph.D. in social history who had become a History Division research associate, revised and expanded for publication by Deseret Book in 1976.[16] The thesis of the book was twofold: first, that communitarianism was a native part of the American cultural heritage that had been preserved and developed by Mormonism and that thus, divorced from any Marxist revolutionary overtones, it was nothing to be feared; to the contrary, it represented the best in American altruism and social obligation. Also, Mormon communitarianism represented a continuity of tradition in which Joseph Smith's Law of Consecration of the 1830s, Brigham Young's United Order of Enoch in the 1870s, and Harold B. Lee's Church Welfare Plan developed in 1936 were only successive phases in the same movement as the church attempted to devise a communitarian plan that would, on the one hand, meet the economic circumstances of the time, and on the other, reflect the degree to which human nature was capable of embracing such a goal. "Church Doctrine has held that the Saints would come to live a higher Order, but no one has ever detailed just what that Order would be like," Arrington wrote to the playwright Carol Lynn Pearson, who was currently writing a musical about Orderville, Utah. "The United Order is, of course, different from Joseph Smith's Law of Consecration. The welfare plan—which is our modern version—is still different. My own reaction is that we come about as close to living the Revelations as stated under our present system as we have done in other Orders."[17]

Building the City of God is an impressive piece of scholarship and, as the multiple authorship indicates, an authentic collaboration: using Fox's pioneering research as the base, Arrington added data from recently available sources while May applied methods and insights of contemporary social history. Among the virtues of the book were its greater coverage of early Mormon communitarianism than Arrington had accomplished in *Great Basin Kingdom*, which had focused on the Utah period of Mormon history to 1900. Another was its detailed study of individual communities that, once again, Arrington had previously done but this time was devoted to a major example of each type of communitarian experiment; thus, the diversity of the movement came into view clearly. As a comprehensive study of the whole sweep of Mormon communitarianism, it immediately became a standard work, and when the authors released a second edition in 1991 they found that scholarship in the intervening fifteen years had necessitated no essential changes.[18]

That is not to say that the book met with a universally enthusiastic reception, for in fact both ends of the thesis aroused ire in various quarters. Although conservatives like Ernest Wilkinson and J. Bracken Lee were no longer factors to be reckoned with, there were others much more dangerously placed—within the church hierarchy—who both literally and figuratively saw red at what they perceived as the authors' attempt to naturalize communitarianism as part of the American tradition and even to baptize it into the Mormon Church. For old Red-baiters like Elders Mark E. Petersen and Ezra Taft Benson, "communitarianism" sounded too close to "communism." "For that reason," Arrington speculated, "it caused them to shudder." Also, because of a perceived risk that it "might encourage unauthorized communal endeavors" (hippie and other communes were still fresh in the public mind in 1976) and because the book, after all, chronicled the failure of the United Order, one of the "major initiatives" of church leaders in the 1870s, it quickly lost any chance of a favorable reception at church headquarters. As a matter of fact, coupled with several related developments, the book provoked a major retaliation against Mormon scholars and liberals: the *Church News* was not allowed to review the book, Deseret Book was not allowed to issue a second printing, and writers affiliated with liberal Mormon publications like *Sunstone* and *Exponent II* were effectively silenced.[19]

Reviews in both academic and popular publications were much more positive, though not uncritical. While all praised the scholarship of the book in its intricate dissection of Mormon communal ideology and its application in a wide variety of institutions and circumstances, criticism generally focused on the authors' interpretation of the meaning of Mormonism's communitarian heritage and their thesis that the modern church welfare program is the culmination of that heritage. Nancy McCormick, writing in *Utah Holiday*, praised the authors for their elaborate reminder to their Mormon audience that communitarianism was a fundamental, essential part of Mormon history. However, she charged that the book "fades out in a wave of Mormon patriotism . . . [and] fails to bring together for us an overview of Mormon communal principles and history in relation to the nation as a whole. . . . Is the United Order, after all, merely an important episode in Mormon history, or does it also have a larger significance and influence on U.S. history?"[20] In other words, she seems to be saying, is the modern welfare system, and indeed the entire communitarian heritage, simply grounds for Mormon self-congratulation ("the Mormons take care of their own" is a proverbial assessment), or should it be an inspiration and example as well to reformers who want to see all unfortunate members of American—not just Mormon—society taken care of as a public obligation?

Similarly, James Clayton of the University of Utah history department observed that "if 19th century communitarianism was a failure, this book is not. Superbly researched and broadly conceived, *Building the City of God* is one of the best books within the genre of the New Mormon History." On the other hand, he asserts, "Including a discussion of the Church's Welfare Plan of the 1930's and contemporary food storage programs—which comes decades after the demise of the last United Order—stretches the concept of the original stewardship idea a bit far. There is not the slightest desire to achieve greater economic equality within the Church today, and cooperating with the secular government which was then attempting to destroy the Kingdom is hardly what the Mormons of that day had in mind. Nor is the 'sharing of burdens' in depressed times an exclusively Mormon idea." Linking the modern welfare system to nineteenth-century communalism, he concludes, is ahistorical, "trying to tack current efforts onto experiments long since discontinued."[21]

Clayton's point is well taken. As we have seen in chapter 3, Arrington ten years later seemed to make the claim that Mormonism had somehow prepared the way for the welfare state in its insistence that "federal and state governments, as agents of the people, have a responsibility to provide relief from disaster and, insofar as possible, maintain the economic health of the nation and its constituent parts."[22] The claim was absurd, as we have also previously noted, because the welfare state grew, historically, out of the same American communal tradition in which Mormonism had its roots, but independently, with little or no reference to Mormon influence or ideas. The claim was also ironic, because at the same time—the Great Depression—in which Arrington saw the Mormons leading the way toward corporate responsibility for relief from economic disaster, they were in fact exhibiting the very failure of their own communitarian resources by signing up in greater numbers than almost any other group in the country for the relief programs of the New Deal.[23]

Rather than addressing the question of how Mormonism had

saved the nation by paving the way to the welfare state, the authors of *Building the City of God* were faced with the much less expansive, but equally thorny, question of whether Mormon communalism had even saved Mormonism: in view of the abject failures of its first two communal experiments—the Law of Consecration and Stewardship and the United Order of Enoch—had the last one, the Church Welfare Plan, preserved enough of the old cooperative ethos to maintain Mormonism's uniqueness?[24] With even the church itself throwing its resources into capitalism by the turn of the twentieth century, it looked as though American individualism and corporate greed had triumphed over Mormon communalism and corporate obligation rather than the other way around. From that perspective, Mormons might well have rejoiced at the onset of the Great Depression, with its revelation of the bankruptcy of unbridled capitalism, which forced Mormons back upon their nineteenth-century communal heritage in their establishment of the Church Welfare Plan.

Toward the end of *Building the City of God*, Arrington admitted that the church welfare system, although an ambitious and universally admired program even outside the Mormon world, is only a pale reflection of the communitarian ambitions of Joseph Smith and Brigham Young:

> The present welfare system has a near-negligible effect upon the functioning of the whole economy in Mormon-dominated areas. It does not provide the central direction for regional economic development, which was an essential part of the economic orders preached by both Joseph Smith and Brigham Young. But it does provide an effective means of drawing a surplus from the community to provide for the poor, also an essential part of the systems taught by the earlier Mormon prophets. In the scale of its activities it is unquestionably the most successful of all the Mormon cooperative experiments.[25]

Minor though its actual economic role might be in the perspective of Mormonism as a whole, the welfare system has a

The Mormon Experience was Arrington and Davis Bitton's collaborative general history directed to a non-Mormon audience. *Image of front cover used by permission of Alfred A. Knopf, a division of Random House, Inc.*

powerful symbolic and emotional function in reminding Mormons of their communitarian heritage. In one of the most memorable passages he ever wrote, Arrington offered an example of that symbolic function. Toward the end of the last chapter he wrote for *Building the City of God* he reminisced of an evening spent in an apple-sorting shed helping process fruit produced for welfare distribution by farmers in the Wells Stake in Cache Valley:

> There seemed something wholesome about an event that put urbanites—factory workers, truck drivers, college professors, and mailmen—in touch with processes that bring forth the sustenance of human life. . . . An intangible spirit of community solidarity mingled in the sorting shed with the restrained, aristocratic scent of Delicious apples. . . . [The apple-sorting session] was one product of 150 years of effort to efface human selfishness and build a harmonious, equitable society. It did not seem modest when we reflected that here, at least, the visions of 1831 still intruded upon the meanness of men's lives, keeping alive the promise that a city of God just might one day be built on earth.[26]

In terms of where the center of gravity of the Mormon economy really lies, Arrington's evening in the apple-sorting shed seems as quaint as a horseshoe-pitching contest. But man does not live by bread alone.

In 1979 *The Mormon Experience: A History of the Latter-day Saints* appeared under the authorship of Arrington and Davis Bitton.[27] The book had been a long time coming, for Arrington had been working on it, or at least thinking about it, since 1966 when Rodman Paul, acting as Alfred A. Knopf's agent, had solicited it during Arrington's year as a sabbatical replacement at UCLA.[28] Arrington's response was enthusiastic, and so was that of Apostle N. Eldon Tanner, who agreed to open the church archives without restriction to support the project. "As far as I am aware, this is the first time that such blanket permission has ever been granted a scholar engaged in writing Mormon history," Arrington breathlessly reported to Knopf. "President Tanner made no request for the privilege of seeing the manuscript in advance, or for other limitations. In my application I stated that I had been engaged in writing about Mormon history for some 20 years and that these writings were an indication of the fact that I could handle materials and interpretations responsibly. It now appears possible to make an intimate study of Mormon policy using correspondence, diaries, and financial records which have hitherto not been examined by historians. Needless to say, I am delighted!"[29]

Of course attracting the interest of a publisher and gaining access to the sources were only preliminary steps; writing the book was another matter. Although Arrington inquired about an advance from the publisher and indicated that Utah State University would give him a reduced teaching load to work on the book, he seems to have accomplished little on that project by the time he was appointed Church Historian in 1972. At that point the project became assimilated into the History Division's master plan for research and publication, which meant that both research and writing assistance would be available and that the project could move forward with deliberate speed. Within that plan it fit nicely as a counterpart to *The Story of the Latter-day Saints* by Glen Leonard and James Allen, published for a Mormon audience. *The Mormon Experience*, issued by a commercial publisher, would be directed toward a general audience. Exactly who would be assigned to support Arrington on the latter project became a matter of considerable jockeying (as, also, did the personnel assigned to the other volume); at various times Dean May, John McCormick, Richard Jensen, and Michael Quinn were all discussed as participants, and by the time the book appeared, the list of assistants had both grown and shifted to include most of those employed by the division.[30] Although many shoulders were eventually put to the wheel, Arrington insisted that the final product was his and Bitton's. Though others created drafts of several of the chapters They were all significantly rewritten prior to the final version of the manuscript. [31] *The Mormon Experience*, then, represented Arrington's literary co-op at full function: many hands submitted contributions, but the whole was engineered and assembled by the two coauthors.

It was fitting that so much energy went into the book, for a great deal was riding on its success. With the cancellation of the sixteen-volume sesquicentennial series, the burden of producing a comprehensive reinterpretation of Mormon history now rested on a single volume, *The Mormon Experience*. As the manuscript neared completion, concerns began to build within the division regarding its likely reception by the Quorum of the Twelve, which, led by the conservative elders Benson and Petersen, had raised such opposition to the equally scholarly and circumspect interpretations of *The Story of the Latter-day Saints* three years earlier. Would *The Mormon Experience* meet a similar fate? By now none of the division staff expected Elder G. Homer Durham, the apostle in charge of the church Historical Department, to be any kind of vigorous advocate of the book as it went upstairs for review.

Surprisingly, it was none other than President N. Eldon Tanner, the apostle at whose instigation the entire department had been reorganized and the History Division created in the first place, who came to the historians' rescue. Although Arrington had been told the First Presidency was going to give the manuscript to Elder Neal A. Maxwell for review, to his immense surprise President Tanner arranged for it to be given to one of the *conservatives* instead—Elder Boyd K. Packer! It was a brilliant tactical ploy, as Durham told Arrington, "to get the support of a leading and articulate conservative behind the project, someone whose judgment would be accepted by Brother Benson and Brother Petersen, neither of whom will probably like the book."[32]

As it turned out, Packer had his own reservations about the

book, but he approved it for publication anyway, though he also advised that the First Presidency should not give it an official endorsement and instead simply let it proceed to publication without comment. Almost as surprising as Packer's approval was Durham's vigorous support during two meetings he and Arrington had with Elder Packer to discuss the book. To Packer's objection that he preferred straightforward narrative history to the interpretive style Arrington and Bitton had employed, Durham indicated that he shared Packer's preference but that he also understood that professional scholarly standards had turned the other way, "that there has been an increasing tendency on the part of historians to do interpretive history, and he told Brother Packer he thought historians would not think that Davis and I had done our duty if we did not do interpretive and analytical history." Similarly, Packer urged that only positive facts about church history should be included, so that the faith of young people would not be placed at risk, to which Durham countered that professional standards called for inclusion of both the good and the bad: "Brother Durham seemed to be defending the idea of presenting a balanced view, and Brother Packer himself agreed." But the greatest surprise for Arrington was yet to come, for when Packer gave him his ultimate assessment of the book, "he started out by saying that we have called this a history of the Latter-day Saints. He thought it was more than a history. It was an apology, he thought—at least it was as much an apology as it was a history. I would interpret that now to mean that he regarded this as a kind of sophisticated defense of the Church, its history and its position. For him to say that to me seems flattering."[33]

Although Elder Packer would later become the most implacable opponent of the academic Mormon historians, his approval of *The Mormon Experience* was well received by the authors and was prescient as well, for the book eminently fulfilled its expectations as the showcase and culmination of the efforts of the History Division. Even at the time of this writing, almost thirty years after its appearance, it still holds its own as the best general history of Mormonism. Much of its effectiveness in reaching the intended general audience lies in its organizational scheme, which is more topical than chronological, giving the authors space to introduce Mormonism as a unique American subculture through its institutions and folkways: the role of the ward, the status of women, the Mormon financial empire, and Mormon humor.

Most welcome to readers, especially skeptical ones, is the authors' frank acknowledgment of the reasons why so many people are unable to accept the claims of the Mormon prophet Joseph Smith at face value. Such acknowledgment is rare and unique among books produced within the Mormon Church. Both Joseph Smith's proponents and his detractors have made extreme cases, they point out, to the detriment of real understanding: "Mormon historians have been too ready to cast Smith in the mold of a modern, twentieth-century man sanitized from all superstitions or presently questionable activities; and critics may have been too ready to magnify into dire villainy activities probably as innocent and prevalent in the 1820s as astrology or health food faddism among respectable people today. . . . Both extremes," they reasonably conclude, "miss the heart of the man, whose often contradictory acts and paradoxical rhetoric suggest that the stereotypes ignore his humanity."[34]

The authors even suggest one way in which modern psychology might offer a way for both the faithful and the skeptics to understand Joseph Smith: "A possible key to at least a partial understanding of Joseph Smith lies in recent studies that portray the will to prophesy as the reaction of a few brilliant, conflicted persons to the unbridgeable contradictions of life. Most individuals respond to inconsistencies and injustices by either enduring them or discovering conventional solutions. Others, of a different cast of mind, are called—or call themselves—to prophethood."[35] One can look a long time in the literature of both pro- and anti-Mormonism for such an olive branch as this.

Another laudable section of the book is chapter 12, in which the authors explore the status of women in the Mormon Church. From the beginning of his career as Church Historian, Arrington had championed women's history and had made a prominent place for it in the programs of the History Division. Here, in their examination of polygamy, he and Bitton make it clear that while plural marriage did have some advantages, it also had its tragic side in the hurt experienced by individuals and by the church itself under federal persecution. More recently, the authors acknowledge the dismay with which Mormon women greeted the correlation movement, which robbed their organizations of the autonomy they had once enjoyed and also moved their publication program more under priesthood control. Overall, they conclude, the hopes raised in the larger culture by the feminist movement of the 1960s and 1970s had not been realized very well within Mormonism.

Other aspects of the book were less successful. As one might expect, on the vexed question of the Mountain Meadows Massacre the authors adopt the most conservative position possible—the same one Arrington would later follow in his Brigham Young biography. The interpretation offered by Juanita Brooks had become a bit shopworn in the succeeding three decades since its publication. Arrington and Bitton declined to dig deeper into the affair, admitting what they had to admit, but no more.[36]

Nor was their treatment of "Mormons and Native Americans" in chapter 8 satisfactory, for once again their thesis is based on a venerable myth, this time that the Mormons got along with the Indians better than other white pioneers because of their concept of them as Lamanites, a Book of Mormon people who, although presently degraded, had the potential of exaltation, and also because of Brigham Young's much-vaunted pragmatic policy that it was cheaper to feed the Indians than to fight them.

The idea of the comparative benevolence of Mormon-Indian relations on the western frontier is a difficult proposition to prove or disprove, though the weight of recent historiography has at least cast a shadow over its validity.[37] However, the available historiography in 1979 lacked some of today's clarity, and one obviously cannot hold Arrington and Bitton responsible for work that took place after their book's publication.

The Mormon policy toward the Indians might have been at times gentler than that of the U.S. Army, many of whose leaders believed that the only good Indians were the dead ones. But they certainly lagged behind other missionaries like the Franciscans and the Quakers in accepting the inherent value of the Indian person and the Indian culture.[38] And much of Brigham Young's pragmatic policy of friendship toward the Indians is no doubt better explained as the military strategy of a vastly outnumbered minority than as benevolence. No outnumbered pioneers—Mormon or Gentile—were foolish enough to risk war with the Indians until the demographic balance had shifted from inferiority, through what Richard White calls "the middle ground" where the two groups deal with each other as relative equals, to an ultimate position of numerical and military superiority in which the Indians could be forced into submission. In the end the result for the Indians inside and outside of Mormon country was the same: encroachment, war (even genocide), defeat and dispossession, the reservation system, and impoverishment.[39]

In 1988 Arrington and Bitton produced one final collaborative work, *Mormons and Their Historians*.[40] A slight work of fewer than two hundred pages, it offers a rapid survey of the works of historians of Mormonism from Willard Richards, George A. Smith, and Andrew Jenson to modern scholars like Richard Bushman, Jan Shipps, and Charles S. Peterson. As such, it constitutes a brief and readily accessible introduction to the Mormon historiographical tradition. While its brevity is probably appropriate in the case of the early, untrained historians like Richards, Edward Tullidge, and Orson Whitney, it becomes frustrating in its superficiality in the case of the "amateur" but highly skilled and critical scholars Bernard DeVoto, Fawn Brodie, Dale Morgan, and Juanita Brooks.[41] And, since the two coauthors were themselves two of the greatest scholars in the history of Mormon historical writing, the book suffers from their understandable shyness in critiquing their own work. To their credit, the book was written before the appearance of the excellent biographies of Brodie by Newell Bringhurst and of Brooks by Levi Peterson, but what one most misses is an extended critical look at their works and those of DeVoto and Morgan, for they were prominent among the scholars, as Arrington and Bitton acknowledge, who began propelling Mormon historiography in a critical, scientific direction.[42]

On the positive side, the book gives a valuable insiders' look at the by-then-defunct History Division and its enduring contribution, and it points the way, through its examination of the ongoing work of Bushman, Shipps, and Peterson of the constructive function critical historiography could have within Mormon culture. If the book is now almost completely superseded by Ronald W. Walker, David J. Whittaker, and James B. Allen's *Mormon History*, it fulfilled a valuable transitional function in the days when Mormon historians were only beginning to look within.[43]

Chapter 8

Arrington and the New Mormon History

Leonard Arrington died at his Salt Lake City home on February 11, 1999, of what the obituary referred to as "heart complications." The last decade of his life was a time of contrast: on the one hand, his ambition continued unabated, as he planned a continuous stream of writing projects far into the future; on the other, increasing health problems asserted his mortality. The negative effects of what he called "the Leonard way of life"—his love of rich food and distaste for exercise—compelled open heart surgery and ultimately cost him his life.[1] "Beloved Mentor," surely the most fitting epitaph in the Logan cemetery, is inscribed on his headstone where he lies beside his "Blessed Damozel" Grace.

To most people, Leonard Arrington was sui generis—a one-of-a-kind literary phenomenon who emerged from a most unpromising background to forge a most amazing publication record. *Great Basin Kingdom* alone would have been enough to establish his reputation as one of the great scholars of U.S. history. Its massive documentation in hitherto unused sources, its compelling interpretation of the nature of the Mormon economic experience and integration with Mormon theology and social institutions, and especially its thesis regarding the place of Mormonism within the larger American culture immediately earned it a place among the classics of U.S. historiography. Here was local history—the history of a region and a subculture—that was exhaustively researched, convincingly interpreted, and most unusual of all, placed in a creative interaction with the national history. That such a book could have been produced by an Idaho farm boy, even one with a degree in economics but still mostly self-trained in historical methods, was cause for amazement.

Still more amazing was the fact that he could follow it up with an ever-increasing torrent of books and articles not only on economic subjects but on a wide variety of Mormon-related topics from autobiography and biography to literature, social history, women's history, historiography, the history of technology, and almost anything else one could find in the world of Mormonism. Beyond that, as director of the History Division of the Church Historical Department, he presided over the greatest historical assembly line since Hubert Howe Bancroft's "literary industries" in nineteenth-century San Francisco. He and his associates produced hundreds of publications over a ten-year period, and that activity continues even to this day. Bancroft may have equaled Arrington in ambition and achievement as a historical entrepreneur, but not in sophistication of the output. Finally, the fact that Arrington could produce so much himself and direct so much production from others without, for the most part, being affiliated with a major academic research department is, once again with the notable exception of Bancroft, unique in American historical writing.[2]

Nevertheless, to see Leonard Arrington as an anomalous lone apple tree suddenly sprouting from barren soil and propagating a whole orchard from seedlings around his trunk would be to ignore his context. There was an orchard in which Arrington grew up, not only the literal but also the metaphorical, for the soil of Mormon culture nurtured other tall trees that sprouted far from the orderly irrigated fields but that had somehow tapped into the same aquifer. It was a diverse group of historical scholars with diverse relations to Mormon culture—consider Bernard DeVoto, Fawn Brodie, Dale Morgan, Wallace Stegner, Juanita Brooks, and Leonard Arrington. All sprouted from the same soil, and one can note some common features of bark, branch, and fruit as they matured.[3]

Also, if Leonard Arrington may not exactly have been a creator of the movement known as the New Mormon History, he certainly became its greatest exponent and, through his own prolific output and that of his disciples, its most influential contributor. The New Mormon History, which some have seen as beginning in 1945 with the appearance of Fawn Brodie's much-reviled but widely read and discussed biography of Joseph Smith, *No Man Knows My History*, was "new" in several characteristics.[4] For one thing, it was largely produced by scholars with solid academic training (Brodie herself would be an exception at this point)[5] and familiarity with current methods, not only in history, but also in fields of the social sciences and humanities that could be brought to bear on historical problems. Further, it was grounded in exhaustive exploitation of primary sources, many of which had not been available to previous historians, and the New Mormon Historians' books and articles were elaborately documented. Finally, the New Mormon History largely turned away from the concern of previous Mormon historians with apologetics for the Mormon faith. Although most of the new scholars were practicing Mormons, their interest focused more on establishing a factual record of Mormon history, rather than defending the truth of the religion.[6]

The preceding chapters have focused primarily on the originality of Leonard Arrington's historical work, with its strengths and shortcomings. We will now look at his roots in Mormon culture, his theology and philosophy, the elements he had in common with his aforementioned contemporaries, and his contributions to the New Mormon History.

Transitions in history are never as clean and clearly defined as historians, in their efforts to divide complex historical reality into intellectually comprehensible units, often make them appear. Furthermore, as that historical reality is in a constant state of flux, any historical moment can properly be seen in some way as a time of transition. Historiographically, Leonard Arrington's generation certainly represented a transitional phase in the writing of Utah and Mormon history from a time in which it was written almost entirely by people with no academic training to its current manifestation where it is written at its most sophisticated level, mostly within the academy. In time, the example of those transitional historians spread beyond Utah and Mormon history to raise the quality of western historical writing as well.

Most of what can be said about the background and historiographical characteristics of the other members of that generation applies also to Leonard Arrington and his work. For one thing, their academic training in history and historical method was very thin: though all of them held at least undergraduate degrees (Arrington and Wallace Stegner even held Ph.D.s), none of them could claim even a bachelor's degree in history, for DeVoto's was in creative writing, Brodie's and Brooks's were in English, and Morgan's was in art. The fact can hardly be overemphasized, for although modern historiography has seen some very sophisticated work produced by scholars lacking in graduate training—the examples of Allan Nevins and Arthur Schlesinger, Jr., come readily to mind—the Ph.D. has become conspicuous only in its absence, and the lack of even an undergraduate degree in the field is even more remarkable. The significance of this fact is that none of these historians had any training in history at a philosophical, or at least at an interpretive level. As a practical consequence, while all of them became expert researchers, tirelessly digging new sources and new factual material, and all of them became very competent writers (some, like DeVoto and Stegner were nothing short of literary artists), all of them fell short in some way when it came to interpreting the material they had dug up. DeVoto, for example, reified interpretive concepts like Manifest Destiny until his histories became the kind of metaphysical documents he professed to despise in others' work. At the other end of the spectrum, Morgan eschewed conscious interpretation altogether, professing just to present the facts, out of which their meaning would somehow naturally become clear. Arrington, for his part, tended to claim too much for his material (as DeVoto had done), almost claiming that the Mormon Village and its cooperative irrigation system could have grown sugar beets on the moon, and that the modern American welfare state was a lesson taught by the Mormons to the nation at large. Like Brooks and Morgan, he never developed a concept of depth psychology so that the subjects of his biographies are portrayed only on the rational surface.

If that generation's interpretive skills remained rudimentary, their research skills were honed to a sharp edge. For Morgan and Brooks in particular, both of whom had participated in the New Deal's history programs during the 1930s, the historical revisionism made possible by the immense body of sources collected or generated under those programs was intoxicating and made them indefatigable researchers. For Arrington, it was the virgin land of the archives of the Mormon Church that previous researchers had never exploited. Thus his books, like those of Morgan, bristle with original data gleaned from sources few others even knew existed.

Finally, literary excellence was a hallmark of the generation. Though his novels were wooden, DeVoto's books on the fur trade and western exploration are literary works as much as historical documents, peopled with vividly drawn personalities moved by grand aspirations and working out grand destinies. Stegner's fiction and nonfiction were equally infused by his literary genius. In such company, Arrington ranks, probably with Brooks, at the back of the room. Nevertheless, no doubt by dint of repeated revision, *Great Basin Kingdom* is not literarily dull, for its immense learning is couched in a clear, if matter-of-fact, prose that has sustained the interest of countless readers through its more than four hundred pages. His later books, after he had become Church Historian, are even better, for he had acquired the editorial services of Rebecca Cornwall, Maureen Ursenbach Beecher, and Lavina Fielding Anderson and had placed himself under the literary influence of Davis Bitton and Ronald W. Walker, two of the best writers ever to apply their skills to Mormon history.

Arrington's work as a historian grew out of an integrated world view that included personal values, religious values, and historiographical values. Pride of place among his personal values would have to go to his work ethic, which he had learned on his father's farm under the summer heat of the Idaho sun. We have already noted the joy with which he reminisced of those days, watering and unharnessing his sweaty horses for their noon break, returning to their task only after a hearty meal and continuing until the sun dropped. Later, as a scholar, Arrington was no academic drone lingering over a long lunch at the faculty club or strolling over a golf course in the afternoon. Rather, he was a tireless dynamo of energy who spent his summer months in the church archives, energetically pounding out books, articles, speeches, and reams of letters on his old manual typewriter. Hard work is a basic element in the Mormon ethos, and the History Division was notable for its cadre of tireless workers who threw themselves into their labors as their ancestors had bent their backs to the heavily laden handcart. Leonard Arrington led by example, and most would agree that he outdid them all.

In the fall of 1980, as he was preparing to move to BYU, Arrington wrote a revealing letter to his old friend Martin Hickman, soon to be his academic dean, attempting to establish a mutual understanding of his work habits so that his institutional commitments would interfere as little as possible with his preliminary work on the Brigham Young biography. "In eight years of experience," he wrote, "I have learned that it is impossible for me to do writing at my desk in the office. Many telephone calls come in, many people come by, many administrative matters need to be tended to. All of the talks I have given during the past few years, all of the papers I have prepared, articles written, and books written, have been done while I was at home, using time that other persons my age might have used to golf or travel or serve in the temple. . . . On a trial basis I propose to stay home, working full-time, during the month of January. . . . I want to explain this to you in advance so you will have full knowledge of what I propose to do. I do not ask you to sanction it; that would set a precedent you wouldn't want established. But the fruits of it, I hope, will be obvious when the work is done. You surely know that I am neither a time-waster nor indulgent in non-professional pleasures and concerns."[7] One imagines Hickman, perusing that letter, letting his mind wander back twenty years when he may have opened his crisp new copy of *Great Basin Kingdom* and let his eyes rest on the telling epigraph, a couplet from William Blake:

> Great things are done when men and mountains meet;
> This is not done by jostling in the street.

Few people ever did less street jostling than Leonard Arrington, and few moved as many mountains.

Paradoxically, he could be remarkably self-indulgent in his hours away from the typewriter. His love of eating was always a besetting weakness, and his perennial weight problem as an adult gradually grew into a health hazard as he became older. "Had my annual checkup at the doctor," he wrote his children in 1976. "I had gained 6 pounds since last year's exam, when I was supposed to lose six. So I've got to lose 10 pounds within 3 months. (That's the real reason I'm tired, I guess; weary at the thought of having to cut out pies and chocolates and the other good things that make up the Leonard way of life.)" Nor was he any kind of gourmet. Although he appreciated the excellent cooking of both his first and second wives, quantity always trumped quality in his eating preferences. Introducing his son Carl at a speaking engagement, Leonard referred to himself as a person "who is stupid enough to eat popcorn with sugar and cream; hungry enough to lick his plate clean after he has gotten up everything he can with his knife, fork, and spoon; and boyish enough to have broken two ribs when he tried to out–high jump his son when he, the father, was well beyond fifty." And despite the latter reference, exercise was not a part of "the Leonard way of life." Reporting the death of his high priest teacher and Sunday school superintendent George Johnson, who had been the state handball champion, and who died of a heart attack while playing handball with his son, Arrington ruefully acknowledged that "people used to ask me how I get my exercise now that I am retired. I used to reply, 'I get plenty of exercise going to the funerals of my athletic friends.' It's now a pretty sick joke."[8]

Rural people like Leonard Arrington are often culturally conservative. Although farmers have often, in American history, been in the vanguard of political reform movements, it has usually been because they have felt left behind and exploited in our historical rush toward a Hamiltonian economy of finance and industry, not because they had some vision in mind of an ideal social order toward which they wanted the country to move. But living in harmony with nature's seasonal rhythms tends to impart to rural people a satisfaction with the natural order of things and an inherent suspicion of change and innovation. Certainly it is true that, especially as he grew older, Leonard Arrington felt himself benefiting from the rapid pace of technological development (though he never learned to use a computer) while objecting to the often jarring aesthetics of modern art, music, and literature. Perhaps in order to help himself find a foothold in an increasingly alien culture, on at least a couple of occasions he compiled lists of things he liked and disliked about the modern world. Those lists yield a couple of important insights into the interior Leonard Arrington. For one thing, they show that beneath that always ebullient exterior was a profound degree of alienation, but they also reveal a man struggling with that alienation, unwilling to give in to it by adopting a reactionary personality and a person trying hard to understand what was going on around him and to remain in a creative relationship with it.[9]

Among the "Things I Most Appreciate in the Modern World," he listed, in the first place, "Inventions," such as "the automobile, the airplane, the typewriter, the Xerox machine, the telephone, modern banks, air conditioning, refrigerators, central heating, dental equipment, medical equipment." Public schools, which give the poor access to the same education as the privileged, was another. Finally, he enjoyed public television, "so we can get worthwhile nature programs, geographical and historical documentaries, talk shows, news without editorial slanting."

Among the things he found objectionable were "insistence on special rights for criminals, rights which leave them on the streets to continue their predations and harmful activity," and environmentalists who, "by demagogic tactics, are forcing us to avoid projects of benefit to many citizens just so the 'wilds' can be protected for the benefit of California millionaires." He also objected to what he regarded as excessively high fees charged by doctors: "They don't work any harder than many of us, they didn't invest any more in education, they aren't any smarter." Not unexpectedly, he inveighed against "modern poetry, modern fiction, modern art, modern dance, modern music. Either my upbringing, my age, or my good sense reacts against them. Life is great, people are wonderful, and I find enough enjoyment with the old poetry, the old fiction, the old art, classical dance, and the old music. Let the new reign, but not to my enjoyment," adding at last, "a defect in me, I'm sure." Finally, he wished for "less emphasis on sex in the modern world, less litigation, more emphasis on the community and less on individual freedom to do and say what you please, and [reflecting his and his first wife's southern heritage and his long admiration for the Agrarians] I wish the Tabernacle Choir would occasionally sing 'Dixie' along with that Yankee Civil War song, 'Mine Eyes Have Seen the Glory.' "

But whatever interior alienation that may have developed as Arrington grew older rarely appeared in his political and personal relations, for he was both moderate in his politics and tolerant in his personal life. Writing to fellow historian Richard Poll, a Republican, during the electoral campaign of 1964, Arrington revealed that although he was mostly voting Democratic, he could be persuaded to support a Republican as well: "I feel that both candidates for governor are better than any candidates we have had in many, many years, so I feel that we will be fortunate whichever one is elected. I have not yet made up my mind which one to vote for. I shall, of course, be voting for Johnson and for [Utah Senator Frank] Moss, and suppose that, though you may disagree, at least you would expect this of me."[10]

And on controversial social issues, even one as divisive as homosexuality, where otherwise moderate people often found their toleration tested, Arrington was unjudgmental. On that particular issue, though, he had family reasons for tolerance:

> I never heard of homosexuality until a graduate student at UNC, and then only an overheard remark. I have never had a homosexual experience, but I had one brother who is and another brother who was. And a favorite

nephew who was. . . . A certain percentage of people are born this way and have struggled because of it. . . . I have never had any animosity toward these people—I have treated them just like anybody else. I have been particularly close to Wayne and have never had any problems with him. Same with Ross. Same with Mike Quinn. Same with others I have known, some of them still not generally known. I do not think they have sinned in the sense that they should be blamed, castigated, or criticized.[11]

Much of Arrington's tolerance, as we have previously seen, came from his father. "My father was a very democratic man; that is, he treated every man equally," Leonard recalled, "regardless of color or nationality . . . regardless of social status . . . regardless of belief. . . . He treated everyone with respect, with dignity. My father enjoyed being liked. Did not want to disappoint people. Was not condescending or patronizing. Was not insensitive. Was not cruel. Did not laugh at people's problems."[12]

On one occasion his son Carl accused his father of being tolerant to a fault as he was working on his autobiography, of seeing too much good in people who were clearly doing damage, for example, to the History Division and failing to speak out boldly enough against them.

I don't want the catch phrases and pulled punches and weasel words that need an enigma machine to decipher. . . . Be bold, man. G. Homer Durham was a scumbag and invertebrate. Gordon Hinckley is a shrewd and lying S.O.B. BYU is a bastion of mealy-mouths and apologists. Joseph Anderson was a fog who could be hoodwinked. Okay, I don't expect from you the kind of loaded vituperative language that a 'High Noon' verbal gunslinger like myself would use, but pallid assessments of villains and faint praise for heroes is damnable. . . . If you see yourself as guardian of the middle ground between extremists and that is a repeating theme of your life, I cannot dispute that. . . . But unless we get some feeling for the passion of both sides were are merely left with a portrait in shades of grey. . . . Unless you tell the true tale of skullduggery with names and dates you will not only lose credibility among your peers who know the complete story, but you will shirk your responsibility as an honest historian.[13]

Leonard's response, rejecting the very frankness and passion Carl was calling for, was about as passionate as anything he ever wrote:

> I have always, or nearly always, been a moderate person, going along with whatever seemed inevitable, not trying to reform anybody or anything, not getting angry or neurotically upset. If you were hoping, by getting me to do more writing about my reactions to events, to get some heated remarks about people and happenings, I'm afraid you will be disappointed. If you expected to get some purple language about current happenings and people we read about or deal with, you will be let down. I realize that this is a defect in my character. I am too accepting, too agreeable, too willing to go along with what others propose, too anxious to avoid a fight. Some persons are born to be mediators; I may have been one of them. My father tended to be one of these, and I may have emulated him. Studying about Jesus tends to reinforce that attitude—at least I have felt that it did. Persons who become angry almost never achieve as much as they think they can. If my writing seems calm and unimpassioned, this is not just the result of studied effort, but my natural tone. There are exceptions, I'm sure, but not often.

Nor was that all, for he went on to point out his basic conservatism in that "I tend to be supportive of existing institutions and traditions. . . . In my historical research I attempt to determine what happened and why, but there is no intention to demean, to condemn, or to render it invalid. I am not interested in *proving* or *disproving* as much as making it meaningful, whatever the finding. I try to be creative and responsible, to be constructive in reconciling points of view and differing traditions." Finally, he protested that he always tried not to take himself and his work too seriously, to invest it with the kind of high seriousness that would justify a crusade or even some kind of dramatic gestures to defend it, and that he always tried just to keep his focus on his immediate work and not to become too agitated about the environment in which he was doing that work.[14]

Part of the environment in which he worked was, of course,

the Mormon Church. We have previously noted that the Mormonism with which he grew up in Idaho was largely a theology of the Arringtons' own making, and thus somewhat outside the mainstream. Just how far outside? A long way, according to Leonard's son Carl. "I think I pretty well understand your fidelity to Mormonism," he wrote, "after carefully observing what you say and don't say in your sermons. I can understand your desire to be diplomatic in your expressions of belief since they are clearly unorthodox."[15] Because Mormonism is a religion of action rather than thought, a Mormon orthodoxy is difficult to define, and in fact the religion contains a variety of schools of thought on various issues, some of them mutually contradictory.[16] Certainly Leonard Arrington saw enough flexibility in Mormon theology that he did not consider himself unorthodox.

In an unpublished manuscript dated July 1987 and called "Recollections: My Early Religious Beliefs," Arrington followed J. Frederic Voros, Jr., in identifying two basic strains of thought in Mormon doctrine, which Voros called the "redemptive" and the "progressive" schools. "The redemptive view tends to be theocentric," Voros wrote: "It emphasizes the Fall, rebirth, and redemption by grace. It is skeptical of human effort and insists upon God's active role in the salvation process. Its defenders look primarily to Paul's letters and the Book of Mormon for support." By contrast, "The progressive view tends to be anthropocentric: without denying the supernatural, it focuses primarily on the personal progress of the individual. It is also progressive in the sense that it emphasizes the goodness of human nature, human potential, and human effort; it is skeptical of reliance on God and insists that man can earn salvation. Its defenders look primarily on the King Follett discourse for support."[17] Arrington placed himself solidly within the latter tradition: "Progressive Mormonism, as I was taught it, said that man was innately good; that perfectibility could be achieved by the wise exercise of one's innate power and freedom. It was a theology of self-reliant, self-will, and self-fulfillment. Man is not merely good, he is eternal; he is destined not merely for greatness but for goodhood [*sic*—"Godhood"?]."[18]

"Progressive Mormonism," then, for Arrington, was a theology of possibility, not of certainty, of discovery and not dogma. It was grounded in the idea, which Arrington emphasized over and over again in both his published and his private writings, that faith and intellect were not enemies, that critical thinking, even dissent, were fully compatible with Mormonism. That fundamental principle, as he explained to his children, was basic to his understanding of Mormonism from the very beginning. "The very first book I read on Mormon history, when I was 15, was *Joseph Smith, An American Prophet*, by John Henry Evans, which was given to me as a birthday present by Bertha Mae Thurgood Hansen, a neighbor. The book portrays Joseph Smith as a person with an open mind, a questioning mind, a person in pursuit of education and knowledge. I accepted this as representing the spirit of Mormonism, and still hold to it. This is the way I have always looked at Joseph Smith in a favorable light and still do." Reflecting upon a recent book that asserted that Mormonism discourages questioning minds, Arrington strongly disagreed: "This has not been my experience. I would say that my spirit of questioning arose from my Mormonism. Questions in Sunday School, in MIA [Mutual Improvement Association], in Priesthood quorums. Far more questioning than in school, where we were supposed to accept what the teacher said. And I have possessed a questioning spirit all my life and have never found it to conflict with my Mormonism. On the contrary, it led to my writing books and articles that, if they did not betray a questioning spirit, at least were the result of the pursuit of facts and meaning."[19] To his frustration, he found a very different view entrenched in the Church Educational System:

> It has been a disappointment to me to realize that not all LDS educators, particularly a few in the College of Religion at BYU and in the seminary system, were brought up, as I was, to believe that there is a close relationship between religion and intellect. . . . Faith, we were taught, was consistent with thought, learning, and the use of the intellect. This is still primary in my belief and in the belief of my friends and associates, but I have seen a retraction from it among various younger educators who give greater emphasis to Scriptural literalism. Listen to your heart, not your head; to your ecclesiastical superiors, not to your own mind; to Church publications rather than works of 'outside' scholarship. I regret this tendency.[20]

The Mormonism of Arrington's youth, then, was a religion of optimism, of confident belief in the essential goodness of human nature, of the malleability of human institutions and even of nature itself as history progressed toward the building of Zion on earth:

> From as early as I can remember I had a positive attitude toward people. I had confidence in them, trusted them, felt goodwill toward them. I had a positive attitude toward life as well. Felt cheerful, confident, and expected things to work out well. My obligation was to work hard, plan well, exercise good control over myself, and treat people well. My job as a teacher was to help people understand things; once they understood, they would do the right thing. This attitude was bolstered by Mormonism. Man was a potential god. A child of God with good qualities and the capability of extraordinary goodness.

As he grew older, though, experience began to temper that optimism with a realization that human nature contained a darker side as well. At first it was the student revolts of the 1960s, during which university facilities were burned, access to classrooms was barred, and the general free exchange of ideas and information restricted, that jarred his optimism. However, it appeared to be only a passing storm: "It seemed that there was a streak of orneriness in the human spirit. But it seemed like a temporary thing. We got over it, or so it seemed." Later, though, what he vaguely terms "secularism" brought a resurgence of that older intolerance and self-righteous certainty, and Arrington then seemed to realize that human nature's darker potential could justify a more permanent pessimism. "The secularist attitude partakes of the same arrogance, irrationality, and intolerance that characterized the religious inquisitions of the Middle Ages," he noted. "Secularism is something like a faith with a passion for certainty. . . . Clearly, fanaticism, long associated with religion, is now a characteristic of secularism. Clearly, its roots are deep in human nature."[21]

Late in life, Arrington came to acknowledge what he called "my come-uppance on the matter of optimism and belief in people's goodness," which came from his reading of the Neo-orthodox Lutheran theologian Reinhold Niebuhr's *The Irony of American History*. "As most Mormons, I had never believed in original sin. But I see that he defines it as the self-pride that mistakes the relative for the absolute. I suppose I did believe in that all along. Niebuhr also discusses the ambiguities of human nature, and God's frowning on human pretensions." Having opened that door, Niebuhr proceeded to lead Arrington into an even more non-Mormon direction: "Niebuhr was critical of those whose egotism leads them to suppose that they grasp the purposes of the Almighty. He sees irony in the situation that arises when the consequences of an action are contrary to the intentions of a person because of the weaknesses inherent in the person himself. He thinks we are too reluctant to recognize the evil to which individuals and communities may sink when they try to play the role of God in history." It was a frontal assault on the basic Mormon assumptions of Man's inherent potential and his ability to build the Kingdom of God on earth—assumptions that had been basic philosophical underpinnings of *Great Basin Kingdom* and the rest of Arrington's work. Perhaps not surprising, Arrington had to jump ship at that point: "These are Lutheran thoughts, not Mormon thoughts, and, while they are justified, they should not force one to lose his cheerful, optimistic, hopeful outlook. Certainly, I retain mine." And so he came finally to a ringing affirmation of his youthful optimism: "My study of history . . . has not made me pessimistic. The human capacity for moral grandeur is unquestionable. The lives of good people—the heroes and heroines. Maybe not in the vast majority, but *there.* Lots of good role models. Lots of people we are grateful for. The ordinary social relations fostered in colleges, grade schools and high schools, in study groups, in neighborhoods. Lots of selfless people. The life of reason is still possible!"[22]

Despite his occasional wrestlings with the dark side of human nature, when one steps back and looks at Leonard Arrington's work as a whole, both the way he wrote history himself and the recommendations he made for others, one cannot fail to be impressed with the degree of consistency, with the integrated way in which his personality and his religious and philosophical views are maintained and shine forth. In one of his best (and unfortunately unpublished) essays, Arrington concisely summarized his recommendations for writing Mormon history as he himself practiced it and encouraged others to emulate. Titled "On the Writing of Latter-day Saint History," it discusses five such recommendations.[23]

The first is that "we must avoid a male interpretation of Mormon history." Well aware of the peril, within a church governed by an exclusively male priesthood, of the role of women being ignored or minimized, Arrington was one of the first and strongest advocates of Mormon women's history.[24] Although he wrote little women's history himself, apparently feeling that women should write their own history, he made it possible for them to do so by hiring many of the most talented ones to work in the History Division and made women's history one of the division's major endeavors.

Second, he recommended giving "due emphasis to intellectual, social, and cultural accomplishments." Once again, he led more by precept and encouragement than example, for he recognized that "these contributions are more difficult to discover and trace [than more tangible aspects of history], but they are nevertheless there, and we should be aware of them." Arrington was, after all, an economist by training, and thus more accustomed to the study of irrigation dams and sugar beet factories than of orchestras and artists, but he was also a man of broad culture whose reading included Nabokov and Dostoevsky and who understood the importance of the refining forces of civilization.

His third admonition grew out of his frustration with idealistic visions of Mormon history as the flawless working out of the will of God. "We must acknowledge," he urged, "that not every program, not every organization, proceeded smoothly. Our histories should make us aware of some of the problems, obstacles, objections, and difficulties." Although it is unclear when Arrington wrote this essay, it is easy to see in this admonition some of his frustration with his superiors in the Church Historical Department who disapproved of any but the most triumphal version of history.

His last two recommendations grew directly from his view of human nature, in which people of all stations and occupations were basically good and of supreme value in the eyes of their Maker. "We should give due attention to the so-called ordinary members of the Church. We should be concerned with both the obscure and the famous." In fact, he argued, the lives of such common people often provide a clearer view of human nature and motives than do the lives of the leaders, who "must necessarily preserve the image of their office by showing the world a mask. In doing so, they may conceal their real selves." And finally, he argued for the writing of "biographical and family histories, to recognize the complexity of people." Perhaps through his reading of Niebuhr, but probably even more from his varied life experience and observation, Arrington realized that human nature is not simple. "The man who cannot resist an opportunity to make money may love his family, may be generous, and may have courage. A whole series of qualities, good and bad, may exist in the same person. And sometimes contradictory qualities. The historian is obligated to give some indication of this diversity, this complexity, this contradictory nature of historical persons."

All of these principles were rooted in Arrington's joie de vivre, his great love of life in all its multiplicity, his solid insistence upon the importance of reason, criticism, the intellect, and, above all, his abiding Mormon optimism, with its faith in the basic goodness of human nature, in hard work, and in the ultimate possibility of building an earthly Zion. In them, one can see both the greatness and the shortcomings of his historical work. One could wish, for example, that one could find in his biographies more of Niebuhr's "Lutheran" thinking with its courage to face the darker motives and even the unvarnished evil that human nature can exhibit, particularly in his portrayals of David Eccles and Brigham Young. One might wish, too, that he had found a better example than Madelyn Silver of the tragic effects of a stifling society on a creative person and thus achieved a more searching critique of the dark side of the Mormon group ethos. On the other hand, *Great Basin Kingdom*, *Beet Sugar in the West*, and *Building the City of God* are among the most elaborately researched and deftly interpreted histories of Mormon economic and social history.

And what of Leonard Arrington's larger historiographical significance? How has his work shaped the course of Mormon and western history? Two great Mormon historians, Charles S. Peterson and Ronald W. Walker, who have studied *Great Basin Kingdom* perhaps more closely than anyone else, appear to come to essentially the same general conclusion, that the influence of the book was so great that it harmed the development of Mormon historiography almost as much as it helped it. At the same time as the book opened up the riches of the Mormon documentary record and synthesized it in both an objective and a critical interpretation, it also channeled and stifled further historiographical development beyond the chronological bounds and the themes Arrington had identified; in Walker's words, the book "was responsible for beginning and ending its own historical movement."[25] "It was probably no coincidence," Walker continues on another occasion, "that much of the work of [the New Mormon Historians] lay within the topical and chronological limits set by *Great Basin Kingdom*—the economic, political, and social development of Mormonism in the last half of the nineteenth century. Arrington's influence even went down to the level of facts and interpretation. . . . Not a few scholars found an idea of interpretation in their own work, thought to be original, to have originally been posed by Arrington, so broad and subtle his influence upon the LDS historical milieu."[26] Peterson added that the book's searching examination of uniquely Mormon experiences and institutions created an "exceptionalist" interpretation of Mormon history that had the effect of isolating that history from other fields of study. Mormon culture and institutions were so completely unique, in other words, that Mormon history was relevant only to Mormons.[27] Although *Great Basin Kingdom* was, by universal acknowledgment, Arrington's best and most influential book, one could argue that most of Walker's and Peterson's observations could be applied to a greater or lesser degree to almost the entirety of Arrington's work, so unified was it within his personal and historiographical world view; anyone who got on the Arrington train rode it to the end of the line—and that train had many passengers.

It is also true, however, as Walker and Peterson would most likely agree, that one can scarcely blame Arrington for his disciples' lack of originality. A mind of Leonard Arrington's originality, coupled with his inexhaustible ambition and energy, does not appear every day; in fact, expecting one even in every generation seems asking too much. If Arrington examined Mormon exceptionalism in minute detail, he also showed how Mormonism was relevant to larger themes of U.S. history; if Mormon history needs to move into the twenty-first century and to embrace themes outside the economic, social, and political realms that were his focal points, it was Leonard Arrington who first pointed in those directions. If he himself wrote narrowly focused articles and biographies of persons of minor significance, thus seeming to encourage the introverted gaze of the New Mormon History, it is nevertheless the case that such a monographic infrastructure needed to be created as the base for larger surveys. If he cast a large shadow over Mormon historiography, perhaps it is time for his disciples to step out into the same sunlight that made his shadow possible. Nothing would have pleased Leonard more.

Notes

Chapter 1

1. Lavina Fielding Anderson, "Doves and Serpents: The Activities of Leonard J. Arrington as Church Historian," 205, quoting LJA Diary of 26 June [1979?], Arrington Papers, Series 10.
2. Leonard J. Arrington, *Great Basin Kingdom: An Economic History of the Latter-day Saints, 1830–1900* (Cambridge: Harvard University Press, 1958).
3. LJA fragment, 15 September 1984, Series 10.
4. Carl Arrington to LJA, 28 December 1984, Arrington Papers, Series 10.
5. LJA to Paul and Josephine Phillips, 12 April 1985; and LJA to his children, 6 February 1995, both in Series 10.
6. Biographical data on the Arrington family is available in Rebecca Cornwall, "From Chicken Farm to History: The Life of Leonard Arrington, 1917–1977," unpublished manuscript in Series 10.
7. Leonard J. Arrington, *Adventures of a Church Historian* (Urbana: University of Illinois Press, 1998), 20.
8. LJA to his children, 6 February 1995; LJA, "Life on the Farm," manuscript fragment of 30 March 1975, both in Series 10.
9. LJA draft fragment of autobiography, Series 10.
10. LJA Reminiscence, "The Replacement of Animal Power with Mechanical Power on our Farm in Twin Falls County," 31 October 1991; LJA Recollections, 14 November 1976, both in Series 10.
11. LJA, "The Replacement of Animal Power with Mechanical Power."
12. LJA, *Adventures of a Church Historian*, 19; LJA to his children, 6 June 1997, Series 10.
13. LJA fragment, 28 August 1984; LJA to his children, 21 July 1989 and 6 June 1997, all in Series 10.
14. As we shall see, there is an interesting parallel in Leonard's marriage to Grace Fort Arrington, a North Carolina Baptist who he met while in graduate school. She attempted to retain her ancestral religion but was dissatisfied with the Baptist church in Logan and sought LDS baptism.

15. This account of the Arringtons' church involvement is based on Cornwall, "From Chicken Farm to History," 36. The quotation is from LJA, "Life on the Farm."
16. Cornwall, "From Chicken Farm to History," 70; and LJA diary, 10 January 1984.
17. LJA Diary, 10 January 1984.
18. LJA Recollections, 14 November 1976, Series 10.
19. Cornwall, "From Chicken Farm to History," 197; Carl Arrington to LJA, 28 December 1984, both in Series 10.
20. Anderson, "Doves and Serpents," 816–17, quoting an uncited diary entry, Series 12.
21. LJA, "Learning by Study and by Faith," 13 February 1995, Series 10.
22. LJA, "Schooling," 30 March 1975, Series 10.
23. LJA, "My Experience in Boy Scouts of America," 31 July 1989, Series 10.
24. Ibid.
25. LJA, "Pillars of My Faith," Sunstone Symposium, 1 August 1998.
26. Ibid.
27. Cornwall, "From Chicken Farm to History," 46; Ronald W. Walker, "Introduction to the Illinois Edition," Leonard J. Arrington, *Great Basin Kingdom: An Economic History of the Latter-day Saints, 1830–1900* (Urbana: University of Illinois Press, 2004), xii. Leonard may have been impressed as well with his own precociousness as an economics researcher—as well he should have been—for he loved to tell this story later in life.
28. Cornwall, "From Chicken Farm to History," 38.

Chapter 2

1. F. Ross Peterson, *Idaho: A Bicentennial History* (New York: W. W. Norton, 1976), 139.
2. Ibid., 149.
3. LJA, *History of Idaho* (Moscow: University of Idaho Press, 1994), 2:169–70.
4. Ibid., 2:171–72; LJA, "My Most Influential Teacher," 3 November 1978, unpublished essay, Series 10.
5. Ibid.; LJA, *Adventures of a Church Historian* (Urbana: University of Illinois Press, 1998), 22.
6. LJA, *Adventures of a Church Historian*, 23–24; LJA Diary, 28 January 1978, Series 10.
7. LJA, *Adventures of a Church Historian*, 22.
8. Ibid., 24.
9. LJA, "The Pillars of My Faith," unpublished speech, Sunstone Symposium, 1 August 1998, Series 12.
10. LJA, *Adventures of a Church Historian*, 27–28; LJA, "Memories and Traditions," unpublished address to the Old Main Society, 15 April 1982, Series 12.

11. Rebecca Cornwall, "From Chicken Farm to History," unpublished manuscript in Series 10, 268.
12. LJA, unpublished comments at *Great Basin Kingdom* symposium at Utah State University, 4 May 1988, Series 12. Arrington's comments, which were given in response to seven critical papers celebrating the thirtieth anniversary of the book, were omitted from the published version of the papers: Thomas G. Alexander, ed., *"Great Basin Kingdom" Revisited: Contemporary Perspectives* (Logan: Utah State University Press, 1991).
13. LJA, unpublished comments at *Great Basin* Kingdom symposium; LJA, "Evolution of My Professional Research," unpublished essay, Series 12; LJA, "Memories and Traditions."
14. LJA, *Adventures of a Church Historian*, 12.
15. LJA Diary, 15 January 1977 "Recollections," Series 12; "Reminiscences," 6 December 1976, Series 10.
16. LJA, "The Evolution of My Professional Research."
17. LJA, "Pillars of My Faith." LJA, *Adventures of a Church Historian*, 28–29.
18. A useful concise summary of Marshall's ideas is the anonymous introduction to Alfred Marshall, *Principles of Economics* (New York: Prometheus Books, 1997). On Graue's background and influence on Arrington, see Cornwall, "From Chicken Farm to History," 83–85.
19. See Marshall, *Principles of Economics*, 8th ed. (London: Macmillan, 1920), 3–4.
20. Ibid.
21. Ibid., 4.
22. LJA, "Reflections on Economics and the Church," BYU conference on Economics and the Mormon Church, 7 October 1975, unpublished lecture, Series 12.
23. Cornwall, "From Chicken Farm to History," 85.
24. Marshall, *Principles of Economics*, 9.
25. LJA, *Adventures of a Church Historian*, 26.
26. Richard T. Ely, "Economic Aspects of Mormonism," *Harper's Monthly Magazine* 106 (April 1903): 667–78.
27. LJA, *Adventures of a Church Historian*, 26.
28. "Ely, Richard Theodore," in *Concise Dictionary of American Biography*, vol. 1 (New York: Charles Scribner's Sons, 1997), 355; Henry F. May, *The End of American Innocence: A Study of the First Years of Our Own Time, 1912–1917* (New York: Alfred A. Knopf, 1959), 100, 158–59.
29. "Ely, Richard Theodore," 355. For a discussion of the conservative side of Ely's thought, his skepticism about the New Deal, and a guide to his writings, see Otis L. Graham, Jr., *An Encore for Reform: The Old Progressives and the New Deal* (New York: Oxford University Press, 1967), 78–82.
30. Ely, "Economic Aspects of Mormonism," 669.
31. LJA, *Adventures of a Church Historian*, 26.

32. Twelve Southerners, *I'll Take My Stand: The South and the Agrarian Tradition* (New York: Harper and Brothers, 1930).
33. Dudley Barker, *G. K. Chesterton: A Biography*. (New York: Stein and Day, 1973), 258–59.
34. LJA, "How This Historian Has Benefited from the Study of Rural Sociology," unpublished lecture, Series 12; LJA, *Adventures of a Church Historian*, 25–26.
35. LJA, unpublished comments at *Great Basin Kingdom* symposium at Utah State University, 4 May 1988.
36. LJA, "How This Historian Has Benefited from the Study of Rural Sociology."
37. "Introduction: A Statement of Principles," in Twelve Southerners, *I'll Take My Stand*, xxvi–xxvii.
38. John Crowe Ransom, "Reconstructed But Unregenerate," in Twelve Southerners, *I'll Take My Stand*, 1–27.
39. Andrew Nelson Lytle, "The Hind Tit," in Twelve Southerners, *I'll Take My Stand*, 205.
40. LJA, "How This Historian Has Benefited from the Study of Rural Sociology," Series 12.
41. LJA, *Adventures of a Church Historian*, 32.
42. LJA, *Great Basin Kingdom: An Economic History of the Latter-day Saints* (Cambridge, Mass.: Harvard University Press, 1958).

Chapter 3

1. LJA comments presented at *Great Basin Kingdom* Symposium, Utah State University, 4 May 1988; LJA Papers, Series 12.
2. My own labors in describing the making of *Great Basin Kingdom* have been greatly eased by Ronald W. Walker's definitive treatment of the subject in his "Introduction" to Leonard J. Arrington, *Great Basin Kingdom: An Economic History of the Latter-day Saints, 1830–1900* (Urbana: University of Illinois Press, 2005).
3. Lewis Atherton, *Main Street on the Middle Border* (Bloomington: Indiana University Press, 1954); Edward Chase Kirkland, *Industry Comes of Age: Business, Labor and Public Policy, 1860–1897* (New York: Holt, Rinehart and Winston, 1961).
4. LJA to Herman E. Krooss, 22 November 1976, LJA Papers, Series 2; Ruth Tsotsi to LJA, 18 November 1976, LJA Papers, Series 12; LJA Diary, "Recollections," 15 January 1977, LJA Papers, Series 12. Walker, "Introduction," xxvii, recounts the financial history of the book and comments truthfully that "few best-selling authors ever went so unrewarded."
5. LJA comments presented at *Great Basin Kingdom* Symposium, Utah State University, 4 May 1988; LJA, *Adventures of a Church Historian* (Urbana: University of Illinois Press, 1998), 32–33, 38.
6. LJA, comments at *Great Basin Kingdom* Symposium, 4 May 1988.

7. LJA, *Great Basin Kingdom: An Economic History of the Latter-day Saints, 1830–1900* (Cambridge, Mass.: Harvard University Press, 1958), vii–viii.
8. Ibid., 35; Milton S. Heath, Arrington's dissertation director, had pointed out this similarity ("I have written you already about the striking parallel with the Trustee experiment in Georgia"), thus establishing a link between Heath's study of the southern agrarian tradition and Arrington's study of Mormonism. Heath to LJA, 25 February 1952, Series 12.
9. LJA, *Great Basin Kingdom*, 62–63.
10. Ibid., 63.
11. Ibid.
12. Ibid., 35. The influence of Richard T. Ely's Progressivism is obvious here, but the reader should note, too, that Arrington is giving a nod to Alfred Marshall at the same time he is pushing beyond him. Marshall, it will be recalled, acknowledged the possibility of a centrally planned economy only among a small group of religious devotees committed to a collective destiny. Arrington is saying that the small-scale success of such planning could become a model for a larger application, much as the Puritans had hoped that their Commonwealth could become a model for the larger renovation of English society. See the title essay in Perry Miller, *Errand Into the Wilderness* (Cambridge, Mass.: Harvard University Press, 1956), 1–15. I can recall no evidence of Arrington's awareness of Miller's work, but their ideas are similar.
13. LJA, *Great Basin Kingdom*, 25.
14. Ibid., 25–26.
15. Ibid., 89.
16. Ibid., 53. An idealized model of the Mormon village and irrigation system is shown on p. 225 in a "Diagrammatic Sketch of a 'Typical' Mormon Valley."
17. Ibid., 132–32, 149.
18. Ibid., 195. See also his discussion of the ways in which the Mormons coped with the coming of the railroad on pp. 234–35, 255, and 257.
19. Ibid., 322, 313, 341–42.
20. Dale L. Morgan, "Contemporary Scene," in Utah Writers' Program, *Utah: A Guide to the State* (New York: Hastings House, 1940), 3. See also Thomas G. Alexander, *Mormonism in Transition: A History of the Latter-day Saints, 1890–1930* (Urbana: University of Illinois Press, 1986). LJA, *Great Basin Kingdom*, 409 uses the term "great capitulation," adding, though, that "it can be called that, although induced by coercive federal legislation."
21. LJA, *Great Basin Kingdom*, 411–12.
22. Ibid., 44.
23. Richard Jackson, "Righteousness and Environmental Change: The Mormons and the Environment," in Thomas G. Alexander, ed., *Essays on the American West, 1973–1974* (Provo, Utah: Brigham Young University Press, 1975), 31.

24. Ibid., 26, 34, 38. "Anything drearier than the scene which must have greeted [the Mormon pioneers] when they reached the valleys among the mountains of Utah can scarcely be imagined." Ely had written. "It was apparently a desert waste, covered with sage-brushes." Richard T. Ely, "Economic Aspects of Mormonism," *Harper's Monthly Magazine* 106 (April 1903): 668. See also Richard Jackson, "The Mormon Experience: The Plains as Sinai, the Great Salt Lake as the Dead Sea, and the Great Basin as Desert-cum-Promised Land," *Journal of Historical Geography* 18 (1992), 41–58, and his "Righteousness and Environmental Change: The Mormons and the Environment," in Thomas G. Alexander, ed., *Essays on the American West, 1973–74* (Provo, Utah: Brigham Young University Press, ca. 1975): 21–42.
25. LJA, *Great Basin Kingdom*, 66.
26. Expansion into the Utah and Sanpete valleys during those early years met with less success, but that was mostly because of Indian resistance rather than any inherent problems in the Mormon system. Both of those sites, like Salt Lake Valley, were fertile and well watered (Sanpete less so than Utah) and thus agriculturally auspicious. Salt Lake Valley had the historic advantage, in terms of the interests of the Mormons, of being a buffer zone between the Shoshone Indians on the north and the Utes in the south, so the Mormon presence there was never seriously contested by the indigenous inhabitants. It was a different story to the south, where the Utes and the Mormons fought two bloody wars, the Walker War of the 1850s and the Black Hawk War of the 1860s, over control of the Utes' traditional territory.
27. LJA, *Great Basin Kingdom*, 411–12.
28. Ibid., viii.
29. Ibid., 43.
30. Richard Firmage, *A History of Grand County* (Salt Lake City: Utah State Historical Society, 1996), chaps. 5–6. Grand County—and San Juan and Washington counties to be considered next—are admittedly in the Colorado Plateau Province rather than the Great Basin, but Arrington himself used the term "Great Basin" as a general designation for the Mormon settlement region in the intermountain area.
31. Andrew Karl Larson, *I Was Called to Dixie. The Virgin River Basin: Unique Experiences in Mormon Pioneering* (St. George, Utah: Author, 1961), 143–44, 146.
32. David E. Miller, *Hole-in-the-Rock: An Epic in the Colonization of the Great American West* (Salt Lake City: University of Utah Press, 1959).
33. James M. Aton and Robert S. McPherson, *River Flowing from the Sunrise: An Environmental History of the Lower San Juan* (Logan: Utah State University Press, 2000), 103–104. San Juan cowboys still boast that the county payroll during some years in the early twentieth century could not be met until the Scorup-Somerville cattle company paid its taxes. Aton and McPherson remind us, though, that that

livestock prosperity came at the price of some very poor range management policies that resulted in serious environmental degradation.

34. Most of the discussion that follows is based on Brian Q. Cannon, "Struggle Against Great Odds: Challenges in Utah's Marginal Agricultural Areas, 1925–39," *Utah Historical Quarterly* 54 (Fall 1986): 308–27.

35. Ibid., 312, 316–17, 320. Brian Q. Cannon, personal communication with the author, 31 July 2006.

36. LJA and Wayne K. Hinton, "Origin of the Welfare Plan of the Church of Jesus Christ of Latter-day Saints," *BYU Studies* 5 (Winter 1964): 67–85; Thomas G. Alexander, *Utah: The Right Place* (Salt Lake City: Gibbs Smith, 1995), 332–33; Brian Q. Cannon, "'What a Power We Will Be in This Land': The LDS Church, the Church Security Program, and the New Deal," *Journal of the West* 43 (Fall 2004): 66–75.

37. Dean L. May, *Utah: A People's History* (Salt Lake City: University of Utah Press, 1987), 177.

38. Cannon, "Struggle Against Great Odds," 320; see also Cannon's "'What a Power We Will Be in This Land.'"

39. LJA, "Utah's Great Drought of 1934," *Utah Historical Quarterly* 54 (Summer 1986): 264.

40. LJA, *Great Basin Kingdom*, 411–12.

41. Donald Worster, "The Kingdom, the Power, and the Water," in Thomas G. Alexander, ed., *"Great Basin Kingdom" Revisited: Contemporary Perspectives* (Logan: Utah State University Press, 1991), 29.

42. Dean May, "The Making of Saints: The Mormon Town as a Setting for the Study of Cultural Change," *Utah Historical Quarterly* 45 (Winter 1977): 79; Worster, "The Kingdom, the Power, and the Water," 37. May's comment refers not to Leonard Arrington, but to the non-Mormon journalist William K. Smythe, whose *The Conquest of Arid America* (1899; repr., Seattle: University of Washington Press, 1969) anticipated the moral claims of *Great Basin Kingdom.*

43. LJA to Ernest L. Wilkinson [BYU President], 3 September 1957, Series 2.

44. LJA, "Schooling," 30 March 1975, Series 10: "My impression of the Twin Falls schools is that they were very good. At least I seem to have been well prepared for the various eventualities which came along. The teachers seem to have been of high quality, and well prepared. Knowing, as I do now, of some of the inadequacies of schools in Utah, I can be grateful I was born and raised in a non-Mormon town."

45. Leonard J. Arrington, Feramorz Y. Fox, and Dean L. May, *Building the City of God: Community and Cooperation Among the Mormons* (Salt Lake City: Deseret Book, 1976); Lowry Nelson, *The Mormon Village: A Pattern and Technique of Land Settlement* (Salt Lake City: University of Utah Press, 1952).

46. Lowry Nelson, "The Mormon Village: A Study in Social Origins," *Proceedings of*

the Utah Academy of Sciences 7 (1930): 18; Richard V. Francaviglia, *The Mormon Landscape: Existence, Creation, and Perception of a Unique Image in the American West* (New York: AMS Press, 1978), xvii.

47. Wayne L. Wahlquist, "A Review of Mormon Settlement Literature," *Utah Historical Quarterly* 45 (Winter 1977): 7, 15–16.

48. Ibid., 19. As Brian Q. Cannon finds, though, enough of those settlers on marginal land did doggedly persist in a "religiously motivated tenacity to even submarginal land," that it defeated any general attempt at a resettlement program during the Great Depression. Cannon, "Struggle Against Great Odds," 320

49. Lowell Bennion, "A Geographer's Discovery of *Great Basin Kingdom*," in Alexander, *"Great Basin Kingdom" Revisited*, chap. 7.

50. Marshall E. Bowen, *Utah People in the Nevada Desert: Homestead and Community on a Twentieth Century Farmers' Frontier* (Logan: Utah State University Press, 1994); Evon Z. Vogt and Thomas F. O'Dea, "A Comparative Study of the Role of Values in Social Action in Two Southwestern Communities," *American Sociological Review* 18 (December 1953): 645–54.

51. Nels Anderson, *Desert Saints: The Mormon Frontier in Utah* (Chicago: University of Chicago Press, 1942), 428–29. To be precise, he calls the Silver Reef miners "bonanza-minded, carefree, reckless types portrayed by Bret Harte," who had constructed "a shack town, its main street lined with saloons, gambling places, and other conveniences for sinners." By contrast, St. George was "a community of fields, gardens, and flowers, . . . a moral family town, where the humble domestic virtues were glorified."

52. Stephen L. Carr, *The Historic Guide to Utah Ghost Towns*, rev. ed. (Salt Lake City: Western Epics, 1986), 141, reproduces the Silver Reef plat map of 1879.

53. Larson, *I Was Called to Dixie*, 615–23; 544–52.

54. LJA, *Great Basin Kingdom*, 217–20.

55. Gary Topping, ed., *Gila Monsters and Red-Eyed Rattlesnakes: Don Maguire's Arizona Trading Expeditions, 1876–1879* (Salt Lake City: University of Utah Press, 1997), 108–9.

56. LJA, *Great Basin Kingdom*, 222.

57. Marietta M. Mariger, *Saga of Three Towns: Harrisburg, Leeds, Silver Reef* (St. George, Utah: Washington County News, n.d.), 59, 115.

58. Topping, ed., *Gila Monsters and Red-Eyed Rattlesnakes*, 107.

Chapter 4

1. Dale L. Morgan, review of *Great Basin Kingdom*, *Utah Historical Quarterly* (Spring 1959): 191. On the enthusiastic reception of the book among historical scholars and within the Mormon Church, see Ronald W. Walker, "Introduction to the Illinois Edition," Leonard J. Arrington, *Great Basin Kingdom: An Economic His-*

tory of the Latter-day Saints, 1830–1900 (Urbana: University of Illinois Press, 2005): xxiii–xxiv.

2. Arrington's service, while in Logan, as president of the Young Men's Mutual Improvement Association, as a president of his Seventies Quorum, and as a member of the Utah State University Stake High Council are all detailed in his *Adventures of a Church Historian* (Urbana: University of Illinois Press, 1998), chap. 3.
3. LJA to Rodman Paul, 4 January 1968, Series 10; LJA, *Adventures of a Church Historian*, 75.
4. LJA to Merrill Jensen, 1 February 1959, Series 10.
5. LJA to Rodman Paul, 26 December 1968, Series 10.
6. LJA and Davis Bitton, *The Mormon Experience: A History of the Latter-day Saints* (New York: Alfred A. Knopf, 1979).
7. LJA to Thomas G. Alexander, 20 September 1966, Series 10.
8. LJA, *Adventures of a Church Historian*, 77.
9. Ibid.
10. LJA to Merrill Jensen, 1 February 1959, Series 10. Rebecca Cornwall, "From Chicken Farm to History," 331. On p. 336 Cornwall says BYU had been making offers of a faculty position since 1960.
11. LJA Diary, 23 November 1971, Series 10.
12. Davis Bitton, "Ten Years in Camelot: A Personal Memoir," *Dialogue: A Journal of Mormon Thought* 16 (Autumn 1983): 9–10.
13. Fawn M. Brodie, *"No Man Knows My History": The Life of Joseph Smith* (New York: Alfred A. Knopf, 1945); Douglas Alder, "Thoughts Concerning the Book, *The Story of the Latter-day Saints*, by Glen Leonard and James Allen," (1976), LJA Papers, Series 2 (this document is in the James Allen correspondence file).
14. Bitton, "Ten Years in Camelot," 10.
15. Ibid., 11.
16. Davis Bitton, ed., *Guide to Mormon Diaries and Autobiographies* (Provo, Utah: Brigham Young University Press, 1977).
17. LJA, *Adventures of a Church Historian*, 82.
18. LJA to James Allen and Davis Bitton, 6 May 1977, Series 2.
19. LJA, *Adventures of a Church Historian*, 85–87. These pages give brief biographical sketches of some of the more prominent staff members, but others are omitted.
20. Ibid., 8–85; Bitton, "Ten Years in Camelot," 13, 11. Bitton's recollection does not name Dean Jessee as one of the participants in the prayer.
21. LJA comments at *Great Basin Kingdom Symposium*, Utah State University, 4 May 1988, Series 12.
22. Laurel Thatcher Ulrich to LJA, 3 May 1982, Series 2.
23. LJA to George Mitton, 7 July 1969, Series 2.
24. LJA, *Adventures of a Church Historian*, 83.

25. Bitton, "Ten Years in Camelot," 12–13. The following chapter will show that this idea of cooperative history writing was more than just an experimental idea, for Arrington had already been practicing it to some degree at Utah State University by subcontracting research and writing out to assistants and other scholars.
26. LJA to Wendell J. Ashton, 19 April 1977, Series 2; Bitton, "Ten Years in Camelot," 14. This cooperative ethos continued even after the History Division was abolished in 1982 and its staff members transferred to Brigham Young University where they formed the Joseph Fielding Smith Institute (JFSI). In an internal undated memo, Ron Esplin reminded his colleagues of their original commitment to cooperative efforts: "Is there an overriding reason for us to exist unless we do things collectively that individually neither we nor others can do as well? [Try this: more resources devoted to research and publication mean more total output; not only that, our individual works are improved by interaction, shared ideas, and shared resources.]" (Brackets in original) Ron Esplin, "Some Thoughts on Defining our Mission," n.d., concerning the mission of the JFSI. LJA Papers, Series 3.
27. LJA, *Adventures of a Church Historian*, 93–94, lists these and other projects; some of them are also discussed in Bitton, "Ten Years in Camelot," 14–16.
28. LJA to Richard Bushman, 12 February 1964, Series 10, indicates that the multivolume history idea was first proposed by Bushman, a prominent Mormon scholar and professor of history at Columbia University.
29. Bitton, "Ten Years in Camelot," 13–14; "Explanation of Accounts of the History Division," n.d., LJA Papers, Series 3.
30. LJA, *Adventures of a Church Historian*, chap. 6 describes the shifting administrative structure during the division's early years and the relationships, perceived and real, between the administrators and the historians.
31. Bitton's "Ten Years in Camelot," 20–33, includes a partial bibliography of "History Division Publications" compiled by Maureen Ursenbach Beecher, Kathleen H. Anderson, and Debbie Lilenquist.
32. Ibid. 16.
33. Ibid., 15.
34. LJA Diary, 30 January 1973, Series 3. LJA to his children James and Susan, 17 February 1973, Series 10.
35. Lavina Fielding Anderson, "Doves and Serpents," 219–20, LJA Papers, Series 3.
36. On the Correlation Committee, see Robert Gottlieb and Peter Wiley, *America's Saints: The Rise of Mormon Power* (New York: G. P. Putnam's Sons, 1984), 59–61.
37. Anderson, "Doves and Serpents," 219–20.
38. Alder, "Thoughts."
39. Bitton, "Ten Years in Camelot," 12.
40. Dean C. Jessee, *Letters of Brigham Young to His Sons* (Salt Lake City: Deseret Book, 1974).

41. LJA, *Adventures of a Church Historian*, 115–21.
42. James B. Allen and Glen M. Leonard, *The Story of the Latter-day Saints* (Salt Lake City: Deseret Book, 1976).
43. As one might have expected, the same objection arose when *Building the City of God: Community and Cooperation Among the Mormons*, by Arrington, Feramorz Y. Fox, and Dean May appeared hard on the heels of *The Story of the Latter-day Saints*. Here was an entire book that examined Mormon communitarian projects in detail. While it was favorably reviewed in non-Mormon scholarly publications, Arrington learned that the utter silence of the *Church News* section of the *Deseret News*, where such works were reviewed for church members, was ordered by one member of the Twelve. Arrington, Fox, and May, *Building the City of God: Community and Cooperation Among the Mormons* (Salt Lake City: Deseret Book, 1976); LJA, *Adventures of a Church Historian*, 152.
44. LJA, *Adventures of a Church Historian*, 140–49; Bitton, "Ten Years in Camelot," 17.
45. LJA, *Adventures of a Church Historian*, 154. Both Arrington and Bitton recognized the collusion of one of the spies in the History Division in this conspiracy to denigrate the faithfulness of the historians. He "was instructed by Elder Mark Petersen to inform him of things we wrote—questionable things. So he would xerox pages of things we had published, underline them with yellow pencil, and send them to Elder Petersen. Elder Petersen never once talked to me, interviewed me, asked me about the things I wrote, but he complained in meetings of the Twelve. I felt he was insecure, evil, and vindictive. Unfair and judgmental." LJA fragment, Series 10, Box 11, Folder 5.
46. LJA to his children, 29 April and 7 May 1977, Series 10.
47. Carl Arrington to LJA, 28 December 1984; LJA to James and Susan Arrington, 17 February 1973, Series 10.
48. LJA, *Adventures of a Church Historian*, 160, 159.
49. Ibid., 160–62.
50. "On Feb. 1978 the First Presidency wrote to me that they were altering the circumstances of my work. I was being released as Church Historian, and the publications and projects of my staff and I were curtailed." LJA to the First Presidency, undated, Series 10, referring to an oral notification he had received from Elder G. Homer Durham, 24 February 1978.
51. LJA Diary, 31 December 1980, Series 3.
52. Anderson, "Doves and Serpents," 205, quoting LJA diary, 26 June 1980, Series 10.
53. Anderson, "Doves and Serpents," 787.
54. Ibid.
55. "Statement on the Brigham Young Biography Based on a Review of My Diary, 1972–1985," Series 10. Though he never lived to see it, Arrington's hope that the exiles might someday return came true in 2005 with the abolition of the Smith

Institute and the reassignment of its staff to work on the massive project of publishing the papers of Joseph Smith at church headquarters in Salt Lake City. Their work, however, which is confined to that one project, bears little resemblance to the old History Division. *Salt Lake Tribune*, 25 June 2005, C1.

56. Anderson, "Doves and Serpents," 787.
57. LJA to his children, 28 April and 6 September 1982, Series 10.
58. LJA to his children, 25 November 1985, Series 10.
59. LJA, *Adventures of a Church Historian*, 199–200.
60. Boyd K. Packer, "The Mantle is Far, Far Greater Than the Intellect," BYU *Studies* 21 (Summer 1981): 267, 269.
61. Lavina Fielding Anderson, "DNA Mormon: D. Michael Quinn," in John Sillito and Susan Staker, *Mormon Mavericks: Essays on Dissenters* (Salt Lake City: Signature Books, 2002), 329–63.
62. Bitton, "Ten Years in Camelot," 17.
63. LJA, *Adventures of a Church Historian*, 226; Bitton. "Ten Years in Camelot," 20.

Chapter 5

1. Davis Bitton, "Introduction" to Bitton and Maureen Ursenbach Beecher, eds., *New Views of Mormon History: Essays in Honor of Leonard J. Arrington* (Salt Lake City: University of Utah Press, 1989), xv. Bitton admits the possible exception of the Brigham Young biography.
2. The reader should understand that in calling for greater psychological depth in biography, I am not necessarily asking for psychobiography or even extensive employment of clinical concepts or terminology, though in the hands of competent craftsmen those approaches can yield impressive results. Scholars lacking such training, though, can still produce insightful biographies, I think, simply by employing common sense analysis based on an awareness of interior forces. Arrington's books tend to be exclusively rational—and thus superficial—in their delineation of character and personality.
3. Or tried to. We shall see that he was defeated in his attempt to get credit as coauthor for Rebecca Cornwall, who had written virtually all of the Edwin D. Woolley biography, for the sponsor of the book demanded that Arrington's name alone appear as author.
4. Stephen W. Gibson, "Attorney's Pioneer Traits Lead Him to Success," *Deseret News*, 13 November 1971, 5–6.
5. Daniel Mark Epstein, *Sister Aimee: The Life of Aimee Semple McPherson* (New York: Harcourt Brace Jovanovich, 1993), 300.
6. This abduction tale is the main subject of her campy autobiography, *In the Service of the King: The Story of My Life* (New York: Boni and Liveright, 1927).
7. See Epstein, *Sister Aimee*, 313. Author Lately Thomas's hostile *The Vanishing*

Evangelist: The Aimee Semple McPherson Kidnapping Affair (New York: Viking Press, 1959) is the only published account of the trial that discusses Woolley's role. See also Carey McWilliams, "Aimee Semple McPherson: 'Sunlight in My Soul,'" in Isabel Leighton, ed., *The Aspirin Age, 1919–1941* (New York: Simon and Schuster, 1949), 50–80.

8. William L. Roper and Leonard J. Arrington, *William Spry: Man of Firmness, Governor of Utah* (Salt Lake City: Utah State Historical Society and University of Utah Press, 1971); Miriam B. Murphy, "William Spry," in Allan Kent Powell, ed., *Utah History Encyclopedia* (Salt Lake City: University of Utah Press, 1994), 527–28; this narrative is also based on Murphy's unpublished "The Governors of Utah", 26–38; manuscript in my possession.
9. Robert C. Mitchell [*Deseret News*] to Dennis McCarthy, 1 August 1968; Reed Stout to LJA, 12 June 1969, both in Series 12.
10. Roper and Arrington, *William Spry*, 179.
11. Woolley's own draft of the dedication text was even more effusive: "This book is dedicated to the youth of America and to the untold thousands, who like William Spry, through their own hard work and integrity and self-respect have reached the great heights and achievements that are only possible in this chosen land by the liberties and opportunities that this great country of ours makes available to all its citizens." Woolley to LJA, 2 December 1969, Series 12. Fortunately, he allowed Arrington to cut and recast his text into its final form.
12. Roper and Arrington, *William Spry*, 225.
13. Ibid., xi.
14. *Pacific Historical Review* 41 (November 1972): 543–44.
15. LJA, *Charles C. Rich, Mormon General and Veteran Frontiersman* (Provo, Utah: Brigham Young University Press, 1974).
16. "Agreement of Understanding" between Woolley and Arrington, 1 September 1970, Series 12.
17. LJA to Dennis Lythgoe, 13 March 1975, Series 2. Lythgoe's review appeared in the *Utah Historical Quarterly* 43 (Winter 1975): 86–87.
18. A table of contents in Series 12 give the participants and the chapters each produced: Richard Jensen—1–4; Ron Watt—5; Richard Daines—6–7, 9–10, 13–14; JoAnn Bair—11–12; Ross Peterson—15–18; Chris Rigby—19–20. The author of chapter 8 is not given. This at least was the plan; Rigby is credited in the book only with transcribing family documents. LJA, *Charles C. Rich*, xiv.
19. LJA, *Charles C. Rich*, xvi.
20. Ibid.
21. LJA to Dennis Lythgoe, 13 March 1975, Series 2.
22. LJA, *Charles C. Rich*, 14–17. Describing his first meeting with Joseph Smith, founder of the religion to which Rich would devote the rest of his life, Rich's diary merely states, "It was at this time that I made my first acquaintance with the Prophet" (20).

23. Ibid., xv.
24. *Journal of American History* 62 (June 1975): 123; *BYU Studies* 15 (Summer 1975): 537–41. LJA, *Adventures of a Church Historian*, 125.
25. Anderson, "Doves and Serpents," 259; copy in LJA Papers, Series 3.
26. LJA, *From Quaker to Latter-day Saint: Bishop Edwin D. Woolley* (Salt Lake City: Deseret Book, 1976).
27. Ibid., ix. The term "middle wagon" was adapted from a talk at the 1947 General Conference of the Church by J. Reuben Clark, who paid tribute "To Them of the Last Wagon," among the Mormon pioneers, i.e., those at the bottom of the social and economic scale who were followers rather than leaders. Woolley was somewhere in the middle—a bishop, but never an apostle.
28. LJA to Roland Rich Woolley, 28 August 1974, Series 5.
29. "Agreement between Leonard J. Arrington and Mrs. Rebecca Cornwall," 9 September 1974; see also LJA to Roland Rich Woolley, 9 September 1974 (both documents in Series 2), where Arrington asks Woolley to deposit $2,500 in the Mormon History Trust Fund to cover Cornwall's salary and supplies.
30. Becky Cornwall to LJA, 28 August [1974], Series 12. Note that the date of her response is the same as the date of Arrington's letter to Woolley in which he speculates about hiring a graduate student or a housewife, indicating that he already had Cornwall in mind for the job.
31. LJA to Roland Rich Woolley, 17 October 1974, Series 12; LJA to Rebecca Cornwall, 21 April 1975, Series 2.
32. LJA to Roland Rich Woolley, 14 October 1974, Series 5.
33. Roland Rich Woolley to LJA, 17 and 21 October 1974, Series 5.
34. LJA, *From Quaker to Latter-day Saint*, ix.
35. Richard W. Etulain, "Re-visioning the Mormons: *Great Basin Kingdom* As Historical Literature," in Thomas G. Alexander, ed., "*Great Basin Kingdom" Revisited: Contemporary Perspectives* (Logan: Utah State University Press, 1991), 48. I admit to taking Etulain's comments slightly out of context here; his intention is to contrast Arrington's measured prose with "torrid, sensational, or biased accounts of the Mormons," which is certainly a valid point. I am arguing that such prose, on the other hand, can be contrasted unfavorably with the genuine eloquence of a Becky Cornwall.
36. LJA to Ernest L. Wilkinson, 2 December 1976, Series 2.
37. LJA, *Adventures of a Church Historian*, 136–37.

Chapter 6

1. The appendices to LJA, *David Eccles: Pioneer Western Industrialist* (Logan: Utah State University Press, 1975), 205–73, list Eccles's businesses with a brief history of each.

2. To the shock of those two families, during the settlement of the estate upon David's death, it came out that there was a third family as well, located in Salt Lake City. Eccles had secretly married Margaret Geddes, a widow of one of his business partners, and they had a son, Albert. Albert's claims to a share of the estate were sustained by a court, though neither of the other branches of the family ever agreed with the decision. LJA, *David Eccles*, 183.
3. LJA, *Adventures of a Church Historian* (Urbana: University of Illinois Press, 1998), 125–26; S. J. Quinney to Wallace Stegner, 3 April 1973, Stegner papers, Marriott Library, University of Utah. Quinney, a prominent Utah lawyer, married into the Logan branch of the Eccles family and was asked by Nonie Harrison to represent her interests in the biography project. This letter to Stegner, who Harrison had asked to critique the manuscript, reports a meeting between Quinney and Arrington in which Quinney assembled the facts of the project's history and his understanding of each family's position.
4. Cleone Eccles to LJA, 4 November 1970; LJA to Cleone Eccles, 12 November 1970; and "Memorandum of Understanding" between LJA and Nora Treadwell, n.d., but probably late 1970, all in Series 12. Treadwell was the name of Nonie Eccles's first husband, who died during the biography project; she later married Dick Harrison.
5. Stegner's Utah works included, among others, *Mormon Country* (New York: Bonanza Books, 1942); *The Big Rock Candy Mountain* (New York: Duell, Sloan and Pearce, 1943); *The Preacher and the Slave* (Boston: Houghton Mifflin, 1950); and *Beyond the Hundredth Meridian: John Wesley Powell and the Second Opening of the West* (Boston: Houghton Mifflin, 1954). At the time he was asked to be involved in the Eccles project, his novel *Angle of Repose* (New York: Doubleday, 1971) had just won the Pulitzer Prize.
6. LJA to Stegner, 25 January 1973; LJA to Stegner, 16 February 1973, in which Arrington even offered Stegner coauthorship, which Stegner declined; S. J. Quinney to Stegner, 3 April 1973, in which Quinney advised Stegner "not to cash the check until you receive a more definite understanding as to your function and your obligations" so as to avoid the kind of entanglement Arrington was already in. All letters are in the Stegner Papers, University of Utah.
7. LJA, *Adventures of a Church Historian*, 126; there are copies of the critique in the Stegner Papers at the University of Utah and in the LJA Papers, Series 12.
8. Stegner to Fawn Brodie, 13 March 1973, Brodie Papers, University of Utah.
9. Stegner to LJA, 25 April 1973, Series 12.
10. Ibid.
11. LJA to O. N. Malmquist, 16 June 1975, Series 2.
12. Lee Scamehorn review of *David Eccles*, in *BYU Studies* 17 (Autumn 1976): 119–21.
13. Craig L. Torbenson, "The Promontory-Curlew Land Company: Promoting Dry Farming in Utah," *Utah Historical Quarterly* 66 (Winter 1998): 4–25.

14. LJA, *David Eccles*, 2; *Adventures of a Church Historian*, 126.
15. Fawn M. Brodie, *No Man Knows My History: The Life of Joseph Smith* (New York: Alfred A. Knopf, 1945); Stanley P. Hirshson, *The Lion of the Lord: A Biography of Brigham Young* (New York: Alfred A. Knopf, 1969).
16. Donna Hill, *Joseph Smith: The First Mormon* (Garden City, N.Y.: Doubleday, 1977).
17. LJA to Paul Edwards, 28 May 1970, Series 10; LJA to Bruno Marberger, 29 November 1972, Series 2.
18. LJA, "The Writing of Biography," p. 13, Series 12.
19. Hirshson, *The Lion of the Lord*, ix.
20. LJA, *Adventures of a Church Historian*, 113–14.
21. LJA to his children, 12 September 1975, Series 10: "Not churchy, not orthodox, [Adamson] nevertheless represented wonderful human and intellectual values.... More driven out than deliberately walking out of the community of Saints, he nevertheless remained sweet and not bitter.... I will not say that I wish we had more like him, because he died essentially outside the faith, but I wish we had more inside the faith who had his humanity and his love of beautiful thoughts and imagery."
22. LJA to Wendell Ashton, 22 February 1973, Series 2; LJA to Joan Nielsen, 15 August 1988, Series 10.
23. Sapient Mormon readers might also have seen the Brigham Young biography as the completion of a process of redemption for the firm, which had previously published both the Brodie and Hirshson biographies (ironically, Ashbel Green, supervising editor on the project, had also edited the Hirshson volume). That process of redemption might have been seen as starting with Knopf's 1979 publication of Arrington and Bitton's *The Mormon Experience*.
24. LJA, *Brigham Young: American Moses* (New York: Alfred A. Knopf, 1985), xi–xiii.
25. Ibid., 65, 250, 407, 188.
26. Ibid., 407.
27. Juanita Brooks, *The Mountain Meadows Massacre* (Palo Alto, Calif.: Stanford University Press, 1950). Brooks followed essentially the same line in her *John Doyle Lee: Zealot—Pioneer Builder—Scapegoat* (Glendale, Calif.: Arthur H. Clark, 1962).
28. Of course I refer here to Will Bagley, *Blood of the Prophets: Brigham Young and the Massacre at Mountain Meadows* (Norman: University of Oklahoma Press, 2002). My own *Utah Historians and the Reconstruction of Western History* (Norman: University of Oklahoma Press, 2003), 207–19 suggests a reinterpretation of the massacre.
29. Stephen J. Stein, "Arrington's Moses," *Journal of Mormon History* 12 (1985): 111–12.
30. LJA, *Harold F. Silver: Western Inventor, Businessman, and Civic Leader* (Logan: Utah State University Press, 1992); *Utah's Audacious Stockman: Charlie Redd* (Logan and Provo: Utah State University Press and Charles Redd Center for Western

Studies, 1995); and *Madelyn Cameron Stewart Silver: Poet, Teacher, Homemaker* (Salt Lake City: Publishers Press, 1998).

31. LJA, *Harold F. Silver*, viii.
32. LJA, *Madelyn Stewart Silver*, xii.
33. Ibid., 296–97.

Chapter 7

1. Henry Steele Commager, *The American Mind: An Interpretation of American Thought and Character Since the 1880s* (New Haven, Conn.: Yale University Press, 1950); Gustive O. Larson, *The "Americanization" of Utah for Statehood* (San Marino, Calif.: Huntington Library, 1971).
2. Henry Adams, *The Education of Henry Adams* (1906; New York: Modern Library, 1931).
3. LJA to Rodman Paul, 4 January 1968, Series 10; LJA, *Adventures of a Church Historian* (Urbana: University of Illinois Press, 1998), 75.
4. LJA, *Beet Sugar in the West: A History of the Utah-Idaho Sugar Company, 1891–1966* (Seattle: University of Washington Press, 1966).
5. Ibid., vii.
6. Ibid., viii.
7. Ibid., 21.
8. Ibid., 27–32.
9. Ibid., 53.
10. Samuel Eliot Morison and Henry Steele Commager, *The Growth of the American Republic*, 6th ed. (New York: Oxford University Press, 1969): 2:65.
11. LJA *Beet Sugar in the West*, 55.
12. Ibid., 157.
13. LJA to Alvah Perry (Deseret Book), 30 April 1964; LJA to Richard Poll, 6 October 1964, Series 12.
14. LJA to Richard Poll, 6 October 1964; Arch Egbert to LJA, 7 November 1964, Series 12.
15. LJA to Everett Cooley, 6 April 1964, Series 12. Wilkinson, president of BYU, and Lee, governor of Utah, were both conservative Republicans active in the anti-communist movement; George Rapp and Robert Owen, German and Scottish communitarian theorists respectively, were responsible for the creation of American communities during the early nineteenth century.
16. Leonard J. Arrington, Feramorz Y. Fox, and Dean L. May, *Building the City of God: Community and Cooperation among the Mormons* (Salt Lake City: Deseret Book, 1976).
17. LJA to Carol Lynn Pearson, 10 July 1969, Series 2.
18. Arrington, Fox, and May, *Building the City of God*, 2nd ed., (Urbana: University of

Illinois Press, 1991). The "Preface to the Second Edition," xi–xiii, contains a useful reflection on the history of the first edition as well as subsequent historiography.

19. LJA, *Adventures of a Church Historian*, 152–55. One of the "related developments" precipitating the retaliation was circulation among church leaders of a master's thesis from the University of Utah that purported to link Mormon scholars with the apostate publishers Jerald and Sandra Tanner and offered fabricated statements that suggested disloyalty to the church.
20. Nancy McCormick, review in *Utah Holiday*, February, 1970.
21. James Clayton, review in *Dialogue: A Journal of Mormon Thought* 10 (Autumn 1977): 134.
22. LJA, "Utah's Great Drought of 1934," *Utah Historical Quarterly* 54 (Summer 1986): 264.
23. Dean L. May, *Utah: A People's History* (Salt Lake City: University of Utah Press, 1987), 177: "Utah received much more New Deal aid per person than most states because the need was so great. . . . Only eight states of the then forty-eight received more help per person than did Utah."
24. The Law of Consecration and Stewardship and the United Order were basically economic experiments with social implications. Irrelevant to *Building the City of God* but hardly irrelevant to Mormon history was the equally conspicuous failure of Mormonism's great social experiment—polygamy—which its contemporary defenders had claimed was just as essential to Mormonism as its communal economy. With both its basic economic and its basic social institutions having run aground by the early 1890s, one might well have asked what was left of Mormonism itself. Preserving Mormonism's unique identity in the face of those and other disintegrative developments was the basic challenge faced by Mormon leaders around the turn of the twentieth century. Thomas G. Alexander, *Mormonism in Transition: A History of the Latter-day Saints, 1890–1930* (Urbana: University of Illinois Press, 1986).
25. Arrington, Fox, and May, *Building the City of God*, 355–56.
26. Ibid., 356–57.
27. LLA and Davis Bitton, *The Mormon Experience: A History of the Latter-day Saints* (New York: Alfred A. Knopf, 1979).
28. LJA to Alfred A. Knopf, 5 December 1966; LJA to Norris Hundley, 5 December 1978, Series 2. Rodman Paul to LJA, 12 December 1966, Series 2 indicates that Paul was originally thinking of a history of Utah, assuming that Utah history and Mormon history were one and the same. LJA to Rodman Paul, 29 December 1966, Series 2 shows that Arrington was thinking of a general Mormon history from the beginning. In the preface to the book, Arrington says the negotiations began "in the spring of 1967," but his correspondence indicates that they were already under way in December 1966. LJA and Davis Bitton, *The Mormon Experience*, ix.
29. LJA to Alfred A. Knopf, 17 January 1967, Series 2.

30. LJA Diary, 25 July 1973, Series 2. LJA and Davis Bitton, *The Mormon Experience*, x, gives the complete list.
31. LJA to Richard Poll, 10 July 1979, Series 2. See also LJA Diary, 27 January 1978, Series 2, which lists in detail who worked on which chapters, a list he indicates he is going to submit to Bitton for his corrections.
32. LJA Diary, 19 October 1977, Series 2.
33. LJA Diary, 4 November 1977, Series 2.
34. LJA and Davis Bitton, *The Mormon Experience*, 12, 17.
35. Ibid., 17.
36. "Unfortunately, the most widely used biography in university circles outside of the Church is Fawn Brodie's *No Man Knows My History* and Juanita Brooks' biography of John D. Lee. We surely do not want to be represented by those two books," LJA wrote to Joseph Anderson, 11 April 1973, Series 2.
37. Robert S. McPherson, "Setting the Stage: Native America Revisited," in Forrest S. Cuch, ed., *A History of Utah's American Indians* (Logan: Utah State University Press, 2000), 18–22, indicates some of the ambiguity of the issue, while Sondra Jones, *The Trial of Don Pedro Leon Lujan: The Attack Against Indian Slavery and Mexican Traders in Utah* (Salt Lake City: University of Utah Press, 2000), shows how, paradoxically, Mormon benevolence actually led to their own practice of Indian slavery and to war with the Utes who were the middle men in the New Mexican slave trade that the Mormons tried to stop. Although the Mormons claimed to be "adopting" rather than enslaving the Indians they acquired from the Utes, in fact they were worked as hard as slaves and consigned to a perpetual existence as an uneducated, unskilled, and unmarriageable underclass. On the other hand, Brian Q. Cannon presents evidence that Indian members of Mormon households were not treated that badly. See his "Adopted or Indentured, 1850–1870: Native Children in Mormon Households," in Ronald W. Walker and Doris R. Dant, eds. *Nearly Everything Imaginable: The Everyday Life of Utah's Mormon Pioneers* (Provo, Utah: Brigham Young University Press, 1999).
38. To be sure, the Franciscans had learned their policy the hard way, for in colonial New Mexico their heavy-handed ways with the Pueblo Indians in attempting to destroy the indigenous culture had led to the bloody Pueblo Revolt of 1680. By the late nineteenth century, though, they were leading the way among missionaries in the Southwest in accommodating Christianity to the indigenous cultures. See Elizabeth A. H. John, *Storms Brewed in Other Men's Worlds: The Confrontation of Indians, Spanish, and French in the Southwest, 1540–1795* (College Station: Texas A&M Press, 1975), chaps. 1–3; and Ross Enochs, "The Franciscan Mission to the Navajos: Mission Method and Indigenous Religion, 1898–1940," *Catholic Historical Review* 92 (January 2006): 46–73.
39. Richard White, *The Middle Ground: Indians, Empires, and Republics in the Great Lakes Region, 1650–1815* (Cambridge: Cambridge University Press, 1991).

40. LJA and Davis Bitton, *Mormons and Their Historians* (Salt Lake City: University of Utah Press, 1988).
41. I employ the term "amateur" here as I do in my *Utah Historians and the Reconstruction of Western History* (Norman: University of Oklahoma Press, 2003) not in a pejorative sense, but only as an acknowledgment that none of them had academic degrees in history. Neither did Arrington, for that matter, yet all of them practiced the historian's craft at a very high level of competence.
42. Levi S. Peterson, *Juanita Brooks: Mormon Woman Historian* (Salt Lake City: University of Utah Press, 1988); Newell G. Bringhurst, *Fawn McKay Brodie: A Biographer's Life* (Norman: University of Oklahoma Press, 1999).
43. Ronald W. Walker, David J. Whittaker, and James B. Allen, *Mormon History* (Urbana: University of Illinois Press, 2001).

Chapter 8

1. *Salt Lake Tribune*, February 12, 1999; LJA to his children, 3 April 1976, Series 10.
2. It is true that *Great Basin Kingdom* was written, and the early biographies begun, while Arrington was a professor at Utah State Agricultural College and also that he held a chair in the Brigham Young University history department during his years as Church Historian and thereafter until his retirement, but his greatest output came not through those affiliations but rather in his role as Church Historian and his directorship of the scholars in the History Division.
3. Readers unfamiliar with the other scholars named here are referred to my *Utah Historians and the Reconstruction of Western History* (Norman: University of Oklahoma Press, 2003), to which the present book may be seen as something of a supplement.
4. Fawn M. Brodie, *No Man Knows My History: The Life of Joseph* Smith (New York: Alfred A. Knopf, 1945). Robert B. Flanders, "Some Reflections on the New Mormon History," *Dialogue: A Journal of Mormon Thought* 9 (Spring 1974): 34–41, is one who suggests Brodie's book as the originator of the New Mormon History.
5. As Brodie held only a master's degree in English, her academic qualifications in history were thin. Nevertheless, she eventually held an academic appointment in the history department of the University of California at Los Angeles and developed a major, if controversial, reputation as an exponent of the new method of psychobiography. Newell G. Bringhurst, *Fawn McKay Brodie: A Biographer's Life* (Norman: University of Oklahoma Press, 1999).
6. It is also true, though, that a significant quotient of the New Mormon History has been written by non-Mormon scholars. While one risks placing people in categories they may not themselves embrace, the New Mormon History has enjoyed major contributions from non-Mormons like Jan Shipps, William P. MacKinnon, and Mario S. DePillis, and continues to be influenced by younger

scholars like Dan Vogel and Polly Aird. Brodie herself, of course, was considered an apostate and excommunicated, as have been recent scholars like D. Michael Quinn and Lavina Fielding Anderson.

7. LJA to Dean Martin Hickman, 27 October 1980, Series 3.
8. LJA to his children, 3 April 1976, Series 10; LJA, "Introduction to [sic] Carl Arrington, 27 August 1983, Sunstone Symposium," Series 12; LJA to his children, 29 January 1989, Series 10.
9. LJA to his children, 26 July 1989, Series 10; another such list is LJA to his children, 21 June 1991, Series 5. See also LJA to Jonathan Hughes, 10 June 1991, Series 5, where he gives further reasons why "I find it increasingly difficult to accept the world I'm living in."
10. LJA to Richard Poll, 6 October 1964, Series 12. In that election, the popular Democrat Calvin Rampton won the first of his three terms as Governor against Republican Mitchell Melich. It is not perhaps surprising that Arrington would support Lyndon Johnson against the perceived right-wing radical Barry Goldwater, and in fact the Presidential election was an immense Johnson landslide. Most surprising, though, was his support of Democratic Senator Frank Moss, who won a second term against BYU President Ernest L. Wilkinson, who was a personal friend of Arrington, but whose conservative politics he obviously did not approve.
11. LJA to his children, 20 April 1998, Series 10.
12. LJA to his children, 10 August 1989, Series 10.
13. Carl Arrington to LJA, 28 December 1984, Series 10.
14. LJA to his children, 21 July 1989, Series 10.
15. Carl Arrington to LJA, 28 December 1984, Series 10.
16. See, for example, Brian Q. Cannon's review of my *Utah Historians*, in which he no doubt correctly chastises what he calls my "streamlined reading of Mormon theology," in which I portray "Mormon culture and theology as if they were monolithic." "One cannot accurately speak," he concludes, "of *the* Mormon world view. Church leaders differed in their opinions and that diversity was magnified in the general membership." To illustrate his point, Professor Cannon observes that "in Mormon theology pessimistic elements coexist with optimistic ones"—two mutually contradictory theologies. *The Journal of Arizona History* (Spring 2005): 81–82.
17. J. Frederic Voros, Jr., "Was the Book of Mormon Buried with King Follett?" *Sunstone*, March 1987, 15–18.
18. LJA, "Recollections: My Early Religious Beliefs," Series 10.
19. LJA to his children, 11 February 1990, Series 10.
20. LJA to his children, 21 October 1987, Series 10.
21. LJA to his children, 12 December 1995, Series 10.
22. LJA to his children, 16 January 1998, Series 10. Reinhold Niebuhr, *The Irony of American History* (New York: Charles Scribner's Sons, 1962); LJA to his children, 2 January 1998, Series 10.

23. LJA, "On Writing Latter-day Saint History," Series 10. This essay is not to be confused with the similarly titled, "The Writing of Latter-day Saint History: Problems, Accomplishments, and Admonitions," *Dialogue: A Journal of Mormon Thought* 14 (Autumn 1981): 119–29. Another of his published essays makes some of the same recommendations under different nomenclature: "The Search for Truth and Meaning in Mormon History," *Dialogue: A Journal of Mormon Thought* 3 (Summer 1968): 56–66.
24. See *Utah Historical Quarterly* 38 (Winter 1970), a pioneering project in which the entire issue, edited by Leonard Arrington, was devoted to articles on Mormon women. A similar pioneering work, Claudia L. Bushman, ed., *Mormon Sisters: Women in Early Utah* (Cambridge, Mass.: Emmeline Press Limited, 1976) gives tribute to his inspiration by being dedicated "For Leonard J. Arrington. He takes us seriously."
25. Ronald W. Walker, David J. Whittaker, and James B. Allen, *Mormon History* (Urbana: University of Illinois Press, 2001), 94.
26. Ronald W. Walker, "Introduction to the Illinois Edition," in Leonard J. Arrington, *Great Basin Kingdom: An Economic History of the Latter-day Saints, 1830–1900* (Urbana: University of Illinois Press, 2005), xxvii.
27. Charles S. Peterson, "Beyond the Problems of Exceptionalist History," in Thomas G. Alexander, ed., *"Great Basin Kingdom" Revisited: Contemporary Perspectives* (Logan: Utah State University Press, 1991): 133–51.

Bibliography

Manuscript Collections

Marriott Library Special Collections, University of Utah

Fawn M. Brodie Papers

Wallace Stegner Papers

Merrill Library Special Collections, Utah State University

Leonard J. Arrington Papers

Stewart Library Special Collections, Weber State University

David Eccles Papers

Books

Here, as in the Articles section below, I have listed only those Leonard J. Arrington titles actually cited in the book. An exhaustive Arrington bibliography prepared by David J. Whittaker is available as part of the Register to the Arrington collection at Utah State University.

Adams, Henry. *The Education of Henry Adams.* New York: Modern Library, 1931.

Alexander, Thomas G., ed., *"Great Basin Kingdom" Revisited: Contemporary Perspectives* Logan: Utah State University Press, 1991.

———. *Mormonism in Transition: A History of the Latter-day Saints, 1890–1930.* Urbana: University of Illinois Press, 1986.

———. *Utah: The Right Place.* Salt Lake City; Gibbs Smith, 1995.

Allen, James B., and Glen M. Leonard. *The Story of the Latter-day Saints.* Salt Lake City: Deseret Book, 1976.

Anderson, Nels. *Desert Saints: The Mormon Frontier in Utah.* Chicago: University of Chicago Press, 1942.

Arrington, Leonard J. *Adventures of a Church Historian.* Urbana: University of Illinois Press, 1998.

———. *Beet Sugar in the West: A History of the Utah-Idaho Sugar Company, 1891–1966* (Seattle: University of Washington Press, 1966.

———. *Brigham Young: American Moses.* New York: Alfred A. Knopf, 1985.

———. *Charles C. Rich, Mormon General and Veteran Frontiersman.* Provo, Utah: Brigham Young University Press, 1974.

———. *David Eccles: Pioneer Western Industrialist.* Logan: Utah State University Press, 1975.

———. *From Quaker to Latter-day Saint: Bishop Edwin D. Woolley.* Salt Lake City: Deseret Book, 1976.

———. *Great Basin Kingdom: An Economic History of the Latter-day Saints, 1830–1900.* Cambridge, Mass.: Harvard University Press, 1958.

———. *Harold F. Silver: Western Inventor, Businessman, and Civic Leader.* Logan: Utah State University Press, 1992.

———. *History of Idaho.* 2 vols. Moscow: University of Idaho Press, 1994.

———. *Madelyn Cameron Stewart Silver: Poet, Teacher, Homemaker.* Salt Lake City: Publishers Press, 1998.

———. *Utah's Audacious Stockman: Charlie Redd.* Logan and Provo: Utah State University Press and Charles Redd Center for Western Studies, 1995.

Arrington, Leonard J., and Davis Bitton. *The Mormon Experience: A History of the Latter-day Saints.* New York: Alfred A. Knopf, 1979.

———. *Mormons and Their Historians.* Salt Lake City: University of Utah Press, 1988.

Arrington, Leonard J., Feramorz Y. Fox, and Dean L. May. *Building the City of God: Community and Cooperation Among the Mormons.* Salt Lake City: Deseret Book, 1976.

Arrington, Leonard J., and William L. Roper. *William Spry: Man of Firmness, Governor of Utah.* Salt Lake City: Utah State Historical Society for University of Utah Press, 1971.

Atherton, Lewis. *Main Street on the Middle Border.* Bloomington: Indiana University Press, 1954.

Aton, James M., and Robert S. McPherson. *River Flowing from the Sunrise: An Environmental History of the Lower San Juan.* Logan: Utah State University Press, 2000.

Bagley, Will. *Blood of the Prophets: Brigham Young and the Massacre at Mountain Meadows.* Norman: University of Oklahoma Press, 2002.

Barker, Dudley. *G. K. Chesterton: A Biography*. New York: Stein and Day, 1973.

Bitton, Davis, ed. *Guide to Mormon Diaries and Autobiographies*. Provo, Utah: Brigham Young University Press, 1977.

Bitton, Davis, and Maureen Ursenbach Beecher, eds. *New Views of Mormon History: Essays in Honor of Leonard J. Arrington*. Salt Lake City: University of Utah Press, 1989.

Bringhurst, Newell G. *Fawn McKay Brodie: A Biographer's Life*. Norman: University of Oklahoma Press, 1999.

Brooks, Juanita. *John Doyle Lee: Zealot—Pioneer Builder—Scapegoat*. Glendale, Calif.: Arthur H. Clark, 1962.

———. *The Mountain Meadows Massacre*. Palo Alto, Calif.: Stanford University Press, 1950.

Bowen, Marshall E. *Utah People in the Nevada Desert: Homestead and Community on a Twentieth Century Farmers' Frontier*. Logan: Utah State University Press, 1994.

Brodie, Fawn M. *"No Man Knows My History": The Life of Joseph Smith*. New York: Alfred A. Knopf, 1945.

Bushman, Claudia L., ed. *Mormon Sisters: Women in Early Utah*. Cambridge, Mass.: Emmeline Press Limited, 1976.

Carr, Stephen L. *The Historic Guide to Utah Ghost Towns*. Rev. ed. Salt Lake City: Western Epics, 1986.

Commager, Henry Steele. *The American Mind: An Interpretation of American Thought and Character Since the 1880s*. New Haven, Conn.: Yale University Press, 1950.

Epstein, Daniel Mark. *Sister Aimee: The Life of Aimee Semple McPherson*. New York: Harcourt Brace Jovanovich, 1993.

Firmage, Richard. *A History of Grand County*. Salt Lake City: Utah State Historical Society, 1996.

Francaviglia, Richard V. *The Mormon Landscape: Existence, Creation, and Perception of a Unique Image in the American West*. New York: AMS Press, Inc., 1978.

Gottlieb, Robert, and Peter Wiley. *America's Saints: The Rise of Mormon Power*. New York: G. P. Putnam's Sons, 1984.

Graham, Otis L., Jr. *An Encore for Reform: The Old Progressives and the New Deal* New York: Oxford University Press, 1967.

Hill, Donna. *Joseph Smith: The First Mormon*. Garden City, New York: Doubleday, 1977.

Hirshson, Stanley P. *The Lion of the Lord: A Biography of Brigham Young*. New York: Alfred A. Knopf, 1969.

Jessee, Dean C. *Letters of Brigham Young to His Sons.* Salt Lake City: Deseret Book, 1974.

John, Elizabeth A. H. *Storms Brewed in Other Men's Worlds: The Confrontation of Indians, Spanish, and French in the Southwest, 1540–1795.* College Station: Texas A&M Press, 1975.

Jones, Sondra. *The Trial of Don Pedro Leon Lujan: The Attack Against Indian Slavery and Mexican Traders in Utah.* Salt Lake City: University of Utah Press, 2000.

Kirkland, Edward Chase. *Industry Comes of Age: Business, Labor and Public Policy, 1860–1897.* New York: Holt, Rinehart and Winston, 1961.

Larson, Andrew Karl. *I Was Called to Dixie. The Virgin River Basin: Unique Experiences in Mormon Pioneering.* St. George, Utah: Author, 1961.

Larson, Gustive O. *The "Americanization" of Utah for Statehood.* San Marino, Calif.: Huntington Library, 1971.

Mariger, Marietta. *Saga of Three Towns: Harrisburg, Leeds, Silver Reef.* St. George, Utah: Washington County News, n.d.

Marshall, Alfred. *Principles of Economics.* 8th ed. London: Macmillan, 1920.

May, Dean L. *Utah: A People's History.* Salt Lake City: University of Utah Press, 1987.

May, Henry F. *The End of American Innocence: A Study of the First Years of Our Own Time, 1912–1917.* New York: Alfred A. Knopf, 1959.

McPherson, Aimee Semple. *In the Service of the King: The Story of My Life.* New York: Boni and Liveright, 1927.

Miller, David E. *Hole-in-the-Rock: An Epic in the Colonization of the Great American West.* Salt Lake City: University of Utah Press, 1959.

Miller, Perry. *Errand Into the Wilderness.* Cambridge: Harvard University Press, 1956.

Morison, Samuel Eliot, and Henry Steele Commager. *The Growth of the American Republic.* 6th ed. New York: Oxford University Press, 1969.

Nelson, Lowry. *The Mormon Village: A Pattern and Technique of Land Settlement.* Salt Lake City: University of Utah Press, 1952.

Niebuhr, Reinhold. *The Irony of American History.* New York: Charles Scribner's Sons, 1962.

Peterson, F. Ross. *Idaho: A Bicentennial History.* New York: W. W. Norton, 1976.

Peterson, Levi S. *Juanita Brooks: Mormon Woman Historian.* Salt Lake City: University of Utah Press, 1988.

Smythe, William E. *The Conquest of Arid America.* New York: Harper and Brothers, 1900. Reprint, Seattle: University of Washington Press, 1969.

Stegner, Wallace. *Angle of Repose*. New York: Doubleday, 1971.

———. *The Big Rock Candy Mountain*. New York: Duell, Sloan and Pearce, 1943.

———. *Beyond the Hundredth Meridian: John Wesley Powell and the Second Opening of the West*. Boston: Houghton Mifflin, 1954.

———. *Mormon Country*. New York: Bonanza Books, 1942.

———. *The Preacher and the Slave*. Boston: Houghton Mifflin, 1950.

Thomas, Lately. *The Vanishing Evangelist: The Aimee Semple McPherson Kidnapping Affair*. New York: Viking Press, 1959.

Topping, Gary, ed. *Gila Monsters and Red-Eyed Rattlesnakes: Don Maguire's Arizona Trading Expeditions, 1876–1879*. Salt Lake City: University of Utah Press, 1997.

———. *Utah Historians and the Reconstruction of Western History*. Norman: University of Oklahoma Press, 2003.

Twelve Southerners. *I'll Take My Stand: The South and the Agrarian Tradition*. New York: Harper and Brothers, 1930.

Walker, Ronald W., David J. Whittaker, and James B. Allen. *Mormon History*. Urbana: University of Illinois Press, 2001.

White, Richard. *The Middle Ground: Indians, Empires, and Republics in the Great Lakes Region, 1650–1815*. Cambridge: Cambridge University Press, 1991.

Articles

Anderson, Lavina Fielding. "DNA Mormon: D. Michael Quinn." In John Sillito and Susan Staker, *Mormon Mavericks: Essays on Dissenters*. 329–63. Salt Lake City: Signature Books, 2002.

Arrington, Leonard J. "The Search for Truth and Meaning in Mormon History." *Dialogue: A Journal of Mormon Thought* 3 (Summer 1968): 56–66.

———. "Utah's Great Drought of 1934." *Utah Historical Quarterly* 54 (Summer 1986): 245–64.

———. *Utah Historical Quarterly* 38 (Winter 1970). Editor of entire issue.

Arrington, Leonard J., and Wayne K. Hinton. "Origin of the Welfare Plan of the Church of Jesus Christ of Latter-day Saints." *BYU Studies* 5 (Winter 1964): 67–85.

Bitton, Davis. "Ten Years in Camelot: A Personal Memoir." *Dialogue: A Journal of Mormon Thought* 16 (Autumn 1983): 9–33.

Cannon, Brian Q. "Adopted or Indentured, 1850–1870: Native Children in Mormon Hoseholds." In *Nearly Everything Imaginable: The Everyday Life of Utah's Mormon Pioneers*, edited by Ronald W. Walker and Doris R. Dant. 341–57. Provo, Utah: Brigham Young University Press, 1999.

———. Review of Gary Topping, *Utah Historians and the Reconstruction of Western History. Journal of Arizona History* (Spring 2005): 81–82.

———. "Struggle Against Great Odds: Challenges in Utah's Marginal Agricultural Areas, 1925–39." *Utah Historical Quarterly* 54 (Fall 1986): 308–27.

———. "'What a Power We Will Be in This Land': The LDS Church, the Church Security Program, and the New Deal." *Journal of the West* 43 (Fall 2004): 66–75.

Clayton, James. Review of *Building the City of God. Dialogue: A Journal of Mormon Thought* 10 (Autumn 1977): 134.

Enochs, Ross. "The Franciscan Mission to the Navajos: Mission Method and Indigenous Religion, 1898–1940." *Catholic Historical Review* 92 (January 2006): 46–73.

Ely, Richard T. "Economic Aspects of Mormonism." *Harper's Monthly Magazine* 106 (April 1903): 667–78.

"Ely, Richard Theodore." In *Concise Dictionary of American Biography*. Vol. 1. 355.New York: Charles Scribner's Sons, 1997.

Flanders, Robert. Review of *Charles C. Rich. Journal of American History* 62 (June 1975): 122–24.

———. "Some Reflections on the New Mormon History." *Dialogue: A Journal of Mormon Thought* 9 (Spring 1974): 34–41.

Gibson, Stephen W. "Attorney's Pioneer Traits Lead Him to Success." *Deseret News*, 13 November 1971. 5–6.

Jackson, Richard. "The Mormon Experience: The Plains as Sinai, the Great Salt Lake as the4 Dead Sea, and the Great Basin as Desert-cum-Promised Land." *Journal of Historical Geography* 18 (1992): 41–58.

———. "Righteousness and Environmental Change: The Mormons and the Environment." In *Essays on the American West, 1973–74*, edited by Thomas G. Alexander. 21–42. Provo, Utah: Brigham Young University Press, ca. 1975.

Lythgoe, Dennis, Review of *Charles C. Rich. Utah Historical Quarterly* 43 (Winter 1975): 86–87.May, Dean L. "The Making of Saints: The Mormon Town as a Setting for the Study of Cultural Change." *Utah Historical Quarterly* 45 (Winter 1977): 75–92.

McCormick, Nancy. Review of *Building the City of God. Utah Holiday*, February, 1978.

McPherson, Robert S. "Setting the Stage: Native America Revisited." In *A History of Utah's American Indians*, edited by Forrest S. Cuch. 18–22. Logan: Utah State University Press, 2000.

McWilliams, Carey. "Aimee Semple McPherson: 'Sunlight in My Soul.'" In *The Aspirin Age, 1919–1941*, edited by Isabel Leighton. 50–80 New York: Simon and Schuster, 1949.

Morgan, Dale L. "Contemporary Scene." In *Utah: A Guide to the State*, by Utah Writers' Program. New York: Hastings House, 1940.

———. Review of *Great Basin Kingdom. Utah Historical Quarterly* (Spring 1959): 191.

Murphy, Miriam B. "William Spry." In *Utah History Encyclopedia*, edited by Allan Kent Powell. 527–28. Salt Lake City: University of Utah Press, 1994.

Nelson, Lowry. "The Mormon Village: A Study in Social Origins." *Proceedings of the Utah Academy of Sciences* 7 (1930): 11–37.

Packer, Boyd K. "The Mantle is Far, Far Greater Than the Intellect." *BYU Studies* 21 (Summer 1981): 259–78.

Paul, Rodman. Review of *Charles C. Rich. BYU Studies* 15 (Summer 1975): 537–41.

Scamehorn, Lee. Review of *David Eccles. BYU Studies* 17 (Autumn 1976): 119–21.

Shipps, Jan. Review of Roper and Arrington, *William Spry. Pacific Historical Review* 41 (November 1972): 543–44.

Stein, Stephen J. "Arrington's Moses." *Journal of Mormon History* 12 (1985): 111–12.

Torbenson, Craig L. "The Promontory-Curlew Land Company: Promoting Dry Farming in Utah." *Utah Historical Quarterly* 66 (Winter 1998): 4–25.

Vogt, Evon Z., and Thomas F. O'Dea. "A Comparative Study of the Role of Values in Social Action in Two Southwestern Communities." *American Sociological Review* 18 (December 1953): 645–54.

Voros, J. Frederic, Jr., "Was the Book of Mormon Buried with King Follett?" *Sunstone*, March 1987. 15–18.

Wahlquist, Wayne L. "A Review of Mormon Settlement Literature." *Utah Historical Quarterly* 45 (Winter 1977): 4–21.

Walker, Ronald W. "Introduction to the Illinois Edition." In *Great Basin Kingdom: An Economic History of the Latter-day Saints, 1830–1900*, by Leonard J. Arrington. Urbana: University of Illinois Press, 2004.

Index